RENÉ DESCARTES
The Essential Writings

RENÉ DESCARTES
The Essential Writings

Translated and with Introductions
and a Conceptual Index by

JOHN J. BLOM

Foreword by Paul Oskar Kristeller

HARPER TORCHBOOKS
Harper & Row, Publishers
New York, Hagerstown, San Francisco, London

The Essential Writings of the Great Philosophers is published under the editorship of Charles M. Sherover.

RENÉ DESCARTES: THE ESSENTIAL WRITINGS. Copyright © 1977 by John J. Blom. All rights reserved. Printed in the United States of America. No part of this book may be used or reproduced in any manner whatsoever without written permission except in the case of brief quotations embodied in critical articles and reviews. For information address Harper & Row, Publishers, Inc., 10 East 53rd Street, New York, N.Y. 10022. Published simultaneously in Canada by Fitzhenry & Whiteside Limited, Toronto.

Designed by Eve Callahan

First edition: HARPER TORCHBOOKS, 1977

LIBRARY OF CONGRESS CATALOG CARD NUMBER: 75–39930

ISBN: 0–06–131909–0

77 78 79 80 10 9 8 7 6 5 4 3 2 1

For Arlette

Contents

Foreword

Descartes is generally recognized as one of the greatest philosophers and as the founder of modern philosophy. Few if any of his teachings have been accepted without criticism by later thinkers, but his problems have dominated subsequent thought for centuries, and he has been the object of important philosophical criticism, not all of it fair or justified, up to the present day. A study of his major works is indispensable for the beginning as well as the advanced student of philosophy, and it also provides an important background for all those readers who are interested in French literature and history.

Dr. Blom's selection of Descartes's writings is a welcome addition to the continuing study of Descartes and to the literature dealing with him. Having devoted much time and effort to a detailed study of Descartes's metaphysics, Dr. Blom is well acquainted with his writings in the original Latin and French texts and well equipped to present some of them in a new and accurate translation. Combining the *Regulae*, the *Discours*, and the *Meditationes* in a single volume, he provides the student and reader with Descartes's most important philosophical writings. At the end, an important section from Descartes's replies to the objections to his *Meditations* has been added, which contains his definitions of many basic terms. The understanding of the texts, not always easy either in the original or in translation, is also helped by the introductions, by the notes, and by a conceptual index.

It is to be hoped that this new translation will find many readers among students of philosophy and of other subjects and will arouse their curiosity to read Descartes in some of his other writings and in his original text. For the study of philosophy should not be based exclusively on the writings of contemporary thinkers, however valuable, but should include the work of earlier thinkers who continue to provide us with a broader perspective and with a variety of significant problems and solutions that deserve to be studied and pondered—if not to be accepted or repeated.

PAUL OSKAR KRISTELLER

Columbia University

Preface

A volume of modest size intended to present Descartes's essential writings dictates its own contents. The *Rules for the Direction of the Native Talents*, the *Discourse concerning Method*, the *Meditations concerning First Philosophy*—these are his fundamental and metaphysically most crucial works, and each is included complete in this volume. Besides benefiting from having these three works together, the reader will, I hope, benefit also from the new translations, the separate explanatory introductions, and the device of a conceptual index that divides and interrelates important elements in Descartes's thought.

The *Rules* and *Meditations* are translated from their Latin originals, the *Discourse* from its French original. I resisted the familiar temptation to base a translation of the *Meditations* upon a combination of the Latin original and an early French version thereof. I have aimed at fidelity in translation. In the case of Descartes a faithful translation needn't be a cumbersome one; so whatever obscurities the reader finds herein, let him suspect my abilities as a translator, not the clarity of Descartes's original texts. I have, however, felt under no obligation to use a too-modern English in these translations. Rather, I have permitted myself to be led by the original texts—by nuance of word and flow of phrase. I have come up with an English equivalent that seems to me clear and that would have lost in faithfulness, subtlety, and style had I artificially restricted myself in English vocabulary and sentence structure. In matters of paragraphing I have followed the standard

edition of Messieurs Adam and Tannery on which these translations are based.* I have also adhered quite closely to the punctuation in their edition—it is not difficult to grasp, and to further
modernize it would often obscure the logical connection of
Descartes's thoughts or mean the loss of his dramatic manner
of presentation. For ease of reference, I have numbered the para-
graphs of each of the works.

René Descartes (1596–1650) is often called the "father of modern philosophy." The profound controversies that his doctrines
have engendered are alone sufficient to establish his eminence.
Yet if this father of modern philosophy is to be paid due respect,
then it is necessary to understand him on his own terms—to distinguish his doctrines from myriad notions labeled "cartesian."
Now, the quest for certainty may be the constitutional imperative
for every philosopher; in the case of Descartes it was an acknowledged passion. Thus there is no more fitting approach to him than
to study seriously his claims to having attained certainty in what
he took to be the two foremost questions of metaphysics—namely,
the questions of the existence of God and of the nature of the
human mind. My introductory essays to the works contained in
this volume have been undertaken in this spirit of exegesis. I have
tried to clarify basic concepts and explain their role in Descartes's
metaphysics. The interpretations that I offer of his "proofs" of
the existence of God and the nature of the human mind are, I
believe, defensible on the basis of the textual evidence, although
I have been unable to provide extensive documentation in a volume of so modest a size.

The use of a conceptual index in an anthology is, as far as I
know, a new idea. The major topics and their subordination to one
another will be easy to grasp. The significance of the further divisions of these subject matters, if not immediately apparent, will
become clear in light of the introductory essays and, most importantly, in light of Descartes's texts themselves.

The notes on pages 257–259 refer to works of Descartes not

* René Descartes, *Oeuvres*, 11 vols., ed. Charles Adam and Paul Tannery
(Paris: Vrin, 1964–1974), *Regulae ad directionem ingenii*, vol. X (1966);
Discours de la méthode, vol. VI (1965); *Meditationes*, with "Objectiones
doctorum aliquot virorum in praecedentes meditationes cum responsionibus
authoris," vol. VII (1964).

included in this volume or to sources he might have used. This conforms to the spirit of the introductory essays, which is to use a limited space to help clarify Descartes's own views. As for his influences, almost the entire subsequent history of philosophy is part of his bibliography, and the interested reader will want to look to Spinoza, Leibniz, Locke, Peirce, Husserl, and many others. The scholarly bibliography is enormous; rather than provide a list that could only be very partial, I refer the reader to Gregor Sebba's *Bibliographia Cartesiana.** Much of the contemporary interest in Descartes in British and American circles† stems from the provocative *Concept of Mind* by the late Professor Gilbert Ryle.‡ However interesting Ryle's own views—reminiscent in many ways of Aristotle's *De Anima*—they seem to me to propogate some serious myths concerning Descartes's position. But perhaps the eventual effect, which I am sure Professor Ryle would heartily endorse, will be to renew our research into the actual doctrines of the "father of modern philosophy."

The many defects in this volume are, of course, my responsibility. But whatever its virtues, the credit must in very large part go to my teachers. I am vividly aware that the labors of many people over the years have combined to provide me with the skills required for this project. I am especially grateful to Professor Paul O. Kristeller of Columbia University: the seriousness with which he devoted himself to the chore of supervising my doctoral thesis has, I hope, nourished some of that same seriousness in myself; he is a scholar completely generous in teaching scholarship to others.

Throughout this project, Drs. William Bryar and Alice Jourdain of Hunter College have been a daily source of pointed criticisms and encouragement. From Anne Marie Weissman I received incisive advice concerning the subtleties of Descartes's French.

I should like to thank Ms. Susan Metcalff for her assistance in preparing the typescript. Mike Robinson of Harper & Row has made many valuable suggestions which, I am confident, have en-

---

* Gregor Sebba, *Bibliographia Cartesiana: A Critical Guide to the Descartes Literature 1800–1960* (The Hague: Martinus Nijhoff, 1964).

† References to some of the British and American literature are to be found in Willis Doney, *Descartes* (New York: Doubleday, 1967), pp. 371–386.

‡ Gilbert Ryle, *Concept of Mind* (New York: Barnes & Noble, 1967).

hanced this volume. I would like to express my warm thanks for the care with which he has managed the production of this volume.

J.J.B.

Brooklyn, New York

Abbreviations

References to works and the selection in this volume are made by the following initials, plus paragraph numbers:

R = *Rules for the Direction of the Native Talents*
D = *Discourse concerning Method*
M = *Meditations concerning First Philosophy*
Re = "Reasons Proving the Existence of God and the Distinction of the Soul from the Body"

I
RULES

Introduction

In the *Discourse concerning Method* (1637) and the *Meditations concerning First Philosophy* (1641), Descartes insists that whatever his success at metaphysics, it is due to the application of a general method for acquiring new knowledge. He maintains that he originally discovered this general method in conjunction with his mathematical studies and already successfully applied it to certain problems in the sciences. Fortunately, Descartes's earliest but incomplete treatise, *Rules for the Direction of the Native Talents* (1628), contains a formal statement of this method as he had developed it by 1628.[1] This treatise was not published during his lifetime, and it is possible that he wrote it to serve as a handbook summarizing the method he had discovered over a number of years.[2]

The *Rules* merits careful study. In it Descartes explicitly identifies and explains distinctions and procedures that are present, but not explicitly named or explained, in all his later works. However, by its nature the *Rules* is unlikely to be an immediately convincing work. It aims to teach, or summarize, a general method or logical procedure that directs us in the acquisition of new knowledge in every area of investigation. Understanding such a method, or logic of discovery, is inseparable from practicing it— Descartes himself became convinced of his method only by its success for him. Accordingly, if the *Rules* is read in isolation from Descartes's subsequent treatises, it will be difficult to anticipate how its various directives can be applied so as to fashion the sys-

tematic metaphysics that finally emerges in the *Meditations*. However, when his later treatises are read in light of the *Rules*, then
the later doctrines are greatly clarified and the persistent influence
of the *Rules*, and the suggestiveness and versatility of its directives, become much more obvious.

The title of the treatise, *Rules for the Direction of the Native
Talents*, nicely captures its purpose. The rules of method that
Descartes lays down are not intended to make men rational.
Rather, they are intended to prescribe procedures whereby men
can make maximal use of their inherent rationality. Descartes
insists that the two basic and inborn operations of reason—intuition and deduction—must be presupposed even to understand his
rules of method. An analogy to the syllogistic logic (of which he
was no devotee) may help. On one level it is highly useful to distinguish a syllogistic rule—for example, the formula "All A are B;
therefore, if something is not B then it is not A." Although it is
useful to distinguish this rule, because there are circumstances
under which someone may inadvertently neglect it, it is obvious
that anyone who can recognize the truth of so basic a rule is
already fully able to reason syllogistically—for to explain to a
person why he ought to follow the rule, one would have to use
the rule in formulating the explanation.

Before discussing intuition and deduction and the rules of
method whereby Descartes directs them, it is extremely helpful to
understand the general conception of mind to which he adheres
in the *Rules*. It must be stressed that he did not undertake to
prove this general conception of mind until he wrote his later
treatises: the *Treatise on Man* (1633), the *Dioptrics* (1637), and
most important, the *Meditations*.

Descartes considers the human mind as capable of acting upon
the human body (for example, in voluntary motions) and as
capable of being affected by the body (for example, when light
rays cause us to see color, or when particles in motion allow us to
hear noises that we recognize as intelligent speech). Nevertheless,
he considers the human mind and human body to be distinct
things. According to him the human body—brain, muscles, nervous system, and so on—is a material thing that is extended in space,
whereas the human mind is not material or extended in space.
Furthermore, he considers the human mind to be much more
easily known than the human body. Perhaps the best way to lead

up to Descartes's conception of the mind is by cursorily examining his conception of the human body. The details of his physiological theory are undoubtedly antiquated; but we can gain some understanding of why he believes the mind is easier to know than the body and of why he thinks no theory can be correct that identifies reasoning, or even sense experiences—such as colors, feelings, smells, and so on—with physiological processes.

In the *Rules* Descartes works with the outline of a physiological theory he is to develop more fully in subsequent treatises. In rudimentary form it goes something like this. The human body is composed of many organs that themselves are composed from fundamental physical particles. The only force that one particle can exert upon another is the force of physical impact by means of collision (action at a distance is not allowed). Thus the external sense organs can be affected only when they are impinged upon by particles that, in accordance with the laws of motion governing collisions, are suited to move certain of the many nerve fibers present in them. These fibers are enclosed in nerve tubes, and both tubes and fibers extend to the interior of the brain. When a fiber is pushed by external particles impinging upon a sense organ, the end of its encasing nerve tube at the interior of the brain is opened to some degree. At this point certain particles, called animal spirits, do their work. These animal spirits originally got to the interior of the brain by a complicated process we cannot describe here. Suffice it to say they derive from the blood that makes its way to the brain after it has passed through the heart. These animal spirits follow certain laws of motion governing floating bodies—and when one or more nerve tubes are opened, the animal spirits rush toward them.

Some of these animal spirits pass into the nerve tubes and go to muscles, thus tending to create motions that are reflex reactions to the external stimuli. For example, when the optic fibers are violently pushed by intense light rays, the nerve tubes in the brain will open so much that many animal spirits pass into them; these animal spirits will then proceed to the muscles of the eye and cause the eyelids to shut. Moreover, when a number of nerve tubes are opened, as is always in fact the case, the animal spirits rush to them in a pattern corresponding to the distribution of the opened nerve tubes. This pattern in turn corresponds to differences in the particles impinging upon the external sense organ. Some of the animal spirits that rush in pattern to the opened nerve tubes create impressions among the fibers of the brain in the region of the nerve tubes. These impressions lay the foundation for memories and imaginations; they constitute what Descartes calls the corporeal fantasy or the corporeal imagination.

Finally, we come to the crucial point. Descartes considers that sense experiences—such as color, smell, feeling, and so on—occur, not in the brain, but in the mind—they are not the same as the brain movements that determine them. Nevertheless, these sense experiences always correspond to a cerebral activity; in his particular physiological theory they correspond to a motion of the animal spirits toward the nerve tubes opened by physical particles impinging upon the sense organs. Similarly, Descartes believes that sensuous imaginations and memories are mental experiences and do not occur in the brain. Nevertheless, they always correspond to cerebral motions; in his particular physiological theory they correspond to motions of the animal spirits into those corporeal memories and imaginations that have been implanted among the fibers of the brain during the previous processes of sensation.[3]

I hope I have said enough to indicate why, from Descartes's point of view, the mind is better known than the body. All familiar sensuous experiences (colors, smells, feelings, and so on), even those we normally describe as portraying or belonging to our body, are considered to be mental effects of highly complicated physiological processes—processes whose nature is by no means immediately revealed by the familiar colors, smells, and feelings produced by them. Indeed, Descartes emphasizes that one of the major and extremely difficult tasks of human reason is to pierce the veil of sense experiences and see through to its external causes. But this process of seeing beyond sense experience can obviously never be a seeing with the eyes; rather it requires us to use what is the most intimately known thing of all—namely, the mind's essential and nonsensuous power, which at various times he calls reason, intellect, or inborn wit. Thus, although sensations and imaginations are indeed mental experiences, they are by no means the only mental experiences. It is the essential feature of mind—namely, reason, intellect, or inborn wit—that alone enables us to think about, understand, or perceive any object, including even those sensations and imaginations that we recognize as among our experiences.

Descartes speaks of this reason, intellect, or inborn wit as "spiritual," implying that it is immediately discerned as something that does not take up space and therefore, according to him, is not material. The most generic description he applies to this reason, intellect, or inborn wit is the "knowing force." He emphasizes that this knowing force is not only spiritual but unitary. By this he means that the mind does not become more than one mind just because the reason, in addition to attending to sense experiences and imagination, also attends to its own nonsensuous nature or to its ideas of very many things—such as its ideas of God or other minds—that have no reference to the senses.

Occasionally Descartes draws finer distinctions in talking of reason or the knowing force. These distinctions turn on specific applications that the knowing force can make of its power to understand. We will learn something more about Descartes's conception of mind by attending to these distinctions.

The knowing force has power over the body, in particular, power over what Descartes calls the common sense and corporeal fantasy. By virtue of this power the knowing force can sense various things. Moreover, the knowing force also has power over the corporeal fantasy* whereby it can resurrect implanted memories. In so applying itself the knowing force is remembering. Furthermore, the knowing force is capable of devising new imaginations out of previously implanted memories, perhaps to serve the purposes of illustrating some idea of reason—e.g., devising a diagram appropriate to illustrating that $a^2 = 8$. In so applying itself the knowing force is imagining, conceiving, or exercising inborn wit or talent. Lastly, when the knowing force is considering some idea that has no reference to the senses (e.g., an idea that represents a contradiction, in which case there could not be a sensuous example, or the idea that represents its own nonsensuous nature), then the knowing force is said to be exercising pure intellect. It is imperative to note that whenever the knowing force applies itself in any of the above-mentioned ways, the reasoning, understanding, perceiving, or use of ideas occurs—for want of a better expression—"in" the reason or intellect. The sensible images about which we may reason are never identical with the nonsensuous activity of reasoning about them.

---

* *phantasia.*

Finally, we need to note the subtle nuance Descartes sometimes confers upon the phrase "inborn wit" or "inborn talents." As pointed out, he suggests that in its proper sense the phrase refers to the cases where the reason, intellect, or knowing force makes purposive use of certain images or diagrams to help illustrate its ideas. This proper sense of "inborn wit" or "inborn talents" sheds some light upon the complete title of the *Rules*—namely, *Rules for the Direction of the Native Talents*. Toward the end of the *Rules*, after explaining the method for using intuition and deduction, Descartes shows us how disciplined use of the imagination aids in preventing certain obscurities in the conceptions of both mathematicians and philosophers.[4]

Now, after this quick look at Descartes's general conception of mind, we are able to discuss the basic operations of reason—that is, intuition and deduction. After that we can proceed to the rules of method. But first we need to note the organization of the entire *Rules*, for its plan of organization is not readily apparent. On the basis of internal evidence the *Rules* is divided into three parts.[5] But unless one is already immersed in the subtleties of the treatise, Descartes's manner of indicating the function of a particular part is of little help. The more basic organization seems to be fourfold:

1. Rules I–IV: preliminary to the basic rules of method
2. Rules V–XII: explanation of the basic rules of method (rules I–XII constitute part one of the treatise)
3. Rules XIII–XXI: applications of the basic rules of method (rules XXII–XXIV, believed never to have been written, were intended for part two of the treatise[6])
4. Rules XXV–XXXVI: believed never to have been written but intended to be the third part of the treatise; they would have applied to "imperfectly understood" questions*[7]

RULES I–IV: PRELIMINARY TO THE BASIC RULES OF METHOD

Under rules I–IV Descartes (*a*) explains intuition and deduction and indicates his definition of knowledge, and (*b*) emphasizes the

---

* My discussion will concern only nos. 1–3.

need for a method to direct intuition and deduction and explains the criteria by which a method is judged to be sound.

INTUITION AND DEDUCTION AND THE DEFINITION OF KNOWLEDGE

By "deduction" Descartes does not mean syllogistic deduction. He considers deduction to be a process of inferring some new consequence or predicate from what is previously cognized. Moreover, a deduction is always necessary deduction—that is, the consequence inferred by deduction must follow necessarily from what has been previously cognized. For example, if one cognizes a line, then by necessary deduction one can infer that the line is necessarily divisible. By contrast, one could never infer that whatever is red must be hard. And as will be pointed out, Descartes argues that the operation of necessary deduction is also required to judge contingency—that is, that something is neither necessarily true nor necessarily not true. In order to know a consequence reached by necessary deduction, the deduction must ultimately begin from something that is capable of being known nondeductively, or "intuitively."

Whatever is known by intuition is called a "certain and evident" cognition. According to Descartes all knowledge is certain and evident cognition. Yet for some purposes he will stretch this definition, and for other purposes he will not. Sometimes the consequence deduced from an intuition can be reduced to an intuition—that is, once the deduction is made, the entire cognized complex can sometimes be understood or known as certainly and evidently as was the original object from which the deduction first proceeded. For example, after divisibility is inferred as necessarily true of a line, then the divisibility of a line is as clear and evident an object of intuition as was the line alone before the deduction took place. However, in the case in which deductions proceed so far that all the evidence for the final consequence cannot be reduced to intuition, or cannot be made all "evident" at once, we must presuppose the trustworthiness of memory when we consider ourselves to know the final consequence. In such a case the consequence is certain but not evident. Among his rules of method Descartes lists a rule of enumeration that is designed to guide us in the best possible manner in those circumstances in which deduced consequences become so far removed from basic intuitions that we cannot reduce them to intuitions.

For practical purposes, which include the ordinary purposes of mathematics, Descartes considers deduced consequences of this certain but not evident kind to be knowledge. Yet when the question of absolutely firm knowledge or metaphysical certitude will be broached, as in his *Discourse* and *Meditations*, deductive consequences of this certain but not evident kind are not accepted as knowledge. Instead, in his *Discourse* and *Meditations* Descartes will endeavor to devise arguments for God's existence that have no or minimal reliance upon the memory.[8] By contrast, he will emphasize that knowledge of deduced consequences in the sciences depends upon knowledge of God—that is, upon the knowledge that a good and infinite God guarantees our memories.

Descartes lists "experience" and "deduction" as the two sources of knowledge. Doing so in no way contradicts his claim that intuition and deduction are the fundamental operations of human reason. Rather he is accentuating the fact that intuition, which must be the starting point for worthwhile deductions, must grasp its object in a clear and evident experience. Since intuition is the fundamental operation whereby the mind grasps what is certain and evident in experience, it is useful to look at Descartes's definition of experience. The definition reminds us of the circumstances under which, instead of confining ourselves to what is certain and evident in experience, we might hastily rush on to make unwarranted assumptions about what experience shows us.

"We experience whatever we perceive by sense, whatever we hear from others, and generally whatever reaches our intellect either from elsewhere or from reflective contemplation upon itself."[9] Thus, in addition to sense experience and imagination, experience also includes our many ideas about innumerable things (for example, numbers, God, physical particles, and so on), whatever the source of these ideas, and however convincing or questionable we find them.

Indeed, there is little or no difficulty in knowing that we have ideas, even ideas about things whose nature or existence we doubt. The existence of our ideas in this sense—that is, of our ideas as our experiences—is a most readily available fact for intuition, and it plays a paramount role in Descartes's subsequent metaphysics.

The crucial difficulty is that the various things, natures, or objects represented in our ideas (what in the *Meditations* Descartes calls the "objective realities" in our ideas) are ordinarily so complicated and obscure that we cannot clearly and evidently understand them. They are not simple enough things or natures to be objects of intuition. Hence if ever we are to understand them, or see through to their nature, we must reach them through a process of reasoning that commences from the simple objects grasped by intuition and proceeds by necessary deductions to arrive at the point where we do comprehend them.

It must be kept in mind that the process of clarifying a complicated idea and the process of reaching it by necessary deductions from simple objects of intuition are one and the same; moreover, until the complicated idea is understood in this way, we will never be in a firm position to judge the existence of an object outside the intellect corresponding to the nature represented in the complicated idea. Thus, for example, if one does not understand why a triangle has 180 degrees, then one is never in a position to know with clarity and evidence that some object exists that is a triangle —that is, something with 180 degrees included under three closed straight lines in a plane. Moreover, until a complicated idea has been deduced from intuition by necessary steps, there is always a danger that what is represented by the complicated idea is contradictory and thus impossible. Thus since mathematical concepts would have to be known not to involve contradictions before one could know the existence of matter described by them, it should be more obvious why, as said above, Descartes considers the intellect or reason as easier to know than the body.

Lastly, it should be emphasized that Descartes views the criterion of necessity, presumably provided by his concept of necessary deduction, as so vital to human reason that without it we cannot definitively construe the notion of mere possibility, or contingency. Necessary deduction ipso facto provides a criterion of impossibility. For example, if it is deduced that a line is necessarily divisible, then an indivisible line is impossible; or if it is deduced that divisibility can attach only to an extended magnitude, then a nonextended magnitude is necessarily not divisible. What is recognized as not necessarily true of something and also as involving no denial of what is necessarily true of that thing is thereby known as being merely possibly, or contingently, true of that thing. For example, if a line is recognized as not necessarily opposite to an angle and not necessarily not opposite to an angle, a line is thereby known as being merely possibly, or contingently, opposite to an angle. We will find the relation between necessity and possibility highly relevant to understanding Descartes's principal proof of God's existence in the *Discourse* and *Meditations*.

Furthermore, for Descartes sense experience or imagination provides no basis for definitively construing the notions of necessity, impossibility, and contingency—as is made clear in the wax experiment in the Second Meditation and in other of his writings.[10] For the present, a brief discussion of the matter must suffice. Attention shows that when we describe the data of sense or imagination, concepts are always involved in our description; and to comprehend these concepts requires that we reason about them by necessary deductions. If, for example, one describes a seen color, it is likely that one would think of it as something extended in space. If so, then one is assuming that its essence (quiddity, whatness, or formal cause) necessarily involves spatiality. Hence to understand what a colored thing is, and certainly to individuate such a thing, one would have to understand how to reason about spatiality. But to reason about spatial things, one would have to use the inborn skill of *intellect*, which, through necessary deductions, discerns what is necessarily true of, impossible for, and consequently what is contingent about, spatial or geometrical objects of various kinds, such as squares, circles, and so on. For how could sense or imagination account for such reasoning? Indeed, sense experience and imagination never display impossibility and never isolate necessity; and since the mathematically contingent can be appreciated only when we understand these former things, the presentations of sense, although they are indeed possible, cannot explain our understanding of the possibilities they exemplify.

NEED FOR A METHOD TO DIRECT INTUITION AND DEDUCTION AND CRITERIA BY WHICH SUCH A METHOD IS JUDGED TO BE SOUND

The need for a method to direct intuition and deduction is manifest. To be sure, if we have already reached the complicated object by necessary deductions from intuition, there is no problem in comprehending it. However, the genuine difficulty in the case of any complicated object that confronts us is to find which intuitions, and which of the sometimes numerous possible necessary deductions from them, will best help us either to reach the complicated object or to discern that knowledge of it is beyond the realm of human reason.

Thus the complicated object is like a question. The directives of a sound method would tell us the procedures by which we would best avail ourselves of the resources of intuition and deduction in order to arrive at the answer to the question or determine that the answer is beyond our capability. In speaking of a sound method Descartes says: ". . . by a method I understand certain and easy rules such that whoever has employed them exactly never supposes anything false as true, and without uselessly consuming his mental effort but rather always gradually increasing his knowledge, will arrive at a true cognition of all those things of which he will be capable."[11] He calls his method "universal mathematics" only because he discerned its rules in conjunction with his studies of algebra and geometry. But he is insistent that the rules of his method constitute a generally applicable logic of discovery: ". . . this discipline ought to contain the first rudiments of human reason and extend itself to drawing out truths from every subject matter. Freely speaking, I am persuaded that this mathematics is more powerful than every other cognition humanly handed down to us, since it is the source of all of them."[12]

The emphasis upon directing the mind at the beginning and throughout the process of acquiring new knowledge is essential to Descartes's conception of sound method. And before turning to his rules of method, it is helpful to note why Descartes thinks naïve reliance upon syllogistic logic becomes an impediment to sound method and blinds one to accessible truths.

According to Descartes syllogistic logic does not enable us to discover new knowledge—it does not allow us to infer new predicates such as those that issue from his operation of necessary deduction. Consequently, syllogistic logic provides no sufficient criterion for determining what is universally necessary, impossible, or contingent; nor does it provide a sufficient criterion for deciding which nonuniversal propositions express a connection of terms that is necessary, impossible, or contingent. Hence syllogistic logic is not sufficient to enable us to decide what evidence is required to verify existential propositions—for example, the proposition "I see red (or seem to see red); therefore space exists"; or

"I exist, and there is no cause of my existence"; or "I decide on the basis of the evidence; therefore I have a free will." The danger Descartes perceives is that if someone forgets these severe limits to syllogistic logic, he will be tempted to feign premises that confer the illusion of probability or verisimilitude upon the denial of truths that an adequate method would enable us to intuit or reach by necessary deduction from intuited truths.[13]

RULES V–XII: EXPLANATION OF THE BASIC RULES OF METHOD

We can now consider the rules of the method Descartes uses to direct the inborn operations of intuition and deduction. Let us recall that a sound method would direct one to the proper object from which to proceed by necessary deduction to the complicated object whose true nature is in question. From the outset we should be aware that Descartes is not suggesting that every complicated object can be understood by human reason; rather, he is asserting that with a sound method we shall be able to decide which complicated objects (objects whose natures are obviously not immediately self-evident) must always escape our complete comprehension. As a consequence of a sound method we will be left with a better understanding of what must remain merely probable and problematic for human intelligence. Furthermore, we should be aware that Descartes in no way intends his rules of method to take one mechanically to the solution of a question. He criticizes syllogistic logic because it does not demand the skill required in making the proper deductions of new predicates relevant to the solution of a proposed question. Indeed, his rules of method require that we cultivate "perspicacity" and "sagacity"—that is, that we first practice separating simple things from complex things, thus fostering finesse in using intuition, and then practice making deductions, so that we acquire finesse at recognizing which of many possible deductions are most relevant to the solution of a proposed question. William James once noted that the same premises in two persons' mouths do not come to the same thing. Descartes had that in mind.

It is best first to discuss Descartes's rules of method without referring to the subtleties of his examples. Later, we can concern ourselves with these aspects. As stated, Descartes treats any complicated object like a question or a proposition to be proved. He presumes nobody is so deprived of reason that he cannot recognize more basic questions that must be faced before he can answer the proposed question and comprehend the complicated object. Thus, by reductive analysis, we set up a series: the simplest or absolute element is at one end, the complicated object is at the other end, and in between are the steps through which we must pass. We cannot know the complicated object unless we can proceed by necessary deductions from the simplest or absolute element all the way up to the complicated object.

As we move away from simple or absolute elements by necessary deductions, we often arrive at a point at which we can no longer intuitively grasp all the evidence linking the absolute element to the point at which we have arrived: we cannot reduce deduction to intuition, and the most we may have is certain but not evident cognition. When we have no way of reaching a complicated object (or solving our major question, which is to discern its nature) without relying upon the memory, Descartes then employs the technique he calls "enumeration" or "induction." At times he seems to mean different things by enumeration; hence, we must understand the range of his meanings.

In its most basic sense enumeration requires us to identify fastidiously the things we must comprehend and establish before we can comprehend the nature of the complicated object that is our major question. These subordinate things will all be in a continuous chain or they will not. If they form one chain, then we simply try to move from the absolute element of intuition to the first thing to be proved or comprehended or solved. If we succeed, we write that fact down to aid our memory, and we proceed until we are either stopped or arrive at the complicated object. If some or all of the things that must be proved are disjoint, then we must examine different chains leading from an absolute element or elements of intuition.

Descartes uses the concept of enumeration in another sense that accentuates the crucial role played by necessary deduction in answering questions about a thing's essential nature. If the question to be solved is whether any A is a B, we do not always have to start counting A's. If we enumerate the properties that necessary deduction shows to be in any A, and if we find one property always in any A that necessary deduction shows is impossible for any B, then we know that no A could be a B. For example, suppose we are inquiring whether a material thing (brain) could be a mind. If in enumerating the properties necessarily in a material thing we find one property (for instance, the property of divisibility) that necessary deduction shows is incompatible with the nature of a mind, then we know that no material thing could be a mind. Descartes, after some elaborate preliminaries, uses such an enumeration in his *Meditations* in order to show that mind and body are different substances.[14]

In introducing these rules of method Descartes defines the "absolute nature," and he also defines what he calls "relative natures." The absolute nature is a simple nature, grasped by intuition, and it is the starting point in the chain of necessary deductions leading to the complicated object or nature in question. Relative natures are all those natures or things along the chain of necessary deductions from the absolute nature. Relative natures presuppose the absolute nature (participate in it) and have peculiar relations to it. For example, if a line is the absolute nature, then a square is a relative nature, because it is derived from the line in a specific manner and therefore contains peculiar relations to the line.

Some relative natures are more complicated than others, and the more complicated relative natures are those farther away from the absolute nature. For example, the cube is a more complicated nature than the square. In the chain of necessary deductions from the line, the cube is further away than the square. Because the square enters into the construction of the cube, the cube has more relations to the line than the square has. To take another example, reasoning is an absolute nature and doubting a relative nature. That is so because doubting presupposes an idea that is doubted, whereas to have the idea it is not necessary to be doubting about it—the same idea may be contemplated, affirmed, or denied. Hence doubting involves a peculiar (and certainly not a geometrical) relation to an idea. Descartes notes that the absolute nature is that which is required in solving questions—e.g., without the line we could not understand the relations that make a square, a cube, and so on. In like fashion Descartes regards equality as an absolute nature required for answering questions about unequal things. In other words, our ability to determine that $x \neq y$ demands that we have a notion of unity whereby we can at least determine that *x* and *y* do not contain this unity in the same amount.

The relations, or proportions, that relative things have to an absolute nature can themselves be simple natures and easily grasped by intuition.[15] For example, a triangle is a relative thing constructed from lines. One of the relations that may exist in a triangle is that the line constituting some side of the triangle is oblique to another line of the triangle. This obliqueness can itself be a simple element of intuition and enter into very many relative things. Descartes insists that all the most simple natures that the mind can divide no further are either material, spiritual, or common. Moreover, whatever ultimate subject we conceive must be conceived as composed either from common natures and the necessary and contingent connections of simple material natures or from common natures and the necessary and contingent connections of simple spiritual natures. For example, such natures as obliqueness, motion, figure, and so on, can be conceived only as composing things, such as triangles or rhombuses, that are material or bodily. By contrast, spiritual or thinking subjects are composed from such natures as reasoning, doubting, affirming, and so on. One of the major goals of Descartes's metaphysical treatises, especially of the *Meditations,* is to prove that this division of finite subjects into two ultimate kinds, material and spiritual, is irreducible. In the *Meditations* he argues that it is absolutely false to suggest that minds could be the same as matter. From his point of view it is equally false and equally foolish to suggest that a mind could be material or that bodies could be mental. And, as we shall soon see, there is further evidence that even as early as the *Rules* Descartes is inclined to assert this dualism of simple subjects or substances.

Speaking of those common natures or common notions mentioned above, Descartes says:

> Finally those things are said to be common that are attributed both to corporeal and to spiritual things, such as existence, unity, duration, and similar things. To this group are referred all those common notions that are like bonds joining some simple natures to others and provide the evidence for whatever we conclude when reasoning. Examples of such common notions are these: that things that are the same as a single third thing are the same as each other; that things that cannot be referred in the same way to

the same third thing have some difference between them, and so on. And, indeed, these common notions can be known either by the pure intellect or by the intellect when it intuits images of material things.[16]

It is useful to glance at Descartes's list of common notions having to do with causality.[17] One of the crucially important elements in his proofs of the existence of God in the *Discourse* and *Meditations* is to show that, in light of these intuitively known common notions or axioms governing causality, God must necessarily exist. These common notions or axioms may be difficult to understand without a knowledge of the *Discourse* and *Meditations;* I will comment upon the technicalities involved in my introductions to those works.

RULES XIII–XXI: APPLICATIONS OF THE BASIC RULES OF METHOD

As mentioned, in its most proper sense Descartes uses the expression "inborn wit" (or "native talents") to designate the circumstances under which human reason purposively devises certain imaginations to better clarify certain of its ideas and thus avoid mistakes. In this way the imagination is brought into a partnership with reason and made its useful tool.

In this section of the *Rules* Descartes illustrates how, and the extent to which, well-chosen figures aid reason in discerning general formulas that reveal the true natures of geometrical figures. Moreover, he is interested to show that with the help of certain figures represented in the imagination, reason will not inadvertently postulate numbers or figures that in reality it does not understand.

Descartes also launches, it seems to me, a critique of doctrines similar to those contained in Thomas Aquinas's important treatise *On Being and Essence.*[18] Furthermore, what Descartes has to say here (together with many refinements contained in his subsequent treatises) provides an indication of how he is to develop his own doctrines regarding substances and their real distinction from each other. But to understand his argument in this section of the *Rules,* it is first necessary to recall what we have already discussed. In his treatment of simple natures, Descartes points out that although the intellect of man can consider these simple natures separately from others, it is nonetheless true that some of them necessarily presuppose others and that they cannot be conceived to exist except in a specific kind of subject—that is, either in a material subject or a spiritual subject. For example, "figure" can be understood independently from another simple nature such as "motion"; yet both figure and motion presuppose "extension," which cannot be conceived to exist except in the subject that Descartes calls "body" or "the extended."

Now, Descartes argues that inattention or inadvertence has caused certain philosophers to conclude that extension itself, which is presupposed by figure, motion, and so on, can be conceived to exist without whatever thing or body is the "subject" of extension (and presumably he means to imply that these philosophers have also thought that the body or subject of extension could exist without its extension).

Descartes insists that, if any extension exists, there is some "thing"—that is, some "subject," or as he eventually calls it, some "substance"—in which that extension inheres. He also insists that we can in no way conceive this thing, subject, or body in which extension inheres except by its extension—in short, according to him extension is not just a mode of an extended thing that need not in fact be in the extended thing at all; rather, it is the necessary attribute of the extended thing and therefore inseparable from it. Descartes suggests that the reason why philosophers have been led to falsely believe that extension need not always be in the extended thing is simply because they can intellectually consider extension without attending to the thing that is extended. However, if they were correct in saying that the extension could exist without an extended subject, presumably they would have some idea of this extension as it would be without its subject. And it is here that Descartes recommends a use of the imagination. He insists that if one attends to the image by which one pictures extension, one will notice that one cannot imagine the extension without imagining an extended subject. Hence, one will no longer believe that this extension might fail to be in an extended subject. Similarly, Descartes thinks that this ingenious use of the imagination will also make it more obvious that the "thing" or "subject" that has extension cannot be clearly understood or conceived to exist without its extension.

It is this general point—namely, that the "thing," "subject," or "substance" cannot be understood except through an essential property and, furthermore, that an essential property cannot be conceived to exist without its subject and, vice versa, that its subject cannot be conceived to exist without it—that becomes crucial to Descartes's later doctrine of substances and their real distinction from each other. For since we cannot, for example, represent the thing that has extension without its extension, it follows that this thing that has extension cannot be the same thing (or substance) as that thing (or substance) in which there inheres a property other than extension—such as the property of thinking, which can indeed be conceived to exist without extension. Thus mind and matter cannot be identical, and man is a composite of two different things or substances. These important matters undergo much refinement in the *Discourse* and *Meditations,* and I will place a special emphasis upon the strategies that Descartes employs to distinguish substances.[19] However, I must add here that while Descartes does not believe that any two substances could be identical, it is another question whether any substance could cause its own existence or explain all its modifications. And we shall find in examining his later treatises and in developing our comments upon those common notions or axioms governing causality that Descartes argues, first, that all things or substances other than God must depend for their existence (and indeed for their very nature) upon God and, second, that finite substances, such as the human mind and matter, can interact.

SOURCES FOR THE LATIN TEXT

The *Rules* is first mentioned in an inventory of Descartes's papers made at Stockholm in 1650. These papers were transported to Paris under the auspices of the French ambassador to Sweden, Chanut, who consigned them to the care of his brother-in-law, Clerselier. The original Latin manuscript of the *Rules* was seen by Arnauld and Nicole in connection with the preparation of the second edition of the *Logique* of Port Royal (1664). Clerselier eventually left the papers to the care of the abbé Legrand, who made the original manuscript of the *Rules* available to Descartes's biographer, the abbé Baillet. After Legrand's death in 1704 the original manuscript of the *Rules* was lost.

Two manuscript copies of the *Rules* were originally in Holland. One manuscript copy, now lost, seems to have been in the possession of a Cartesian, Jean de Raey, who apparently made it available to serve as the basis for the first printed edition of the *Rules* contained in the *Opuscula Posthuma*, published at Amsterdam in 1701. The second manuscript copy, still extant, was acquired by Leibniz at Amsterdam in 1670. It is now at Hanover. Adam and Tannery rely principally upon the published Amsterdam text of 1701, but they take into account the Hanover manuscript in arriving at their Latin text of the *Rules*.* I have followed the Adam and Tannery Latin text except in a few cases that I note. "A" is used to signify the Amsterdam published text, and "H" signifies the Hanover manuscript.

---

* *Regulae, Oeuvres*, vol. X, pp. 351–357.

1 # Rules for the Direction of the Native Talents

2 <center>RULE I</center>

The goal of studies should be to direct the inborn talents toward producing solid and true judgments concerning everything that presents itself.

3 Each time men recognize some similarity between two things, it is their habit to judge, even as regards that in which the things differ, that what they have learned true of one is true of both. Thus they mistakenly compare the sciences, all of which consist in the cognition of the reason, with the arts, which require a specific condition and use of the body. And since they have seen that all of the arts should not be learned at the same time by the same person, but that he who works at one art only will more easily develop into the best artist—because the same hands cannot be so easily trained for cultivating fields and plucking the cithara or for many different tasks of this kind as for one of them —they have also believed the same thing concerning the sciences. And distinguishing the sciences from each other by the diversity of their objects, they have decided that individual sciences should be researched separately, omitting all the others. In that they are certainly deceived. For since the sciences taken together are nothing but human wisdom, which always remains one and the same however much it is applied to different objects, and since this human wisdom derives no greater distinction from these objects than does the light of the sun from the variety of things it illumi-

nates, there is no need to restrain our inborn talents within any limits. The cognition of one truth unlike the practice of one art does not hinder us from discovering another, but rather helps. And indeed it seems astonishing to me that most people very diligently examine the customs of men, the effects of plants, the motions of the stars, the transmutations of metals, and the objects of similiar disciplines, and yet in the meanwhile almost nobody thinks about the good mind, or this universal wisdom—for in the end every other thing is to be esteemed not so much because of itself as because it relates to this. And accordingly it is not without merit that we propose this rule as the first of all the rules, because nothing sooner leads us away from the right way of searching after truth than to direct our studies not to this general goal but to some particular goals. I am not speaking of perverse and damnable goals, such as empty glory or dishonorable gain: in respect to them it is obvious that specious reasonings and chicaneries suited to the native bent of common people suggest a journey that is far more of a shortcut than the solid cognition of the truth can allow. Rather I mean to speak of honest and praiseworthy goals, because often we are more subtly deceived by these—for example, when we search for sciences useful either for the comforts of life or for that pleasure found in the contemplation of the truth, which is about the only happiness in this life that is complete and untroubled by pain. Now, we can indeed expect these as the legitimate fruits of the sciences; but were we to think of them as among the things we ought to study, the effect would often be to omit many things that are necessary for the cognition of others, either because at first they seem to us of little utility or because they seem of little interest. Thus we should believe that all the sciences are so connected among themselves that it is far easier to learn all at the same time than to separate one from the others. Therefore if someone earnestly wishes to investigate the truth of things, he should not hope to find any isolated science—for all the sciences are joined together and dependent upon each other. Rather let him think only of increasing the natural light of reason, not to resolve this or that difficulty of the school, but in order that in the individual contingencies of life his intellect shall point out to his will what ought to be chosen. Thus in a brief period of time he will be astonished that he has made far greater progress than those who study particular sciences and that he has become adept, not only at everything others long after, but even at things loftier than they are capable of anticipating.

4   RULE II

*It is proper to deal only with those objects concerning which
our inborn talents seem sufficient to achieve a certain
and indubitable cognition.*

5 All knowledge is certain and evident cognition. He who doubts about many things is not more learned than one who has never thought about them; on the contrary, he seems less learned if he has conceived a false opinion about any of them. Thus, by similar reasoning, it is better never to study than to deal with such very difficult objects that, being unable to distinguish what is true from what is false, we are forced to admit what is doubtful as certain—for in dealing with such objects the prospect of increasing our learning is not so great as the danger of decreasing it. And so by this proposition we reject all those merely probable cognitions and declare that only those things should be believed that are perfectly known and incapable of being doubted. And although those who have derived their education from much reading may perhaps persuade themselves that there are indeed very few such cognitions—because, sharing a common fault of human beings, they neglect to reflect upon such cognitions as too easy and obvious to everyone—nevertheless I warn them that there are far more such cognitions than they believe and that these suffice for demonstrating with certainty innumerable propositions about which they, until this very day, have been able to speak only with probability. Indeed, since they have thought it unworthy in a man of letters to admit that he does not know something, they so accustomed themselves to embellish their contrived reasonings that afterward they gradually convinced themselves and thus peddled these reasons to others as truths.

6   Truly, if we employ this rule well, very few things present themselves to which it is proper to turn our attention in order to learn about them. For there is hardly any question in the sciences over which talented men have not often disagreed among themselves. Yet whenever there is a difference in the judgments of two talented men regarding the same thing, it is certain that

at least one of them is deceived, and it furthermore seems that not even one of them has knowledge: for if the reasoning of one of them were certain and evident, he could explain it to the other in such a manner that he would finally also convince the other's intellect. Therefore we seem unable to acquire perfect knowledge of any probable opinions of this kind, because we cannot without rashness hope for more from ourselves than others have achieved; so it follows that if we are placing our wager correctly, there remain only arithmetic and geometry, from among the sciences already discovered, to which the observance of this rule reduces us.

Nevertheless, we do not on that account condemn what others 7 have thus far discovered—namely, the technique of philosophizing and those instruments for inflicting pain, so useful in waging wars, the probable syllogisms of the scholastics. These undoubtedly give exercise to the native talents of boys and instill in them a certain drive to excel; and it is far better to develop their talents by opinions of this kind—even if these opinions are uncertain since they are disputed among the learned—than to leave the boys to themselves. For perhaps without a guide boys would proceed straight to the precipice; whereas as long as they follow the footsteps of their teachers, although sometimes they may turn away from the truth, they nevertheless will be undertaking a journey that is more secure at least in this sense, that it will already have been tried by the more prudent. And we ourselves rejoice that in former days we were instructed in the schools; but because we are already freed from the obligation that bound us to the words of the master, and because at last upon attaining sufficient maturity we have withdrawn our hand from their rod, if now we seriously wish to propose rules for ourselves by whose help we may ascend to the height of human cognition, this rule must certainly be admitted among the first of our rules: namely, we must be on guard lest we misuse our free time as do many who, neglecting situations where things are easy, occupy themselves only with difficult things concerning which they ingeniously trumpet what certainly are very subtle conjectures and very probable reasonings—but after many labors, finally, and late in their lives, recognize they have only added to the multitude of their doubts, gaining nothing in the way of knowledge.

8   We have said a little bit above that from among the disciplines
familiar to others only arithmetic and geometry exist as free of
every stain of falsity or uncertainty. In order that we may more
diligently set forth the reason why this is so, it must be noted that
we arrive at the cognition of things in a twofold way, namely,
through experience and deduction. Moreover, it is to be noted
that our experiences of things are often mistaken, but deduction,
or the pure inference of one thing from another, although it can
be neglected if it is not recognized, can never be wrongly performed by an intellect rational in the least degree. And for this
purpose those fetters of the dialecticians by which they suspect
that they govern human reason seem to me to do little good,
although I do not deny that they are very suited to other uses.
Surely all deception that can befall men—I speak of men, not
beasts—never results from wrong inference, but only because experiences that are insufficiently understood are falsely accepted,
or judgments are rashly and without foundation maintained as
certain.

9   From this it is evidently gathered why arithmetic and geometry
exist as far more certain than all the other disciplines—namely,
because they alone deal with an object so pure and simple that
they obviously do not falsely suppose anything that experience
has rendered uncertain, but rather totally consist in rationally
deducing consequences. They are therefore the most easy and
perspicuous of the disciplines and have an object such as we require, since in these two sciences it seems that a human mind
is scarcely able to err except by inadvertence. Nevertheless, we
should not be astonished if the native talents of many people are
spontaneously directed to other arts or to philosophy rather than
to arithmetic and geometry. This happens because everyone more
confidently allows himself the license to play the seer in obscure
matters than in evident ones; and it is far easier to conjecture
something by way of answering any question whatever than to
come to the very truth itself concerning a single question however
easy that question is.

10   Certainly, from all this it is to be concluded, not indeed that
arithmetic and geometry alone are to be learned, but only that
those who seek the correct path of truth ought not occupy themselves with any object concerning which they cannot have a certainty equal to the demonstrations of arithmetic and geometry.

RULE III   11

*As regards the objects proposed for our study, we ought to inquire
into what we can clearly and evidently intuit or deduce with
certainty, and not into what others have opined or into
what we ourselves conjecture—for in no other
way is knowledge acquired.*

The books of the Ancients should be read because it is an enor-   12
mous benefit for us to be able to make use of the labors of so many
men. In this way we become acquainted with those things that
were already correctly discovered in past times, and we also bring
ourselves to recognize what further remains to be thought out in
all the disciplines. Yet in the meanwhile there is the strong danger
that perhaps those stains of error contracted from an excessively
attentive reading of the ancients will remain with us, however
unwanted and however much we guard against them. For authors
are accustomed to be of such a native bent that whenever, because
of some ill-considered belief on their part, they themselves have
relapsed into assuming the very thing that is crucially at issue in
some difference of opinion, they will then attempt with very subtle
arguments to draw us along the same path. Indeed, on the other
hand, whenever they have luckily discovered anything certain and
evident, they never display the thing except as complicated by
various intricacies—either because they fear that the dignity of
their discovery will be diminished by the simplicity of the explanation or because they begrudge us any easily accessible truth.

However, even if authors were all truthful and candid and   13
never thrust dubious things upon us as though they were true, but
instead explained everything in good faith, still, since there is
nevertheless hardly anything said by one author whose contrary
is not asserted by another, we would always be uncertain which
of them should be believed. And it would be of no value to count
opinions in order to follow that held by most [authors]: for in the
case of a difficult question it is much more credible that the truth
could be discovered by a few rather than by many. But even if all
agreed among themselves, nevertheless their doctrines would not
suffice for us: for example, we shall never become mathematicians,
even though we hold in memory all their demonstrations, unless
our native talents are suited for solving mathematical problems of
whatever kind; likewise, we shall never become philosophers if,

having read all the arguments of Plato and Aristotle, we are yet unable to produce a firm judgment concerning the topics proposed. In such cases we would seem to have learned history, not the sciences.

14   We furthermore warn that conjectures are never to be admitted into our judgments concerning the truth of things. Attention to this matter is of no small importance: for there is no more telling explanation why nothing is found in the common philosophy so evident and certain that it cannot be shown controversial than the fact that those who first study, not being content to become acquainted with things that are perspicuous and certain, have dared even to assert obscure and unknown things that they arrived at by probable conjectures only; and then they gradually came to bestow total trust upon these things and, mixing them indiscriminately with true and evident things, they finally have been unable to conclude anything that did not seem to depend upon some proposition of this probable kind and that for that reason was not uncertain.

15   But in order that we in turn do not fall into the same error, we here list all the acts of our intellect through which we can arrive at a cognition of things without any fear of deception; and only two such acts are admitted, namely, intuition and deduction.*

16   By *intuition* I understand, not the fluctuating testimony of the senses nor the deceiving judgment of an imagination that constructs things badly, but so easy and distinct a conception of the pure and attentive mind that there remains no further doubt concerning that which we understand; or what is the same thing, I mean an indubitable conception of the pure and attentive mind that is born from the light of reason alone and is more certain even than deduction because it is simpler—although deduction, as we noted above, also cannot be wrongly performed by man. Thus everyone can intuit with his reason that he exists, that he thinks,

---

* Adam and Tannery give *inductio* rather than *deductio*. A and H contain *inductio*, although the phrase & *inductio* is stroked over in H. There is reason to conclude that *inductio* is a copyist's error and that *deductio* is to be substituted: Descartes proceeds to contrast intuition and deduction (R 19); moreover, R 78–79 makes it clear that in Rule III deduction is contrasted to intuition. The substitution of *deductio* for *inductio* has been proposed by others; see *Regulae, Oeuvres*, vol. X, p. 694. It should be noted, however, that deduction not reduced to intuition is called induction (R 46, 79); hence intuition and induction do exhaust our ways of knowing (R 46).

that the triangle terminates in three lines only, that the sphere has a single superficies, and similar things—things far more numerous than very many people have noticed because they have disdained turning their mind to such easy things.

Furthermore, lest anyone is strongly disturbed by the new usage 17 of the word *intuition* as well as of other words that in the following pages I will try to remove from their common signification, I here warn generally that I plainly do not pay attention to the manner in which this vocabulary has been usurped by the schools in recent times, because it would be most difficult for me to use these very names and at the same time inwardly to suppose a different meaning for them. Rather I attend only to what each word signifies in Latin, so that whenever appropriate words are lacking I bestow upon those words that seem best suited a meaning of my own.

And indeed this evidence and certitude of intuition is required 18 not merely in single propositions but also in any process of rational connection. For example, if the conclusion is that 2 and 2 makes the same as 3 and 1, it must not merely be intuited that 2 and 2 makes 4 and that 3 and 1 also makes 4; but it must further be intuited that that third proposition, namely, the conclusion, is necessarily concluded from these two propositions.

At this point there can be a doubt why besides intuition we 19 have added another manner of knowing that is accomplished through *deduction*—by which we understand everything that is necessarily concluded from other things known with certainty. But this had to be done because many things, although not evident themselves, are known with certainty provided only they are deduced from true and known principles through a continuous and wholly uninterrupted movement of thinking that includes a perspicuous intuition of each thing. This is not different from how we know that the last link of some long chain is connected with the first: for even if we do not contemplate in one and the same intuition of the eyes all the intermediate links upon which this connection depends, we may nevertheless know the connection provided only we have run through each link successively and remember that each of them adheres to the next from first to last. Therefore we here distinguish an intuition of the mind from a certain deduction by the fact that in the latter some motion or some succession is conceived, while in the former this is not the case. Furthermore, a present evidence is not required for deduction such as for intuition; rather it derives its certitude in a certain manner from the memory. From all of this it can be gathered that certainly those propositions that are immediately concluded from first principles can be said, from different points of view, to be capable of being known sometimes by intuition and sometimes by deduction; however, those first principles themselves can be known only through intuition and, on the contrary, distant conclusions can be known only through deduction.

20   Thus these are the two most certain paths to knowledge, and we ought not admit that any others lie open to our native talents; on the contrary, all others are to be rejected as suspect and as pervious to errors. But nevertheless, this in no way prevents us from believing that things divinely revealed are more certain than every cognition, since faith in them and faith in whatever is obscure is not an action of our native wits but of the will; and if they have foundations in the intellect, those foundations can and ought to be discovered best of all by one of the two paths already spoken of, as perhaps one day we shall more amply show.

21   RULE IV
        A method is necessary for investigating the truth of things.

22   Mortals are gripped by such blind curiosity that often they lead their native talents down unknown paths; and they do so without any reason for hope but merely to make an experiment to see whether what they seek lies there. It is as if someone were burning with so foolish a desire of discovering a treasure that he constantly roamed the streets seeking whether he would by chance find something lost by a traveler. This is the way in which nearly all the chemists, very many of the geometers, and not a few of the philosophers study. I do not indeed deny that occasionally they wander so fortunately as to find something of the truth; nevertheless I do not on that account concede they are more industrious but merely that they are then more fortunate. It is truly far more preferable never to think of seeking the truth about anything than to do so without a method: for it is most certain that the natural light is confounded and our native talents blinded by obscure meditations and unsystematic studies of this kind. Furthermore, whoever thus become accustomed to walk in the darkness

likewise debilitate the keenness of their eyes, so that afterward they cannot bear the unobstructed light: and this experience again confirms when very often we see people who never devoted industry to letters judge far more solidly and clearly about obvious things than those who have remained perpetually in the schools. Hence by a method I understand certain and easy rules such that whoever has employed them exactly never supposes anything false as true, and without uselessly consuming his mental effort but rather always gradually increasing his knowledge, will arrive at a true cognition of all those things of which he will be capable.

But these two points must be stressed: never indeed to suppose   23
anything false as true, and to arrive at a cognition of everything [capable of being known by us]. For if we are ignorant of any one of those things that we can know, that occurs only because either we have never noticed any way that would lead us to such a cognition or we have lapsed into the contrary error. And if the method rightly explains how the intuition of the mind is to be used so that we do not lapse into the contrary error, and if it rightly explains how deductions are to be discovered so that we come to a cognition of all the things of which we are capable, then it seems to me that nothing else is required for the method to be complete—for, as said above, no knowledge can be obtained except through intuition of the mind or deduction. Neither can this method be extended to teaching how these operations of intuition and deduction are to be performed, because they are the simplest and primary; they are so much so that unless our intellect were already able to use them beforehand, it would not even comprehend any of the precepts of this very method, however easy they are. Moreover, the other operations of the mind which dialectic undertakes to direct with the aid of those just mentioned are here useless; or rather they are to be enumerated among obstacles, because nothing can be added to the pure light of reason that does not have the effect of obscuring it in some fashion.

Therefore, since the utility of this method is great, so that with-   24
out it it seems that attention to letters shall be harmful rather than profitable, I easily persuade myself that its utility has in some manner already formerly been seen by people of greater inborn talents who were indeed led to it by nature alone. For the human mind has something I know not what divine about it in which the first seeds of useful thinking are implanted in such manner that,

despite being suffocated by the brambling effect of certain studies, they often produce spontaneous fruit. This we experience in the easiest of sciences, arithmetic and geometry: for we can fairly reliably notice that the old geometers have used some kind of analysis that they extended to the resolution of all problems, although they begrudged divulging it to posterity. And at present there thrives a kind of arithmetic, which they call algebra, whose purpose is to operate upon numbers in the manner that the old geometers did upon figures. Moreover, these two disciplines [arithmetic and geometry] are nothing but the spontaneous fruits issued from the inborn principles of this method. Furthermore, I am not astonished that to date they have more successfully developed their very simple objects than happens in the other arts wherein greater obstacles are accustomed to suffocate them; yet even in these latter arts, provided only they are cultivated with the greatest care, they undoubtedly are capable of attaining to a perfect maturity.

25   Indeed, that is what I principally undertook to do in this treatise. For I certainly would not have made a great ado about these rules if they sufficed only for resolving inane questions such as the calculators or geometers are accustomed to play at during their leisure. In such a case I would have believed myself to have excelled in nothing except that I trifled more subtly than the others. And although in this treatise I shall be speaking a great deal about figures and numbers, because from no other disciplines can so evident and so certain examples be asked for, still, whoever will have attentively looked at my meaning will easily perceive that I have least in mind the common mathematics. On the contrary, I explain another discipline of which they are the outer garment rather than parts. And this discipline ought to contain the first rudiments of human reason and extend itself to drawing out truths from every subject matter. Freely speaking, I am persuaded that this mathematics is more powerful than every other cognition humanly handed down to us, since it is the source of all of them. I indeed spoke of the outer garment, not because I wish to conceal this doctrine and complicate it in order to ward off common people, but in order to so outfit it and adorn it that it can be better accommodated to the native talents of human beings.

26   When I first applied my reason to the mathematical disciplines,

I read through forthwith most of those matters that are customarily treated of by the mathematical authors. Above all, I cultivated arithmetic and geometry because they are said to be the simplest and, as it were, the paths to the others. But the writers on both these topics whose works then fell into my hands were not such as to greatly satisfy me. Certainly, I read a great deal by these authors concerning numbers, which I proved true by calculation. It was similar in regard to figures. In a certain manner they displayed many figures to my eyes, and from particular features of these figures they drew inferences as to consequences. However, they did not seem to show well enough to my very mind why these consequences follow and how they were discovered. And therefore I was not astonished that very many natively gifted and learned people after tasting of these arts quickly neglect them as childish and useless or, on the contrary, are deterred at the very outset from learning them—which happens whenever the beginning of something is filled with difficulties and intricacies. For there truly is nothing more inane than so to occupy ourselves with bare numbers and imaginary figures that as a result we seem to wish to repose in the cognition of these kinds of trifles; neither is there anything more vain than to so encumber ourselves with those superficial demonstrations—which are more often discovered by chance than by art and pertain more to the eyes and imagination than to the intellect—that as a result we in a certain manner become disaccustomed to use our very reason. At the same time there is nothing more intricate than to disentangle by such manner of examination new difficulties that are complicated by confused numbers. Indeed, when afterward I reflected about why therefore in former times the first discoverers of philosophy wished to admit nobody inexperienced at mathematics to the study of wisdom—as though this discipline seemed the easiest of all and the most necessary for instructing and preparing the inborn talents for grasping all the greater sciences—I clearly suspected that they had been familiar with some particular mathematics very different from the one common to our age. I am not of the opinion that they had known it perfectly, for the insane exultations and the sacrifices offered for the least impressive discoveries manifestly show that they were inexperienced. Nor would I alter this view because of particular machines of theirs celebrated by the historians: for it is possible that those machines were perhaps quite simple and yet could easily have been extolled to the character of miracles by an ignorant and wonder-prone multitude. But I am persuaded that those particular first seeds of truths implanted by nature in our inborn wits, which we have extinguished in ourselves by the daily reading and hearing of so many different errors, were of great strength in that inexperienced and pure antiquity; so that with the same light of the mind by which they saw that virtue is to be preferred to pleasure and honor to the useful, although they were ignorant of why these things are so, they also recognized the true ideas of mathematics and even of philosophy, although they were not yet able to pursue these sciences perfectly. And, indeed, particular vestiges of this true mathematics seem to me to appear even as late as Pappus and Diophantus* who did not live in the earliest age but nevertheless lived many centuries before the present. I believe that later on this true mathematics was suppressed by these very same writers out of some pernicious cunning. They strongly feared that because of the very great easiness and simplicity of what they had discovered the common people would vilify them. Hence they did what many artisans are known to have done with their own discoveries. In short, in order that we would come to admire them, they chose to show us as the effects of their art particular sterile truths already subtly demonstrated from their principles—this rather than to teach us the very art by which they deduced them, which obviously would have dispelled our wonder. Finally, in this century there have been some very natively gifted men who have attempted to resuscitate this same art. For that art which they call by the barbarous name algebra seems to be the same thing—if only it can be so purged of the many numbers and inexplicable figures with which it is obscured that afterward it would not lack that perspicuity and greatest facility that we suppose ought to be in true mathematics. When these reflections had called me back from the particular studies of arithmetic and geometry to some general mathematics, I sought at first to determine what precisely others understood by the name of "mathematics," and why not only those mentioned above, but even astronomy, music, optics, mechanics, and very many other studies are

---

* Pappus, mathematician of Alexandria during the reign of Theodosius I (379–395). Diophantus, mathematician, native of Alexandria. The age in which he lived is uncertain. Some place him in the reign of Augustus (27 B.C.–A.D. 14), others under Nero (54–68) or the Antonines (138–180).

called parts of mathematics. In this undertaking it does not suffice to consult the etymology of the word; for since the name "mathematics" signifies merely the same thing as does the name "discipline," these latter studies would with no less right than geometry itself be assigned to mathematics. However, despite that fact, there is nobody who having once set foot in the schools fails to distinguish easily in any subject matter presented to him between what pertains to mathematics and what pertains to the other disciplines. Considering this more attentively it finally became apparent that all and only those things in which order or measure are examined are to be referred to mathematics; nor does it make a difference whether such measure is sought after in numbers, figures, stars, sounds, or whatever object you wish; and accordingly I realized that what explains all these subject matters must be some general science that can search after order and measure as linked to no special matter; and this general science is named—and not with a novel word, but with one already inveterate and of received usage—universal mathematics, for in this universal mathematics is contained everything on account of which the other sciences are called parts of mathematics. Indeed, just how much this universal mathematics excels the other sciences subordinated to it in both utility and simplicity is manifest from the fact that it applies to all the same matters to which they apply as well as to a greater number of others. Also, if this universal mathematics contains certain difficulties, then the same difficulties exist even in these subordinate sciences; moreover, the subordinate sciences contain still further difficulties stemming from their specific objects that do not exist in universal mathematics. Now since everyone is certainly acquainted with the name of "universal mathematics," and since everyone understands it even if they do not attend to what it treats of, whence then does it happen that very many people laboriously pursue other disciplines that depend upon it and yet nobody cares to learn this very discipline of universal mathematics? This indeed would have astonished me had I not known that everyone considers universal mathematics the easiest of disciplines, and had I not long since noticed that human wit just premises whatever it believes can easily be presumed and then immediately hastens on to new and greater things.

By contrast, conscious of my limited powers, I decided to observe steadfastly such an order in my search for a cognition of

27

things that by always beginning with the most simple and easy things I would never proceed to others unless it seemed to me that there remained nothing more to hope for in these beginning things. For this reason I have cultivated till now as best I could that universal mathematics precisely so that afterward I would deem myself able without premature zeal to deal to some extent with the higher sciences. But before I move on from here I will attempt to collect in one place and to arrange in order whatever of my former studies I perceive to be more meriting of mention. I do this both so that when my memory diminishes with mounting years I can easily review from this book those studies made in previous years, and also so that with my memory relieved of these particulars I can more freely turn my reason to other matters.

28   RULE V

All method consists in the order and disposition of those things toward which the keen vision of the mind must be turned in order to discover any truth. Undoubtedly, we shall exactly employ this rule if we reduce by steps complicated and obscure propositions to simpler ones and thereafter try to ascend through those same steps from an intuition of the simplest of all things to a cognition of all the others.

29   In this method alone is contained the foundation of all human skill, and it is no less necessary to employ this rule in advancing toward a cognition of things than to use the string of Theseus in making one's way into the labyrinth. But many people either do not reflect upon what it teaches, or obviously ignore it, or presume themselves not to require it; and consequently they often examine very difficult questions without any order. Thus to my mind they act just as if they started at the bottom and attempted by one jump to reach the summit of some edifice, either neglecting the steps of the staircase designed for this purpose or never even noticing them. This is the way all the astrologers act who, without knowing the nature of the heavens nor having indeed observed their motions, nevertheless hope to be able to designate the effects of these motions. And in this way act very many people who, studying mechanics without physics, rashly design new instruments to produce motions. Moreover, in such manner do even those philosophers act who, neglecting experiments, believe the truth is

something that will spring from their own heads as Minerva issued from Jove's.

And certainly all these manifestly sin against this rule. More- **30** over, since the order that is required by this rule is often of a sufficiently obscure and intricate sort that not everyone can easily recognize it, it is hardly possible for such people to guard themselves sufficiently well against error unless they diligently observe what is explained in the following proposition.

RULE VI   31

In order to distinguish very simple from complicated things and to
search out such simple things in an orderly way, it is necessary,
in regard to each series of things in which we have directly deduced
some truths from others, to observe what is the most simple and
how all the others are either more, or less, or equally
removed from this.

Although this proposition seems to teach nothing truly new, it **32** nevertheless contains the principle secret of art; nor is there any more useful in this entire treatise. For it proclaims that all things can be laid out in certain series, not indeed so as to be referred to some genus of being, as the philosophers have divided them under their categories, but inasmuch as some can be known from others. Thus each time any difficulty occurs we can immediately notice whether it would be profitable to examine any others first, and which they are, and in what order.

Finally, to do this correctly it must first be noted that all things **33** considered in the sense in which they can be useful for our pur- pose—where we do not look at their isolated natures but compare their natures among themselves so as to know some from others— can be said to be either absolute or relative.

I call absolute whatever contains in itself the pure and simple **34** nature relevant to the question asked: so that everything that is considered as independent, cause, simple, universal, one, equal, similar, right, or others of this kind, is absolute; moreover, this same first nature I call the simplest and easiest because we use it in resolving questions.

The relative, however, is that which indeed participates in this **35** same absolute nature or at least in something of it according to which it can be referred to the absolute and deduced from it through some series; but furthermore, the relative also involves in its concept other particular features which I call relations—for example, whatever is called dependent, effect, composite, particular, many, unequal, dissimilar, oblique, and so on. The further these relations are removed from the absolute, the more relations of this kind do they contain subordinated one to another; we warn in this rule that all these must be distinguished and their reciprocal relations and natural order so observed that we can go from the last to the most absolute by passing through all the others.

36   And in this consists the secret of all art—namely, that we diligently notice in every series what is most absolute. From one point of view certain things are indeed more absolute than others, but yet from another point of view they are much more relative: as the universal is indeed more absolute than what is particular because it has a more simple nature, but yet it can also be said to be more relative than the particular in that it depends for existence upon individuals, and so on. In this way some things are occasionally truly more absolute than others, but nevertheless they are still not yet the most absolute of all: thus if we consider individuals the species is something absolute; if we look at the genus the species is something relative; among measurable things extension is something absolute; but among extended things length and so on are absolutes. And finally, to make it better understood that we are here considering the series of things to be known and not the nature of each thing individually, we have purposely enumerated cause and equality among the absolutes: for although among the philosophers cause and effect are indeed correlative, certainly here, if we seek for what the effect is, it is first necessary to know the cause and not vice versa. Likewise, equal things correspond reciprocally, but we do not know unequal things except by comparing them to equal ones and not vice versa.

37   It must be noted, secondly, that there are but few pure and simple natures that can be intuited first of all, through themselves, and independently of any others, either because they are themselves experienced or because of some light placed in us by nature; and it is these pure and simple natures that we say must be attended to diligently; for it is these same natures that in each series we call most simple. Moreover, all the other natures can only be perceived as deduced from these, either immediately or proxi-

mately, or through the use of two or three or more different conclusions; and the number of these conclusions is to be noted so that we recognize whether they are removed from the first and simplest proposition by many or fewer steps. It is in this way that in every subject matter those connections of consequences are established from which are born those series of things sought after to which every question must be reduced in order that it can be examined by a method that is certain. But because it is indeed not easy to enumerate every series, and furthermore because such series need not be so much held in memory as discerned by a particular acuteness of our inborn wits, we should seek some way of so forming our inborn wits that they will immediately discern what is required whenever the need arises. I have certainly learned that for this purpose nothing is more suitable than to accustom ourselves to reflect with a particular sagacity upon the least things we have already perceived to be derived from particular absolute, or simple and pure, natures.

Finally, it is to be noted, thirdly, that the starting point of studies is not to begin with the investigation of difficult things; rather, in order to prepare ourselves beforehand for undertaking determinate questions, it is first necessary to gather together without distinction all spontaneously obvious truths, and afterward to see gradually whether any others can be deduced from these, and still others from them, and so on. Then when this is done we must attentively reflect upon the truths discovered; and we must diligently think why we were first and more easily able to find some from others and which these are that we could so easily find; and thus when we shall come upon any determinate question, we can judge which other questions it would help us first to devote attention to in order to discover the answer to that question. For example, if it should occur to me that the number 6 is the double of 3, I would then seek for the double of 6, namely, 12: I would seek afterward, if it pleased me, for the double of this, namely, 24; and of that, namely, 48, and so on; and from here I would deduce, as can easily be done, that there is the same proportion between 3 and 6 as between 6 and 12 and 12 and 24, and so on; and accordingly I would deduce that the numbers 3, 6, 12, 24, 48, and so on, are continuously proportional: and undoubtedly after doing this—even if all these things are so perspicuous that properly speaking they are puerile—I understand by attentive reflection the rule by which all questions that can be proposed about proportions or relations are compounded and the order in which such questions ought to be investigated: and this one realization contains the foundations of all the science of pure mathematics.

39   Now, I first notice that it was not more difficult to discover the double of 6 than the double of 3; and it is the same in all cases: once given a proportion between any two magnitudes, it is no more difficult to discover innumerable other magnitudes that have the same proportion between them. Nor is the nature of the difficulty changed if we seek 3 or 4 or more [pairs of magnitudes] of this kind—namely, because each [pair] is to be discovered singly apart from each other and without relation to the others. Next, I notice that given the magnitudes 3 and 6, I will easily find the third magnitude in continuous proportion, namely, 12; but nevertheless it is not equally easy, given the two extremes 3 and 12, to find the mean magnitude 6; and the reason for this lies open for intuition, namely, that here arises another kind of difficulty obviously different from that involved in what preceded: for to discover the mean proportional it is necessary to attend simultaneously to the two extremes and to the proportion between them in order to take something from their division; and this is very different from the former case wherein from two given magnitudes it is required to discover a third in continuous proportion. Proceeding still further I examine whether, given the magnitudes 3 and 24, it would have been equally easy to discover one of the two mean proportionals, namely, 6 and 12; and here at last arises a different kind of difficulty more complicated than previous ones: for indeed here we must attend, not merely to one or to two, but to three different things in order to discover a fourth. I can go further and see whether, given only 3 and 48, it would have been still more difficult to discover one of the three mean proportionals—namely, 6, 12, and 24, which on first appearance do indeed seem more difficult to discover. But immediately afterward it occurs to me that this difficulty can be divided and broken down—namely, by first seeking after only one mean proportional, 12, which lies between 3 and 48; and then by seeking after another mean proportional, 6, which lies between 3 and 12; and finally by seeking after the mean proportional, 24, which lies between 12

and 48; and so the difficulty is reduced to the second kind of difficulty expressed above.

And from everything said above I notice how, from among the 40 different ways in which the cognition of the same thing can be sought after, one way is far more difficult and obscure than another. Thus it will be an easy matter to discover the four magnitudes in continuous proportion—namely, 3, 6, 12, 24—when given two of them in series—either 3 and 6, or 6 and 12, or 12 and 24— we must discover the rest from them. In such a case we will say that the proposition to be discovered is directly examined. If, however, given two magnitudes in alternation—namely, 3 and 12, or 6 and 24—we must discover the remaining magnitudes, then we will say the difficulty is indirectly examined in the first mode. If, correspondingly, the two extremes are given namely, 3 and 24, and the remaining magnitudes must be discovered from them, then we will say the difficulty will be examined indirectly in the second mode. And so I will be able to go further and deduce many other things from this one example; but these suffice for a reader to notice what I mean when I say some proposition is deduced directly or indirectly, and to realize that from some very easy and immediately known things much can be discovered even in other disciplines by whoever reflects attentively and conducts his investigations sagaciously.

Rule VII 41

For the completion of science, it is necessary to survey by a continuous and completely uninterrupted motion of thought each and every one of those things that pertain to our project, and to embrace them in a sufficient and ordered enumeration.

Adherence to everything propounded here is required in order to 42 admit as certain those truths that we said above are not immediately deduced from first and self-evident principles. Occasionally truths are deduced by so long a connection of consequences that when we come to them we do not easily recall the entire route that led us to them; and accordingly we say that it is necessary to assist our infirm memory by a particular continuous motion of thinking. Therefore, if, for example, I have come to know by different operations, first, what the relation is between the magnitudes A and B; next, between B and C; then, between C and D; and finally, between D and E; I will not on that account notice what the relation is between A and E, nor will I be able to understand precisely what that relation is on the basis of those already known unless I remember all of them. For this reason I will run through them several times by a particular continuous motion of the imagination that at the same time intuits each individually and passes to others, until I have finally learned to pass so quickly from the first to the last that, hardly leaving any parts to memory, I seem to intuit the entire thing together. By this means the memory is assisted and the slothfulness of our native wits is corrected and their capacity in some manner extended.

43   Moreover, we add that this motion should in no way be interrupted; for frequently those who attempt with excessive quickness to deduce something from remote principles do not accurately pass through the entire concatenation of immediate conclusions but instead hasten over many such conclusions without consideration. And certainly, when even the least thing is overlooked the chain is immediately broken and the entire certitude of the conclusion is weakened.

44   Furthermore, we here say that enumeration is required in order to complete science: for other precepts do indeed help in resolving many questions, but by aid of enumeration alone can we always make a true and certain judgment about whatever we turn our reason toward; accordingly, by virtue of enumeration alone, nothing completely escapes us; indeed, by enumeration alone we seem to know something about everything.

45   Thus this enumeration or induction is so diligent and accurate an examination of all those things that have reference to any proposed question that from it we may certainly and evidently conclude that nothing has been incorrectly omitted by us. Hence, so long as we have used this enumeration in each case, then, if the smallest thing is wanting, we will at least be more learned in this respect—namely, we will perceive with certainty that it could not be discovered by any path known to us; and if as often happens we have been able to pass through all the paths that lie open to man, then we shall be able to assert boldly that the desired cognition of this thing exceeds all discovery by the native wits of human beings.

46   It is also to be noted that by a sufficient enumeration or induc-

tion we understand exclusively such an enumeration or induction as that from which the truth is concluded with more certainty than from any other kind of judgment except simple intuition. For having rejected all the bonds of the syllogisms, every time any cognition cannot be reduced to intuition, there remains for us only this path of enumeration or induction upon which we ought to bestow our complete trust. For wherever we have immediately deduced one thing from others, if the inference was evident, then those things we have thus deduced are already reduced to a true intuition. If, however, we inferred something from many and disjoint things, then often the capacity of our intellect is not so great that all those things can be held together in a single intuition; in this case the certitude of this operation should suffice. In a like manner we cannot with one intuition of the eyes distinguish all the links of a long chain; yet nevertheless if we have seen the connection of each link with the next, that will suffice for us to say that we have noticed how the last is connected with the first.

I said that this operation should be sufficient, because often it can be defective and consequently liable to error. For although upon occasion many of the things we pass over in enumeration are truly evident, still, as long as the least thing is omitted, the chain is broken and the entire certitude of the conclusion weakened. Occasionally we even hold everything together in an enumeration that is certain, but yet have not distinguished each thing from another—and the result is that we know them all only confusedly. 47

Furthermore, this enumeration should sometimes be complete, sometimes distinct, and there are occasions when neither is in order; for that reason it has been said only that enumeration ought to be sufficient. For if I wish to judge through enumeration how many kinds of entities are corporeal and the manner in which they fall under the senses, I will not assert that they are so many and not more unless I have first established that I have already embraced them in an enumeration and have distinguished them from each other. If indeed I wish to show in the same way that the rational soul is not corporeal, it will not be necessary for the enumeration to be complete, but it will suffice if I encompass all bodies together in some few collections so that I can demonstrate that the rational soul can be referred to none of them. If finally I wish to show by enumeration that the area of a circle is greater 48

than all the areas of other figures of equal periphery, it is not necessary to inspect all figures; rather it suffices to demonstrate this
about some figures in particular, so that by an induction I can
conclude the same of all the other figures.

49   I also added that the enumeration should be ordered: I did so
not only because, as regards the defects already enumerated, no
remedy is more available than to search through everything in an
orderly manner; but also because it often happens that if each of
those things relevant to the thing proposed had individually to be
scrutinized, then no man's lifetime would be sufficient, either
because the things are excessively numerous, or more often, because the same things repeatedly present themselves for review.
However, if we dispose all things in the best order, it finally results
that they are reduced to certain classes such that it suffices either
to make an exact examination of one of them, or to examine something from each of them, or particular classes rather than others—
or at least never needlessly to review anything twice. Moreover,
this also helps in that often because of well-designed order many
things are expedited in a brief period of time and are easily accomplished—things that on first appearance seem immense.

50   However, the order of things to be enumerated can frequently
be varied, and depends upon the decision of each person; and for
that reason, in order to consider this matter more keenly it is
necessary to keep in mind what has been said in Rule V. Indeed,
very many of men's more frivolous games depend for their entire
method of solution upon this orderly arrangement of things: thus
if you wish to make the best anagram by transposing the letters
of some name, it is not required to proceed from the easier to the
more difficult, nor to distinguish absolutes from relatives; because
neither of these have any place here; rather it will suffice to set
out for oneself an order for examining the transpositions of the
letters such that the same transpositions are not examined twice
and their number is, for example, distributed in certain classes so
that, as a result, it immediately appears in which classes lies the
greatest hope of discovering what is sought after; and thus the
labor will often not be long, but merely puerile.

51   Finally, these three last propositions are not to be separated, because often they must be reflected upon together, and each equally
contributes to the perfection of method; neither is it important
which proposition was taught first, nor that we have explained

them curtly—for there is hardly anything else to be done in the remaining parts of this treatise except to show in detail what we have here considered in general.

Rule VIII

52

If in the series of things to be sought after anything occurs that our intellect is unable to intuit sufficiently well, there we must stop; neither should the other things that follow be examined, but we should abstain from this superfluous labor.

The three preceding rules prescribe and explain order; this rule, however, points out the circumstances in which order is altogether necessary, and those in which it is only useful. Surely whatever constitutes an entire step in that series by which we have to pass from the relative to the absolute, or the reverse, must of necessity be examined before everything that follows. If, as indeed often happens, many things pertain to the same step, it is certainly always useful to review all of them in order. In this, however, we are not forced to observe order so strictly; and very often even if we do not perspicuously know all, but merely a few or one of these things, it is nevertheless allowable to progress further.

53

This rule follows necessarily from reasons adduced in relation to Rule II; nevertheless it must not be thought that it contains nothing new for enlarging our learning—although it seems only to forbid us from an inquiry into particular things and not to expound any truth. It is true that this rule teaches tyros only that they should not waste their labors, and it teaches this by much the same reasoning as does Rule II. But for those who have perfect acquaintance with the seven preceding rules, this rule shows them by what reasoning they can so satisfy themselves in any science that they desire nothing further: for whoever shall have exactly employed the prior rules to solve any difficulty but is nevertheless ordered by this rule to stop at some point, he will certainly then know that the knowledge sought after absolutely cannot be discovered by any effort—and not because of a fault with his native wits but because the nature of the difficulty itself, or the human condition, prevents the discovery. And this cognition itself is no less knowledge than that which shows the nature of the thing itself; and whoever would extend his curiosity further would not seem to be of sound mind.

54

55   All this should be illustrated through one or another example. If, for example, someone who is a student merely of mathematics seeks to discover that line which in dioptrics they call the anaclastic—namely, the line in which parallel rays so divide that after refraction they all intersect each other in one point—he will easily notice, following Rules V and VI, that the determination of this line depends on the proportion that holds between the angle of refraction and the angle of incidence; but because he will not be capable of tracking this proportion down, since it does not pertain to mathematics but to physics, he will be forced to remain at the threshold of a solution; and it will do him no good if he wishes to hear the correct answer from the philosophers or to learn it from experience: for he would sin against Rule III. For this proportion, moreover, is composite and relative; but experience, however, if it is certain, can be had only of things that are purely simple and absolute, as will be said in its place. It would also be vain for him to suppose that a particular proportion between angles of this kind is the truest of all; for in doing so he would no longer be seeking the anaclastic, but merely that line which follows the rule laid down in his supposition.

56   If someone who is not merely a student of mathematics, but one who in accordance with Rule I wishes to seek the truth about everything that presents itself, has fallen upon the same difficulty, he will further discover that this proportion between the angles of incidence and refraction depends upon the change of these same angles due to a variation in the medium; moreover, he will also discover that this change depends upon the manner in which a ray penetrates the entire diaphanous body, and that a knowledge of this penetration also supposes that the nature of illumination is known; he will finally discover that to understand illumination he must know what a natural potency is in general, because a natural potency in general is the most absolute thing in this entire series. Accordingly, when he shall have clearly seen this by an intuition of the mind, he will return through the same steps, following Rule V; and if he cannot immediately recognize the nature of illumination at the second step, he will enumerate, following Rule VII, all the other natural potencies, so that from the cognition of some others he may understand the nature of illumination at least by analogy, of which I will speak later on; and when this is done, he will seek the reason why the ray penetrates the entire

diaphanous body; and so he will pursue the remaining questions according to order until he comes to the anaclastic itself. Now although the anaclastic has been sought after in vain by many people up until this day, nevertheless I see no reason which can prevent anyone who uses our method perfectly from attaining an evident cognition of it.

But let us give the most noble example of all. If anyone proposes to himself the question of examining all truths for the cognition of which human reason suffices (which seems to me should be done once in their life by all who seriously strive to attain a good mind), such a person will certainly discover by the rules laid down that nothing can be known before the intellect, since the knowledge of all other things depends upon this and not vice versa; moreover, having seen all those things that proximately follow upon the cognition of the pure intellect, he will enumerate whatever other instruments of knowing we possess beyond the intellect—and these are two, the imagination and the senses. Accordingly, he will collect all his efforts to distinguish and examine these three modes of knowing; and seeing that, properly speaking, truth or falsity can exist only in the intellect, although often they take their origin from the other two modes of knowing, he will attend diligently to all those things by which he can be deceived in order to guard against them; and he will exactly enumerate all the paths that lie open to man for attaining to the truth so as to follow one that is certain—and these paths are not so multifarious that he cannot easily discover all of them by means of a sufficient enumeration. And however astonishing and incredible this will seem to the inexperienced, whatever the subject matter, he shall have managed to distinguish those cognitions that merely fill up and adorn the memory from those on account of which someone should truly be said to be more learned, and he will easily understand that distinction . . . :* moreover, he shall certainly not consider himself as ignorant of any further things because of a defective native wit or a defect in his art; nor shall he think that another could know something further that he himself could not know despite the fact that he applied his mind to it in a suitable manner. And although many things can frequently be proposed

57

---

* A and H both remark that something is missing; see *Regulae, Oeuvres*, vol. X, p. 396.

to him that this rule prohibits him from searching after, still, because he will clearly perceive that they exceed all discovery by the
native wits of men, he will not judge himself on that account
more ignorant; indeed, this fact itself, that he knows the things
sought after can be known by no one, will abundantly assuage
his curiosity, provided he is of a balanced temperament.

58   But lest we always be uncertain about what our reason is capable
of doing, and lest our reason labor incorrectly and rashly, we will
prepare ourselves beforehand to know particular things: for it is
fitting once in one's life to have diligently sought after all those
cognitions of which human reason is capable. In order to do this
better, if things are equally easy, one ought to search for those
things that are more useful.

59   This method imitates those of the mechanical arts, which do
not require the assistance of the others, but themselves lay down
the manner in which their instruments are to be made. For if anyone wishes to engage in one of these mechanical arts, for example,
the art of forging hard materials into tools, then, if he lacks all
instruments, he would indeed at first be forced to use a hard
stone or some mass of crude iron for an anvil, to employ a piece
of stone in place of a hammer, to use sticks as forceps, and of
necessity to collect other things of this kind: next, when such
things have been prepared, he would not immediately attempt to
thrash out for other people's use swords, helmets, or any of those
things made from iron; but he would first make hammers, anvils,
forceps, and all those other things that are useful to himself. With
this example we teach that, when at the outset we shall be able
to discover only some disordered precepts that seem natively in-
stilled in our minds rather than prepared with art, we are not to
attempt to use them to immediately break in upon the disputes
of the philosophers or to solve the difficulties of the mathematicians: rather they must first be used for other things that require
the greatest care and are more necessary for the examination of
the truth. And there is no particular reason why it appears more
difficult to discover these other things than to solve any of those
questions customarily proposed in geometry or physics and in the
other disciplines.

60   Certainly, at this point there is nothing more useful about
which to inquire than the nature of human cognition and to what
it extends. And for that reason we now encompass this matter in

a single question that we consider the foremost question to be examined according to the rules already treated; and this should be done once in his life by anyone who loves the truth however little; for in the investigation of this question is contained the true instruments of knowing and the whole of method. Moreover, nothing seems to me more inept than to dispute boldly, as many do, concerning the secrets of nature, the powers exerted by the heavens upon the lower regions, the prediction of future events, and similar things, without ever having inquired whether human reason suffices for finding out these things. Neither does it seem hard or difficult to define the limits of our native talents, which we experience in ourselves, since often we do not hesitate to judge even about those things that are outside of us and exceedingly foreign to ourselves. Nor is it an immense task to wish to embrace in thought everything contained in this universe in order to know how each thing is subjected to the examination of our intellect; for nothing can be so manifold or disparate that it cannot, by means of that enumeration already discussed, be circumscribed within certain limits and arranged under a few headings. However, to show the power of enumeration in regard to the question proposed, we first divide what pertains to this question into two parts: for the question should be referred, either to us who are capable of cognition, or to the things themselves that can be known; and these two we discuss separately.

And indeed we notice in ourselves that only the intellect is 61 capable of knowledge; but it can be helped or impeded by three other faculties—namely, by imagination, sense, and memory. We must therefore look in an orderly way to determine wherein these faculties can be a hindrance, so that we may be on guard; moreover, we must look in an orderly way to determine wherein they can be of benefit, so that we may employ all their resources. And thus we will discuss this part of the question through a sufficient enumeration, as will be shown in the following proposition.

Next, we must come to the things themselves, which are to be 62 regarded only according as they are reached by the intellect; in this sense we divide them into natures that are most simple and natures that are complex or composite. There can be no simple natures except those that are spiritual, corporeal, or that pertain to both; finally, as regards composite natures, some are certainly experienced by the intellect to be composite before the intellect judges anything more determinate about them; however, other composite natures are composed by the intellect itself. All this will be further explained in proposition XII, where it will be demonstrated that no falsity can exist except in these last natures that are composed by the intellect. Thus we distinguish further among these natures composed by the intellect: there are those that are deduced from very simple and self-evident natures, with which we shall deal in the entire book that follows; and there are others that presuppose still others that we experience to be composite in things themselves. Moreover, we intend to devote the entire third book to the exposition of composite natures of this latter kind.

63   In this entire treatise we shall certainly attempt to follow so accurately, and explain so easily, all those paths that lie open to men for the cognition of truth that whoever shall have perfectly learned this entire method, however mediocre his native wits, will finally see that he is not entirely cut off from anything to which others have access; and he will also realize that he is no longer ignorant of anything because of a deficiency of native talent or of art. Instead, every time he applies his mind to the cognition of anything, he will either completely find what he seeks after; or he will recognize that it depends upon some experiment that is not in his power, and for that reason he will not blame his native wits, although he will be forced to stop there; or finally he will demonstrate that what is sought after exceeds all discovery by human wit, and accordingly he will not on that account judge himself more ignorant, because this realization is no less knowledge than the recognition of anything else would have been.

64   RULE IX
*It is fitting to turn totally the keen vision of our inborn wits
toward the least and easiest of things, and to immerse ourselves in
them for a long time, until at length we are accustomed to
intuit the truth distinctly and perspicuously.*

65   Having explained the two operations of our intellect, intuition and deduction, which we said are alone to be used in learning science, we continue in this and in the following proposition to explain by what effort we can become more adept at exercising them and at simultaneously cultivating the two principal faculties

of our native wits—namely, perspicacity, or the intuiting of individual things; and sagacity, which is the artful deducing of some things from others.

And indeed we know the manner in which the intuition of the 66 mind should be used from a comparison with the eyes. For whoever wishes to look with the same intuition upon many objects together sees nothing about them distinctly; and similarly, whoever is accustomed to attend with one act of thought to many things together confuses his native wits. However, craftsmen trained to labor on minute objects have become accustomed to direct the keen vision of their eyes with attention upon individual points, and they have acquired by practice a capacity to distinguish perfectly things however small and thin; and so also people who never perplex their thinking with various objects at the same time, but always totally occupy themselves with considering things that are most simple and very easy, become perspicacious.

It is, however, a common fault of mortals that what is difficult 67 seems to them more beautiful: for very many people think they know nothing when they see a perspicuous and simple cause of something; yet in the meanwhile they admire those sublime and lofty demands made upon their belief by the arguments of the philosophers, even though these arguments very often rest upon foundations that are never sufficiently seen through by anyone; now all such people are certainly unhealthy spirits who hold the darkness dearer than the light. By contrast, it should be noted that those who truly know discern the truth with equal facility whether they have gathered it from a simple subject or from an obscure one: they comprehend each instance of truth with a similar, unique, and distinct act; but the entire difference is in the path to truth, which certainly ought to be longer if it leads to a truth more removed from the first and most absolute principles.

It is proper therefore that everyone become accustomed to en- 68 tertaining so few things at any one time in thought that he never thinks he knows anything he does not intuit as distinctly as what he knows most distinctly of all. Now, certainly some are born more adept at this than others, but with art and practice everyone can make his inborn talents far more adept at it; and it seems to me that one thing must here be stressed as most important of all— namely, that each person firmly persuade himself that it is not from weighty and obscure things, but only from easy and more obvious ones, that the sciences, however recherché, are to be deduced.

69   For example, if I wish to examine whether any natural power can in the same instant pass to a distant place through an entire medium, I will not immediately turn my mind's attention to the force of the magnet, or to the influence of the stars, nor indeed to the speed of illumination, in order to inquire whether such actions are truly accomplished in an instant: for I can tell that this would be more difficult to determine than the thing sought after: rather I will reflect upon the local motions of bodies, because nothing in the genus of very quick motions could be more apparent to sense. And I will take note that a stone certainly cannot pass in an instant from one place to another, because it is a body; yet nevertheless it is true that a power, similar to that which moves the stone, is communicated in an instant if it passes directly from one subject to another. Thus if I move one end of a long stick, I easily conceive that the power that moves that part of the stick necessarily moves all the other parts at one and the same instant, because it is then communicated directly—nor does it consist in any body, such as a stone, by which it is carried along.

70   In the same way if I wish to learn how two contrary effects can be produced simultaneously by one and the same simple cause, I will not rely upon the medicines of the doctors that expel some humors but retain others; neither will I prophesy that the moon heats itself by light and cools itself through an occult quality: but better, I will intuit the scale on which the same weight at one and the same instant elevates one pan and depresses the other, and other similar things.

71   RULE X
*In order that our native wit become sagacious, it ought to be
exercised in seeking after those things that have already been
discovered by others, and we ought to review even the
slightest devices of men, but particularly those that
explain or suppose order.*

72   I admit that I was born with such a native bent as always to place the greatest pleasure from studying, not in hearing the explanations of others, but in discovering explanations by my own efforts.

This one trait led me while still a youth to learn the sciences; and each time any book promised in its title some new discovery, I tested before reading any further whether perchance I might come up with anything similar by some particular inborn sagacity; and I put myself on guard lest precipitous reading would rob me of this harmless delight. This course of action was so often successful that finally I noticed I no longer came to the truth of things as others are accustomed to do—that is, through vague and blind investigations aided more by chance than art. On the contrary, I relied upon certain rules long experience had taught me to be of no little use for this purpose, and it was these rules that I afterward used in considering further topics. And thus I diligently cultivated this entire method and persuaded myself that from the beginning I have followed the most useful manner of studying.

Truly, since everyone's native talents are not so inclined by nature to discover things by their own effort, this rule teaches that it is not fitting to occupy ourselves immediately with more difficult and arduous things, but instead some slighter and simpler arts should be grasped first—and particularly those in which a greater order resides, such as the art of the craftsmen who weave webs and tapestries, or the arts of women who embroider or intermix threads of various textures in countless ways. In the same manner we should grasp all the games of numbers, whatever has reference to arithmetic, and similar things: for they all exercise the native talents to an astonishing degree, provided only we learn to construe them, not from others, but from ourselves. For since nothing remains hidden in these arts, and since they are fit for the capacity of human cognition, they very distinctly manifest to us innumerable orders, each differing from the other but nonetheless regular, in the correct observance of which human sagacity almost completely consists.

Accordingly, we have warned that things must be sought after with method, and method in these more lightsome arts consists in nothing but the constant observance of the order, either in the thing itself as existing or in the thing as subtly contrived by thought: thus if we wish to read a writing concealed in unknown characters, certainly no order is manifest there; yet we nevertheless feign one, firstly, in order to examine all conjectures concerning individual marks, words, or sentences, and secondly, to dispose these marks, words, or sentences in such a way that we can recog-

73

74

nize from an enumeration what can be deduced from them. We must guard most assiduously against wasting time by artlessly and haphazardly divining similarities; for even if such similarities can often be discovered without art, and even if occasionally they are more quickly discovered by luck rather than by method, nevertheless such approaches will finally dull the light of our native wits and so accustom them to boyish and empty pursuits that afterward they will always remain attached to the superficial characteristics of things and never penetrate within. But still we must not in the meantime fall into the error of those who occupy their thinking only with serious and higher matters concerning which, after many labors, they acquire only confused knowledge while they desire a profound knowledge. It is therefore appropriate that we exercise ourselves first in these easier sciences; yet we must do so with a method so that, as if by play, we may accustom ourselves by means of open and known paths to penetrate always to the inmost truth of things. In this manner we shall afterward gradually discover, in a shorter period of time than we could have hoped for, that we find ourselves able, with equal facility, to deduce from evident principles many propositions that appear exceedingly difficult and intricate.

75   However, many people are perhaps astonished that in this place, where we inquire into the plan that renders us more adept at deducing particular truths from others, we omit all the precepts of the dialecticians. It is with these precepts that the dialecticians think they direct human reason by prescribing certain forms of discourse that yield conclusions with such necessity that, in relying upon any one of these forms, human reason is in a certain manner carried along without evident and attentive consideration of that very inference, although in the meanwhile it can nevertheless conclude something with certainty because of the mere force of the form. Now, by all means, we notice that often the truth does emerge from these bonds, although those who use them remain entangled in them. Such entanglement does not so often befall others; moreover, we observe that the most acute sophistries hardly ever have the effect of deceiving anyone who uses his pure reason —and yet they deceive the sophists themselves.

76   For this reason we are here principally concerned that our reason not be carried blindly along when we are examining the truth of any matter; thus we reject these forms of the dialecticians as antagonistic to our project, and by contrast we require all those aids

with which our thought remains attentive, as will be pointed out in what follows. But to make it still more evident that this art of discourse contributes nothing to the cognition of the truth, it is to be noted that the dialecticians are unable to form with their art any syllogism that yields the truth unless they already have its matter—that is, unless they already know the same truth they deduce in their syllogism. From this it is manifest that from such a form they themselves perceive nothing new, and it is therefore manifest that the common dialectic is certainly useless to those desiring to investigate the truth of things; rather it merely helps occasionally in enabling them to explain more easily to others what they themselves have already found out; and accordingly the common dialectic should be transferred from philosophy to rhetoric.

Rule XI 77

After we have intuited particular propositions, if we conclude anything else from them, it is useful to run through these same propositions with a continuous and completely uninterrupted motion of thinking, to reflect on their mutual relations, and as much as possible distinctly to conceive very many of them together: for in this manner our cognition will be far more certain and our inborn wit more greatly augmented.

This is the occasion for more clearly explaining what has already 78 been said concerning the intuition of the mind in Rules III & VII: for in one place we have opposed it to deduction and in another only to enumeration, which we have defined to be an inference drawn from many and disjunct things; indeed, we said in the same place that the simple deduction of one thing from another is done through intuition.

We did this because we require two things for the intuition of 79 the mind: namely, that a proposition is clear and distinct; and after this, that a whole is understood together and not successively. Indeed, a deduction, if we think of performing it as under Rule III, is not completely seen together but involves some motion of our inborn wit that infers one thing from others; and hence we were correct there in distinguishing it from intuition. But certainly if we attend to deduction as already performed, as in accordance with what has been said under Rule VII, then it designates no further motion, but rather the end of motion; and accordingly we suppose a deduction is seen through by an intuition when it is simple and perspicuous, but not when it is multifarious and complicated. To a deduction not seen through by intuition we have given the name "enumeration" or "induction," because at that time it cannot be comprehended simultaneously by the intellect, and its certitude somehow depends upon the memory, wherein judgments concerning the individually enumerated parts should be retained so that from all of them one thing can be extracted.

80   It was necessary to distinguish all these things for the interpretation of this rule; for as Rule IX concerned only the intuition of the mind and Rule X only enumeration, this rule explains the manner in which these two operations mutually assist and perfect each other, so that they seem to coalesce into a single operation by means of a particular motion of thought that attentively intuits single things together and passes over to other things.

81   We point to a twofold usefulness of such thinking: namely, to grasp the conclusion that concerns us with more certainty, and to render our inborn wit more fitted for discovering other conclusions. Now, as we said, it is the memory upon which hangs the certainty of the conclusions that embrace more than we can hold in one intuition. And surely since memory is wandering and infirm, it ought to be scrutinized and strengthened through this continuous and repeated motion of thinking. For example, if by many operations I have first come to know what the relation is between the first and second magnitudes, and then between the second and the third, and then between the third and fourth, and finally between the fourth and fifth, I do not on that account see what the relation is between the first and fifth. Moreover, neither can I deduce this relation from what I already know unless I remember all the relations; for which reason it is necessary for me to run through them with repeated thought until finally I have passed so quickly from the first to the last that, with almost no parts remaining for memory, I seem to intuit the entire thing together.

82   Nobody fails to see that by this operation the slothfulness of the inborn wit is certainly corrected and its conceiving developed. But, moreover, it should be noted that the greatest utility of this rule consists in the fact that, by reflecting upon the mutual dependence of simple propositions, we acquire the habit of immediately distinguishing what is more or less relative and the steps by which it is reduced to the absolute. For example, if I run through some

magnitudes that are continuously proportional, I will reflect upon the following: namely, that by a similar conception, which is neither more nor less easy, I recognize the proportion between the first and second, the second and the third, the third and the fourth, and so forth; however, I cannot so easily simultaneously conceive the dependence of the second upon the first and third; and it is still much more difficult to recognize the dependency of this same second upon the first and the fourth, and so forth. From these things I easily recognize the reason why, if only the first and second magnitudes are given, I can easily discover the third and fourth, and so forth: namely, because this is done through particular and distinct concepts. If, however, only the first and third are given, I will not so easily recognize the mean, because this cannot be done except by a concept that involves the two preceding ones at the same time. If the first and fourth alone are given, it will be still more difficult for me to intuit the two means, because here three concepts are involved simultaneously. As a consequence it might seem even more difficult to find the three means from the first and fifth magnitudes. Yet there is another approach whereby the outcome is different: namely, because even if four concepts are joined together, they can nevertheless be separated, since four is divisible by another number; thus from the first and the fifth, I can look for the third alone; and then from the first and the third, I can look for the second alone; and so on. Whoever has accustomed himself to reflect upon this and upon similar things will immediately recognize, each time he examines a new question, what in the question engenders the difficulty, and what is the simplest method of solving it—all of which is of the greatest aid in attaining a cognition of the truth.

RULE XII

83

Finally, the intellect ought to use every assistance of the imagination, sense, and memory: first, to intuit distinctly simple propositions; second, to correctly unite what is sought after with what is known in order that the former may be distinguished; and third, to discover those things that ought to be so compared among themselves that none of our human capacities is omitted.

This rule embraces everything said above, and in the following   84
manner it teaches in general what had there to be explained in particular:

85   As far as the cognition of things is concerned, only two points must be regarded—namely, we who know and the things themselves to be known. In us there are just four faculties we can use for this purpose: namely, intellect, imagination, sense, and memory. To be sure, only the intellect is capable of perceiving truth, but nevertheless it should be assisted by the imagination, sense, and memory lest by chance we omit something within our capacities. As regards things themselves, it suffices to examine three points: first, that which is spontaneously obvious; next, the manner in which one thing is known from another; and finally, what in particular is deduced from what. This enumeration seems to me to be complete, and in short it does not seem to omit anything within the scope of human capacities.

86   As regards those things that are spontaneously obvious, I should have liked to explain here what the mind is, what the body is, how the body is informed by the mind, what faculties that serve for knowing exist in the entire composite of mind and body, and what each of these faculties does; however, this place seemed to me too limited for encompassing everything requiring advance consideration before the truth of these matters can be made manifest to everyone. For it is my desire to write always in such a manner that I assert nothing that is customarily controverted unless I have first established those reasons that led me into the assertion, and deem them capable of persuading other people as well.

87   But since I cannot do this now, it will suffice for me to explain as briefly as I can the manner most suited to my project for conceiving everything within us that serves for knowing things. Do not believe, unless it pleases you to do so, that these matters stand such as I conceive of them; but nevertheless what is there to prevent you from following these same suppositions if it appears that they do not at all alter the truth but rather render all truths far more clear? This is no different than in geometry, where you suppose particulars concerning quantity that in no way weaken the force of demonstrations, although you often judge differently about the nature of the quantity in physics.

88   Accordingly, we should conceive, first, that insofar as they are parts of the body all the external senses—even if applied by us to objects through an action, namely, by a local motion—properly speaking sense only through a passion, in the same fashion in which

wax receives a figure from a seal. And this should not be taken as said through analogy; rather it ought clearly to be conceived that the external figure of the sentient body is really changed by the object, in the same way as what is on the superficies of the wax is changed by the seal. This is to be conceded, not merely when by touch we feel some body as having figure, or as being hard or rough, but even when we perceive heat or cold and similar things by touch. It is the same with the other senses: the first opaque part of the eye receives the figure impressed upon it by light endowed with various colors; and the first part of the ears, nose, and the skin of the tongue, being impervious to the object, receive in the same way a new figure from sound, odor, and flavor.

To conceive all these things in this manner helps a great deal, 89 since nothing falls more easily under the senses than does figure— for figure is touched and seen.

No more falsities result from making this supposition rather than 90 any other; this can be demonstrated from the fact that the concept of figure is so common and simple as to be involved in everything sensible. For example, suppose whatever color you wish; you nevertheless will not deny that this same color is extended, and as a consequence has figure. Therefore what inconvenience will ensue, if, guarding against uselessly admitting and rashly feigning some new entity, we do not certainly deny whatever it has pleased others to believe about color, but merely abstract from everything concerning color except that it has the nature of figure, and conceive the difference among white, dark blue, red, and so on, as the difference that exists between these or similar figures?

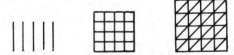

And the same thing can be said about all sensible things, because it is certain that the infinite multitude of figures suffices for expressing all the differences among sensible things.

Second, it is to be conceived that when the external sense is 91 moved by an object, the figure that it receives is transferred to some other part of the body, which is called the common sense, and this happens in the very same instant and without the motion of any real entity from one place to the other: this obviously happens in the same manner in which now, while I write, I understand that not only is the lower part of the pen moved in the same instant in which single characters are written upon the page, but also that no motion, not even the slightest, can be in the pen unless at the same time the entire pen receives this motion; furthermore all these differences of motion are described in the air by the top part of the pen, although I conceive nothing real as traveling from one end of the pen to the other. And who is there who thinks that there is a lesser connection among the parts of the human body than among those of the pen, and what simpler way of explaining the connection among the parts of the human body can be thought?

92   Third, it is to be conceived that the common sense acts in the role of a seal that forms upon the fantasy or imagination,* just as upon the wax, those very figures or ideas that come pure and without body from the external senses; and this fantasy is a genuine part of the body and of such a magnitude that different portions of it can assume very many figures, each distinct from the other, that are customarily retained for a long time: and then this is the same as what is called memory.

93   Fourth, it is to be conceived that the motor force, or the nerves themselves, take their origin from the brain, where the fantasy is located. The nerves are diversely moved by the fantasy, as the common sense is moved by the external sense, or as the entire pen is moved by its lower part. This example even shows how the fantasy can be the cause of many motions in the nerves, although it does not have the images of such motions expressly in itself, but has some other images from which these motions can follow: for the entire pen does not move in the way the lower part does; rather the greater part of the pen seems to follow in a motion that is obviously diverse and contrary. And from this it is possible to understand the manner in which all the motions of the other animals come about, although no true cognition of things, but merely a corporeal fantasy, is conceded to the animals; in this same way we can understand the nature of all those operations that happen in ourselves and that we are engaged in without any direction by reason.

* *phantasia vel imaginatio.*

Fifth, and finally, it is to be conceived that the force through 94
which we properly know things is purely spiritual, and no less distinct from the entire body than is blood from bone or hand from eye; and this force is one thing, whether it receives figures from the common sense together with the fantasy, or applies itself to those things preserved in memory, or forms new images that so occupy the imagination that often the imagination neither suffices for receiving ideas from the common sense, nor for transferring them to the motor force according to the dispositions of the body taken alone. In all these situations this knowing force occasionally is acted upon, and occasionally acts, imitating once the wax and then the seal; however, reference is made here to wax only by way of analogy, for nothing at all similar to this knowing force is found among corporeal things. Moreover, it is a single force, which, if it applies itself with the imagination to the common sense, is said to see, touch, and so on; and if it applies itself merely to the imagination that has assumed many different figures, it is said to remember; and if it applies itself to this same imagination in order to form new figures, it is said to imagine or conceive; lastly, if it acts alone, it is said to understand; furthermore, as to how understanding takes place, I will explain it more amply in its proper location. And accordingly this same knowing force, in relation to these different functions, is called either pure intellect, or imagination, or memory, or sense; however, it is properly called native wit when it forms new ideas in the fantasy, and when it applies itself to those ideas already formed; and we will study this knowing force as it is suited for these different operations, and we will continue to observe the differences among these names in what follows. Thus, by conceiving everything in this manner, the attentive reader will understand what assistance should be sought from each faculty, and how far the skill of men can be extended so as to supplement the defects in our inborn talents.

For since the intellect can be moved by the imagination, or, on 95
the contrary, act upon it; and since in like manner the imagination can act upon the senses through the motor force—by applying these senses to objects—or, on the contrary, be acted upon by the senses—when the senses describe the images of bodies upon it; and since memory, or at least that memory which is corporeal and similar to the recollection of brutes, is nothing distinct from the imagination: it can be concluded with certainty that if the intellect

acts upon those things in which there is nothing corporeal, or similar to the corporeal, then it cannot be helped by these faculties; on the contrary, in order that it not be impeded by these faculties, the senses should be shunned, and insofar as possible the imagination should be stripped of every distinct impression. Indeed, if the intellect does propose to examine something it can relate to body, then the idea of this thing should be formed in the imagination as distinctly as possible; moreover, in order to preserve this image more distinctly, the thing this idea will represent should be displayed to the external senses. Furthermore, many objects cannot help the intellect to intuit individual things distinctly. Indeed, in order to do what often must be done, namely, to deduce one thing from many things, we should reject from our ideas of things whatever does not require present attention so that what remains can be retained more easily in memory; accordingly we will not now hold up before our external senses the things themselves; rather we shall choose small figures of these objects that, provided they suffice for preventing a lapse of memory, are easier to work with because they are more compact and contain what is essential to our concerns. And whoever shall observe all these precepts will, it seems to me, certainly not have omitted anything that is pertinent to this part.

96   And now we enter upon the second point.* We endeavor: first, to distinguish correctly the notions of simple things from those composed from them; second, to detect in each notion where falsity can reside so that we may guard against it; third, to find those things that can be known with certainty so that we may devote ourselves exclusively to them. Following our previous manner, certain things are to be assumed that are perhaps not agreed to by everyone. However, it matters little even if these things are not believed any more true than those imaginary circles with which the astronomers describe their phenomena—provided that with their help you distinguish between what is false and what is true in regard to anything that has been cognized.

97   Thus we say, first, that in respect to the order of our cognition of them, individual things are to be regarded differently than if we speak of these same things according to the manner in which they truly exist. Thus, for example, were we considering some extended

* See R 85.

and figured body, we would indeed admit that, from the point of view of the thing itself, it is something unitary and simple: for in this sense it cannot be said to be composed from the nature of body, extension, and figure, since none of these parts ever exist distinct from the others; but indeed, in respect to our intellect, we call it something composed of these three natures because we first understood the single natures separately before we were able to judge that the three of them are found together in one and the same subject. For this reason, since we are not concerned here with things except insofar as they are perceived by the intellect, we call only those things simple whose cognition is so perspicuous and distinct that they cannot be divided by the mind into further things more distinctly known; such are figure, extension, motion, and so on; finally, we conceive all the remaining things to be composed in some manner from these. All this is to be understood so generally as not even to exclude those things we occasionally abstract from the simple natures themselves, such as when we say that figure is the boundary of the extended thing, conceiving by boundary something more general than figure—because we can also speak of the boundary of duration, of motion, and so on. For at this stage, even if the signification of boundary is abstracted from figure, nevertheless boundary does not seem to be more simple than figure; rather, since boundary is attributed to other things that differ completely from figure, such as the extremity of duration or of motion, it ought to have been abstracted from these also; and accordingly boundary is something composed from many natures plainly different from each other, and is applied to them only in an equivocal sense.

We say, second, that those things that are called simple in respect to our intellect are either purely intellectual, or purely material, or common to both. Those things are purely intellectual that are known by the intellect through some inborn light and without the assistance of any corporeal image: that such things exist is certain, because there can be no corporeal idea that represents to us what cognition is, what doubt is, what ignorance is, what the action of the will is that we may call volition, or similar things; yet we nevertheless truly know these things—indeed, these things are so easily known that it is sufficient only to have reason in order to know them. Those things are purely material that are known only in bodies: such as figure, extension, motion, and so on. 98

Finally, those things are said to be common that are attributed indifferently both to corporeal and to spiritual things, such as existence, unity, duration, and similar things. To this group are referred all those common notions that are like bonds joining some simple natures to others and provide the evidence for whatever we conclude when reasoning. Examples of such common notions are these: that things that are the same as a single third thing are the same as each other; that things that cannot be referred in the same way to the same third thing have some difference between them, and so on. And, indeed, these common notions can be known either by the pure intellect or by the intellect when it intuits images of material things.

99   Furthermore, among these simple natures it is convenient also to number the privations and negations of the simple natures themselves, insofar as these privations and negations are understood by us: for the cognitions by which I intuit what nothing is, or what the instant is, or what rest is, are none of them any less true cognitions than those by which I understand what existence is, or duration is, or motion is. Moreover, this manner of conceiving the privations and negations of simple natures as being themselves simple natures will here assist us in speaking next about all the other things composed from these simple natures: thus if I judge that some figure does not move, I will say my thought is in some way composed from figure and rest; and I will speak in a like manner in other cases.

100   We say, third, that these simple natures are all self-evident and never contain any falsity. This is easily shown if we distinguish that faculty of the intellect by which it intuits and knows a thing from that by which it judges through affirming and denying; for it can arise that we think ourselves ignorant of what we truly know—that is, if we falsely suspect that, beyond what we do intuit in things or reach by thought, something else is in them that is hidden from us. By this reasoning it is evident that we err whenever we judge that any simple nature is not totally known by us: for if our mind attains even the least thing about it—which undoubtedly is necessary, since we suppose we can judge something about it—then it must be concluded that we know it totally; otherwise it cannot be called simple but would be composed from what we perceive in it and what we judge ourselves to be ignorant of in respect to it.

Fourth, we say that the connection between these simple things   101
is either necessary or contingent. The connection is necessary when
one thing is implied in some confused manner in the concept of
the other, so that we cannot distinctly conceive one of the two if
we judge them to be separated from each other: in this manner
figure is connected to extension, motion to duration or to time,
and so on, because one cannot conceive figure devoid of all extension or motion of all duration. Thus if I say that 4 and 3 is 7, this
composite is necessary; for we do not distinctly conceive 7 unless
in some confused manner we include in it 3 and 4. And in the
same way whatever is demonstrated about figures or numbers is
necessarily connected with that of which it is affirmed. This necessity is not found merely in sensible things, since, for example, even
if Socrates says he doubts everything, it necessarily follows that
therefore he at least understands this, namely, that he doubts; in
like manner he also realizes that something can be true or false,
and so on, because these things are necessarily connected to the
nature of doubting. Unquestionably, only a contingent union exists
among those things that are joined together by no inseparable relation: such as when we say that a body is animated, a man is
clothed, and so on. However, very many people often consider
as contingently connected things that are necessarily joined to
each other, because they have not noticed the necessary relation,
such as in this proposition, "I exist, therefore God exists"; or, likewise, as in this proposition, "I understand, therefore I have a mind
distinct from the body," and so on. Finally, it should be noted
that the converses of very many necessary propositions are contingent: thus although from the fact that I exist I conclude with
certainty that God exists, nevertheless from the fact that God
exists it is not correct to conclude that I exist also.

Fifth, we say that we can never understand anything except those   102
simple natures and their particular mixtures or unions. Furthermore, it is indeed often easier to attend simultaneously to many of
these simple natures joined together than to separate them one
from the others: thus, for example, I can cognize the triangle
although I have never thought that the cognition of the angle,
line, the number three, figure, extension, and so on, is also contained in that cognition; yet nevertheless this does not prevent us
from saying that the nature of the triangle is composed from all
these natures, and that these natures are better known than the

triangle, since these very natures are those that are understood in it; furthermore, perhaps many other natures that escape our notice are involved in the same triangle—for example, the magnitude of the angles which are equal to two right angles, and those innumerable relations that hold between the sides and the angles, or the amount of area, and so on.

103   Sixth, we say that these natures we call composite are known to us either because we experience what they are or because we ourselves compose them. We experience whatever we perceive by sense, whatever we hear from others, and generally whatever reaches our intellect either from elsewhere or from reflective contemplation upon itself. It should be noted that no experience can ever deceive the intellect if it intuits a thing precisely as the thing is object to it, whether it has the object in itself or in the fantasy, and provided also that, first, it does not judge that the imagination faithfully records the objects of the senses, or that the senses themselves are endowed with the true figures of things; and, second, it does not judge that external objects are always such as they appear. For were we to make the two sorts of judgments proscribed above, we would be liable to error: just as if, when someone narrated a story to us, we believed that the events took place; or as when someone suffering with the disease of jaundice judges everything to be yellow because his eye is itself tinged with the color yellow; or finally, just as if we were to believe that the troubled fantasy of the victim of melancholy, in whom the imagination is injured, represents true things. However, these same things do not deceive the intellect of the wise man; for whatever he will accept from the imagination, he will indeed truly judge to be depicted in it; yet he will never assert that entirely the same thing, without undergoing any alteration, has traveled from external things to the senses, and from the senses to the fantasy, unless he first knows this fact on some other basis. Moreover, it is we ourselves who compose the things we understand each time we believe something is in them not immediately perceived by our mind through any experience. Thus, if the man with jaundice persuades himself that the things seen are yellow, this thought of his will be composed, both from what his fantasy represents to him, and also from what he assumes about it—namely, that the color yellow appears to him, not because of a defect in his eye, but because the things seen are truly yellow. From this it follows that we can be

deceived only when the things we believe are in some way composed by ourselves.

Seventh, we say that this composition can be effected in three 104
ways—namely, through impulse, conjecture, or deduction. Those
people compose their judgments about things through impulse
who, persuaded by no reason, but determined only by some
higher power, or their proper liberty, or a disposition of the fantasy, are led of their own natural bent to believe something. Now,
the first, that is, a higher power, never deceives them; the second,
that is, their proper liberty, rarely does; and the third, a disposition
of the fantasy, nearly always does. However, the first sort of impulse, that due to a higher power, is not relevant at this place,
because it does not fall within the province of art. Moreover, an
example of conjecture would be the following: when from the
facts that water is further from the center of the earth than earth
itself and is of finer substance, and, likewise, that air is further
from the center of the earth than water and is rarer still, we then
conjecture that above the air there is only some very pure ether
that is far finer than this very air, and so on. Now, whatever we
compose in this manner will not indeed deceive us if we judge it
merely to be probable and never affirm it to be true; yet it is also
true that it will not* render us more learned.

There remains only deduction through which we can compose 105
things in such a way that we are certain of their truth. However,
even in this operation there can be very many defects: such as
when, from the fact that in this space filled with air we perceive
nothing by sight, touch, or any other sense, we then conclude that
this space is empty, mistakenly conjoining the nature of vacuum
with the nature of this space; and this kind of mistake occurs
every time we judge that from something particular or contingent
anything general and necessary can be deduced. It is, however, in
our power to avoid this error, that is, if we never join anything
together unless we intuit that the connection of one with the

---

* Adam and Tannery give *doctiores nos facit* (*Regulae, Oeuvres*, vol. X,
p. 424). A gives *doctiores non facit* (ibid., p. 694); also see *Regulae ad directionem ingenii*, ed. Georges Le Roy (Paris: Boivin et C¹ᵉ, 1902), p. 220, n.
11. Furthermore, Le Roy maintains that the condition of H allows for reading
nos or *non* and maintains the sense of *non* to be preferable (ibid.); cf. *Regulae*,
p. 694.

other is indeed necessary: such as when we deduce that nothing can be figured that is not extended from the fact that figure has a necessary connection with extension, and so on.

106   From all this it can be gathered, firstly, that we have, in my opinion, distinctly shown by sufficient enumeration what initially we were able to show only confusedly and with uncultivated natural ability: namely, that no paths to a certain cognition of the truth lie open to men except evident intuition and necessary deduction; and we have likewise shown what those simple natures are, about which we spoke in proposition VIII. And it is manifest that intuition of the mind extends to all these simple natures, to the cognition of their necessary connections, and finally to all the remaining things the intellect strictly experiences either in itself or in the fantasy. More indeed will be said about deduction in what follows.

107   Secondly, it should be gathered that no effort is called for in cognizing these simple natures because they are sufficiently self-evident; effort is rather to be invested only in separating them from each other and in intuiting each of them singly by means of focusing the sharp vision of the mind. For nobody has such sluggish inborn talents as not to perceive that when seated he in some way differs in his condition from when standing on his feet; however, everyone does not with equal distinctness separate the nature of position from everything else contained in the thought about it, nor is everyone able to affirm that nothing else is now changed except position. We do not point this out without a purpose, for frequently the learned are wont to be so clever as to have found a way of obscuring matters even as regards things that are self-evident and known by the unsophisticated; this happens each time they try to explain self-evident things through something more evident: in effect, either they explain something else or nothing at all. For who does not perceive whatever is involved by virtue of which we are changed when we change place? Yet who would conceive that very same thing by being told that *place is the superficies of the surrounding body*? Who would conceive that very same thing in being told this, inasmuch as this superficies can change although I am immobile and the place is unchanging or, on the contrary, this superficies can be moved along with me in such a way that although the same body surrounds me I am nevertheless no longer in the same place. And truly, doesn't it appear

that these learned ones pronounce magic words that are endowed with some mysterious force and elude the understanding of our native wits when they say that *motion,* which is something very well known to everyone, *is the act of the being-in-potency according as it is in potency*? For who understands these words? Yet who is ignorant of what motion is? Who doesn't confess that these learned ones have looked for a difficulty where there is none? Therefore, in order to avoid apprehending composite things in the place of simple things, it must be said that things are never to be explained by any definitions of this kind; rather only those things that have been separated from all others are to be attentively intuited conformable to the illumination of our native wit.

Thirdly, it should be gathered that all human knowledge consists in this one thing—namely, that we distinctly see how these simple natures join together at the same time to compose other things. It is very useful to note this. For each time any difficulty is proposed for examination, nearly everyone remains fixed at the threshold of the problem because he is uncertain about the thoughts with which he ought to occupy his mind and is convinced that he must seek for some new kind of entity previously unknown to him: hence, if it is the question of the nature of the magnet, because he surmises that the problem is hard and difficult, he immediately turns his mind from all those things that are evident and directs it toward things that are very difficult; thus wandering through an empty space of numerous causes, he looks to see whether by chance something new shall be found. By contrast, the person who thinks that nothing in the magnet can be known that does not consist of some simple and self-evident natures is not uncertain about what must be done: for such a person first diligently collects everything experiments can show regarding this stone, and finally from such experiments he attempts to deduce what the mixture of simple natures has necessarily to be in order to produce all those effects experienced in the magnet; and when this is discovered he can boldly assert that he has perceived the true nature of the magnet insofar as it can be discovered by man from the experimental data.

At last, from what has already been said, it can be gathered, fourthly, that some cognitions of things are not to be deemed more obscure than others, because all cognitions are of the same nature and consist solely in the combining of things that are self-evident. Hardly anybody notices this; rather almost everyone is hindered by the contrary opinion, and the more confident permit themselves to assert their conjectures as if they were true demonstrations; and even in regard to matters about which they are certainly ignorant, these people have the presentment that they often see obscure truths as if through a cloud; furthermore, they do not hesitate to propound these obscurities by tying their conceptions of them to certain words with whose help they are accustomed to dissert on many topics and speak "logically," although in truth neither they themselves nor those who hear them understand these words. Indeed, more modest people often abstain from examining many things, even things that are easy and very necessary for life, just because they deem themselves not up to the subject matters; and since they think that these same things can be perceived by others who are extolled as having greater native wit, they embrace the declarations of those in whose authority they place more confidence.

110 Fifthly*, we say that the only things that can be deduced are the following: either things from words, or cause from effect, or effect from cause, or like from like, or the parts or the whole itself from the parts . . .†

111 For the rest, lest by chance the connection of our precepts escape anyone, we divide what can be known into simple propositions and questions. As for simple propositions, we hand down no precepts other than those that prepare the force of knowing to intuit objects more distinctly and scrutinize them more sagaciously, since such objects ought to present themselves spontaneously and cannot be sought after; this we have explained in the twelve preceding precepts, in which we believe that we have displayed everything we consider capable of in some way rendering the use of reason easier. As regards questions, however, some are perfectly understood even if their solution is unknown, and with these alone we will deal in the twelve rules that follow next; finally, other questions are not perfectly understood, and these we reserve for the last twelve rules.

---

* *Quinto* is a conjecture by Adam and Tannery. A and H give *octavo* (*Regulae, Oeuvres*, vol. X, p. 428). Le Roy does not accept the change; see *Regulae,* ed. Le Roy, p. 220, n. 13.

† There seems to be a gap here. Some of the missing material seems to be paraphrased in the second edition of the *Logique* of Port Royal; see *Regulae, Oeuvres*, vol. X, pp. 470–475.

We have not decided upon this division without a plan. We have chosen it both that we may not be forced to say anything that presupposes knowledge of what follows, and also that we may first teach those things we deem must first be attended to in order to cultivate our inborn talents. It is to be noted that among questions that are perfectly understood we place only those in which we distinctly perceive three things: first, those signs by which what is sought after can be distinguished when it presents itself; second, from precisely what it is to be deduced; and third, the manner in which it is established that these so depend upon one another that under no conditions can one be changed and the other remain unchanged. In this way we have all the premises, and nothing remains to be taught except the manner in which the conclusion is discovered. But indeed this need not be taught in the case where one thing is to be deduced from something simple (for as already said this can be done without any precepts). However, where one thing depends upon many things that at the same time imply it, we must teach how to so artfully extract that thing that no greater capacity of inborn wit is required than is involved in the simplest inference. Questions of this kind, since they are the most abstract and occur almost only in arithmetic and geometry, will seem of little use to the inexperienced; nevertheless, I admonish those who wish to grasp perfectly the following part of this method, in which we shall treat of everything else, that they ought to concern themselves with, and for a long time exercise themselves in, this art.

Rule XIII   112

*If we understand a question perfectly, it must be abstracted from
every superfluous concept, reduced to the greatest simplicity,
and divided by enumeration into as many least parts as possible.*

In this one thing we imitate the dialecticians: namely, just as they,   113
in treating of the forms of the syllogisms, suppose that their terms
or matter are known, so too we here make it a prerequisite that a
question be perfectly understood. However, we do not distinguish
as they do between two extremes and a middle; rather we consider
the entire affair in the following manner: first, in each question
there must be something unknown, for otherwise any search would
be in vain; second, what is unknown must be in some way designated, for otherwise we would not be determined to investigate it

rather than anything else; third, this unknown cannot be so designated except through something that is known. All these three conditions are found even in imperfect questions: thus in searching for the nature of the magnet, what we understand to be signified by these two words "magnet" and "nature" is known; and it is this that determines us to seek for the nature of the magnet rather than for something else, and so on. But in addition, for a question to be perfect we require that it be entirely determined, so that nothing more is sought for than what can be deduced from what is given. Examples of such questions follow: if someone asks me what can be inferred concerning the nature of the magnet precisely on the basis of those experiments that Gilbert* asserts that he has made, whether true or false; or if someone asks me what I judge concerning the nature of sound precisely from the fact that the three chords A, B, C, produce an equal sound, and on the supposition that B is twice A in thickness but not longer than A, and is pulled by twice the weight that pulls A, while C is not at all thicker than A, and only twice the length of A, but yet is pulled by a weight four times as great as that which pulls A, and so on. From these examples it is easy to perceive how all imperfect questions can be reduced to perfect ones, as will be further explained in its place; moreover, it is also apparent how to follow this rule in order to abstract every superfluous concept from a well-understood difficulty, thus reducing the difficulty to a point where we no longer think ourselves dealing with this or that subject only, but rather as dealing generally with particular magnitudes that must be compared with each other: for example, after we have determined that we should attend only to this or that experiment concerning the magnet, there remains no difficulty in removing our thought from all the others.

114   Beyond this, we add that the difficulty must, first, be reduced to its simplest form, namely, according to Rules V and VI, and second, be divided, namely, according to Rule VII: thus, if I examine the magnet on the basis of very many experiments, I will run through these experiments separately one after the other; likewise, if I examine the sound, as already said, I shall separately compare the strings A and B, then A and C, and so on, in order that I may afterward embrace them all simultaneously in a suffi-

* William Gilbert (1540–1603), English physician and physicist.

cient enumeration. Moreover, in respect to the terms of any proposition, only these three present themselves for attention by the
pure intellect before we approach its ultimate solution, if it requires use of the eleven following rules; and as to how this is
carried out, it will be clearer from the third part of this treatise.
Moreover, by questions we understand everything in which truth
or falsity is found; the different kinds of questions should be enumerated in order to determine what we can achieve in respect to
each question.

We have already said that falsity is impossible only in the in- 115
tuition of things, that is, in the intuition either of simple things
or of combinations of them; and in this sense the things are not
called questions, but they immediately acquire the name of questions when we deliberate in order to cast some determinate judgment upon them. Neither do we restrict the name "questions" to
those queries made by others; but that too was a question that
Socrates had concerning his own ignorance—or better, concerning
his doubts—when he first began to inquire whether it was true
that he doubted everything, and indeed asserted that he did.

Moreover, we seek either things from words, or causes from 116
effects, or effects from causes, or a whole or other parts from parts,
or finally we seek several of these at once.

We say that we seek things from words each time the difficulty 117
consists in the obscurity of the language. To this type of difficulty
should be assigned not merely all riddles, such as that posed by the
Sphinx—namely, what animal initially has four feet, then two feet,
and finally afterward becomes three-footed; or that of the fisherman
who, standing on the shore and instructed to catch fish with hooks
and fishing rods, said they no longer had the fish they had cap-
tured, but, on the contrary, had those they had as yet been unable
to capture, and so on: indeed, not merely in such riddles, but also
in the greatest part of the things about which the learned dispute,
the question is nearly always about a name. However, we should
not hold their native wits in such low esteem as to judge they
mistakenly conceive the things themselves that they then proceed
to explain with insufficiently appropriate words. In calling *place*,
for example, *the superficies of the surrounding body*, they indeed do not conceive anything false; rather they only misuse the
name of "place," which in its common use signifies that simple and
self-evident nature by reason of which something is said to be here

or there—a nature that consists totally in a particular relation of the thing said to be in place to the parts of the exterior space. Moreover, some people, seeing the name of "place" thus betsowed upon the surrounding superficies, have then improperly called "place" *intrinsic place*; and they have done likewise in other cases. These questions about names occur so frequently that, were there always uniformity of usage among philosophers, nearly all their controversies would be abolished.

118   We seek causes from effects whenever we investigate whether something exists or what it is. . . .*

119   Furthermore, when some question is proposed to us for solution, we often do not immediately notice what kind of question it is— that is, whether it is a matter of seeking things from words, or causes from effects, and so on: for that reason it seems to me super- fluous to say more about these in particular. It will be briefer and more convenient if we investigate at the same time in orderly fashion everything required for the solution of any kind of dif- ficulty. Accordingly, whatever the question posed, to understand it distinctly we must first distinguish what is sought after.

120   One frequently finds people who are in such a rush when in- vestigating propositions that they do not make a concentrated application of their inborn wit to the solution of these problems, and moreover, they fail to notice beforehand by what signs they would distinguish the thing sought after if by chance it presented itself: such people are no less inept than the boy who, when sent somewhere by his master, was so concerned to please that he ran hastily off without as yet having received his instructions or know- ing where he was ordered to go.

121   In every question something certainly ought to be unknown— for otherwise it would be inquired after in vain. Nevertheless, this unknown must be so designated by means of certain conditions that we are immediately determined to investigate one thing rather than another. And, indeed, it is these conditions with which we say it is imperative to be concerned right from the outset: and we will be acting suitably if we direct the keen vision of our mind to intuiting individual things distinctly, and if we diligently inquire

* There is a gap here. Some of the missing material seems to be paraphrased in the second edition of the *Logique* of Port Royal; see *Regulae, Oeuvres*, vol. X, pp. 470–475.

how much the unknown that we seek is limited by each of these conditions. In this undertaking human wit is accustomed to be deceived in two ways, namely, either by assuming something more than is given for determining a question or, on the contrary, by omitting something.

We must guard against assuming numerically more things, and more detailed things, than are given: and this must be guarded against principally in riddles and other queries that are artfully designed to deceive our native wit, but occasionally even in other questions, where something certainly seems to be required for their solution, although no certain reason but mere inveterate opinion persuades us that this is so. For example, in the riddle of the Sphinx, it should not be assumed that the name "foot" signifies only what are truly feet of animals; but one should inquire whether the name "foot" can be transferred to some other things, as occurs, namely, in the cases of the hands of an infant and in the walking stick of old people, because infants and old people use these things for walking.* In a similar way, in the riddle of the fishermen we must be on guard lest the thought of fish so occupy our minds that it detracts our thought from considering those unwanted animals which the poor frequently carry around upon their bodies and cast off whenever they catch them.† Likewise, suppose we seek to discover how that vessel was constructed that we have occasionally seen—namely, the one in whose middle stood a column upon which was placed a figure of Tantalus trying to drink. Now, the water put into that vessel was very well held by the vessel as long as it did not reach a height where it would enter into the mouth of Tantalus; yet immediately upon coming close to his unfortunate lips, the water in its entirety instantly flowed out of the vessel. At first appearance it indeed seems that the entire craftsmanship was in constructing this figure of Tantalus; nevertheless the construction of this figure in no way determines the question but is merely accessory to the question: for the entire difficulty consists in this one thing—namely, to seek the manner in which the vessel must be constructed so that the water, as soon as it has come to a certain altitude, completely flows out of it, whereas before reaching this altitude it does not

* See R 117.
† See R 117.

flow out at all. Finally, if on the basis of all those observations we have made concerning the stars, we seek to find what can be asserted concerning their motions, we must not along with the ancients gratuitously assume, just because it has always seemed so to us from childhood, that the earth is immobile and situated in the center; rather even this should be doubted, so that we may afterward examine what can be judged as certain in this matter. And we should act similarly in other cases.

123   Truly, we sin by omission each time we fail to reflect upon any condition required for the determination of a question, whether the condition is expressed or must in some way be understood: thus in inquiring whether there is any perpetual motion that, unlike the motion of the stars or springs, is not natural but such as could be made by human skill, some people have believed it possible. Thinking that the earth perpetually moves in a circle around its axis and that the magnet truly retains all the properties of the earth, they believe they will have discovered such a perpetual motion if they adapt this magnetic stone so as to move in an orbit in which it will certainly communicate its motion along with other powers to iron. However, even if someone achieved this, he would nevertheless not have made a perpetual motion by art alone; rather he would only have made use of a natural motion—no differently than if he placed a wheel in the current of a river in such a way that it was always moved along. Accordingly, whoever has thought in this manner has omitted a condition required for the determination of the question, and so on.

124   In a question sufficiently understood, we must see precisely in what the difficulty consists, so that having abstracted it from everything else, it is more easily solved.

125   To understand a question, it does not always suffice to know in what the difficulty consists; but we must furthermore reflect upon the individual things required to solve it, and thus if things that are easy to discover present themselves we may omit them, and with them removed from the question only that of which we are ignorant will remain. In the question of the vessel described a little way above, we indeed easily notice how that vessel must be constructed: a column must be placed in its middle, the bird must be painted, and so on; but when all this is rejected as not helping in the solution, there remains the crucial difficulty—namely, that the water initially held by the vessel, having reached

a certain height, flows completely out; hence what we must seek is why this happens.

Accordingly, we here maintain that the full value of our efforts   126
lies in scrutinizing in orderly fashion everything given in a proposition—that is, in rejecting whatever we shall manifestly see does not pertain to the solution, in retaining whatever is necessary, and in reexamining whatever is dubious with more diligence.

Rule XIV   127

A given question is to be put in terms of the real extension of
bodies and presented as a whole to the imagination by the use of
figures alone: for in this manner the question will be perceived
far more distinctly by the intellect.

Moreover, in order that we may employ the assistance of the   128
imagination, we must note that each time one unknown is deduced from another thing previously known, we do not on that account discover any new kind of being, but merely extend this entire cognition in such a way as to perceive that the thing sought for participates in this or that manner in the nature of those things given in the proposition. For example, if someone is blind from birth, we must not hope ever to bring it about by any arguments that he perceives the ideas of colors such as we have derived them from our senses; however, if someone has indeed previously seen primary but never intermediate and mixed colors, it is nevertheless possible for him to form images of those colors he has not seen by means of some sort of deduction based upon a similarity to those colors he has seen. In the same way, if there is any kind of being in the magnet to which up until this time our intellect has seen nothing similar, it is not to be hoped that we will ever come to a cognition of it by reasoning—because for that to occur it would be necessary to be provided with some new sense or a divine mind. On the contrary, we believe that we have attained whatever human ingenuity can discern about the magnet if we very distinctly perceive which mixture of previously noted entities or natures produces effects the same as those that appear in the magnet.

And indeed all these entities already noted, such as extension,   129
figure, motion, and similar things—which it is not fitting to enumerate here—are cognized in different subjects through the same

idea, since we do not imagine the shape of a crown differently if the crown is of silver rather than gold; and the only way this common idea is transferred from one subject to another is through a simple comparison by means of which we affirm that what we seek after is, in this or that respect, either similar to, the same as, or equal to something given: thus in all reasonings it is only through a comparison that we precisely cognize the truth. As an example, examine the following: All A is B, all B is C, therefore all A is C; now, here, that which is sought after and that which is given, namely, A and C, are compared among themselves according to the fact that both are B, and so on. But since, as we have already often warned, the forms of the syllogisms are of no help in perceiving the truth, it will be useful to the reader if, having completely rejected these forms, he conceives that every cognition that is not attained by a simple and pure intuition of a single thing must indeed be attained by a comparison of two or more things among themselves. And unquestionably almost the entire task of human reason consists in preparing for this operation, since when the application of intuition is manifest and simple the assistance of art is not required—rather all that is then required to intuit the truth is the light of nature, the prerogative of which it is to do this.

130   It should be noted that comparisons are said to be simple and manifest when the thing sought after and the thing given participate equally in a certain nature. The other comparisons, however, all require some preparation, because that common nature is not in both things equally; rather it is in them according to some other relations or proportions in which it is involved. And thus it is clear that the principal part of human effort must be directed to reducing these propositions to a point where there is an equality between what is sought for and something known.

131   It is to be further noted that nothing can be reduced to this equality except what is susceptible to greater and less and that all such things are included under the name of magnitude: consequently we understand that, when once the terms of the difficulty have been abstracted from every subject according to the preceding rule, here only are we at last concerned with magnitudes in general.

132   Even when we have reached that point, let us not use the pure intellect in order to imagine things; but let us use the intellect helped by images depicted in the fantasy: and it is to be noted,

finally, that nothing is said of magnitudes in general that cannot be referred to whatever is in the image.*

From all this it is easily concluded that it will be of no little   133
benefit if we transfer those things we understand to be said about magnitudes in general to that image of magnitude most easily and most distinctly portrayed in our imagination: indeed, that this is the image of the real extension of body, abstracted from everything else except that it is figured, follows from what was said in Rule XII, where we conceived the fantasy itself, together with the ideas in it, as nothing other than a genuine body that is really extended and figured. But this is also evident in itself, since in no other subject are all the differences of proportions more distinctly exhibited than in this image of figured extension; for although one thing can be said to be more or less white than another, and likewise one sound more or less acute than another, and so on, nevertheless we cannot define exactly whether such excess consists in a double or triple proportion, and so on, except through some analogy to the extension of a body having figure. Therefore, it stands, guaranteed and unassailable, that questions that are perfectly determined hardly contain any difficulty beyond that which consists in transforming proportions into equalities; and whenever precisely such a difficulty is discovered, it can and ought to be separated from every other subject and thereupon transferred to extension and figures; consequently, excluding thoughts of anything else, we will treat of extension and figures up until Rule XXV.

At this point we would hope to have a reader disposed to the   134
studies of arithmetic and geometry, although we would prefer him not to be versed in these subjects at all rather than to be trained according to the common manner: for the practice of the rules, which I will here treat, is far easier in learning these sciences— for which it entirely suffices—than in mastering any other kind of question; moreover, the utility of these rules is so great in attaining to a higher science that I do not fear to say that, rather than this part of our method being acquired on account of mathematical problems, mathematics should be learned almost exclusively for the purpose of cultivating this method. Furthermore, I will suppose nothing from these disciplines of arithmetic and geometry

* *in specie.*

except perhaps particular things that are self-evident and obvious to everyone. However, the cognition of these same self-evident things as customarily attained by others—even if it is not ruined by manifest errors—is nevertheless obscured by very many tangential and badly conceived principles which we will try to amend at various places in what follows.

135   By extension we understand everything that has length, breadth, and depth, not inquiring whether it is a genuine body or merely space; nor does this extension seem to require greater explanation, since nothing at all is more easily perceived by our imagination. However, since the learned often use such fine distinctions so as to dissipate the natural light, and since they find darkness even in matters about which the uncultivated are never ignorant, I admonish them that, here, extension does not designate something distinct from its very subject, nor do we generally acknowledge philosophical entities of the kind that do not fall under the imagination. For suppose someone can persuade himself that, if whatever is extended in the world of nature is reduced to nothing, that does not contradict the fact that in the meanwhile the very extension exists alone and of itself; nevertheless such a person is not using a bodily idea for this conception, but rather he is using solely his intellect, which is judging badly. And the person will himself admit this if he attentively reflects upon that very image of extension that he will then be attempting to form in the fantasy: for he will note that he does not perceive it bereft of every subject, but rather imagines it altogether differently from how he judges it; and so those abstract entities (whatever the intellect believes about the truth of the matter) are nevertheless never formed in the fantasy separated from subjects.

136   Indeed, since we will do nothing from here on in without the help of the imagination, the task demanded of us is to distinguish carefully by which ideas the individual significations of words are to be displayed to our intellect. For this purpose we propose for consideration these three manners of speaking: *extension occupies place, body has extension,* and *extension is not body.*

137   The first of these shows how extension is taken for that which is extended: for if I say *extension occupies place,* I manifestly conceive the same thing as if I say *the extended occupies place.* Nevertheless, it is not on that account better to use the word *the extended* in order to avoid ambiguity: for *the extended* would not

have signified so distinctly what we conceive, namely, that some subject occupies place because it is extended; moreover, someone could simply interpret *the extended is a subject occupying place* no differently than if I were to say *the animated occupies place*. This reasoning explains why we have said that we would be dealing here with extension rather than with the extended, even though we think that extension should not be conceived differently than the extended.

Now, we proceed to these words: *body has extension*, where we understand that *extension* does indeed signify something other than body; nevertheless we do not form two distinct ideas in our fantasy, one of body, the other of extension, but rather we form one idea only, namely, that of an extended body; and from the point of view of the thing this is no different than if I were to say *body is the extended*, or better yet, *the extended is the extended*. This is peculiar to those entities that exist only in another and can never be conceived without a subject. But is it different in the case of those that are really distinct from subjects: for if I were to say, for example, *Peter has riches*, the idea of Peter is manifestly different from that of riches; likewise, if I were to say *Paul is wealthy*, I would imagine something completely different than if I were to say *wealth is wealth*. Very many people who do not distinguish such a difference falsely conclude that extension contains something different from what is extended, just as the riches of Paul are something different from Paul.

Finally, if it is said *extension is not a body*, then the word "extension" is taken in a very different way from that already discussed, and in this new signification no particular idea in the fantasy corresponds to it, but this declaration is completely effected by the pure intellect, which alone has the faculty of separating out abstract entities of this kind. Here is where very many people fall into error, because not noticing that extension so taken cannot be comprehended by the imagination, they nevertheless represent it to themselves through a genuine idea; but since such an idea necessarily involves the concept of body, if they say that extension so conceived is not a body, they imprudently imply in that statement that *the same thing at the same time is a body and is not a body*. And it is of great importance to distinguish declarations in which names of this kind—*extension, figure, number, superficies, line, point, unity*, and so on—have so strict a signifi-

138

139

cation that they exclude things from which they are not really distinct, as when it is said: *extension, or figure, is not body; number is not the things numbered; the superficies is the boundary of a body; the line is the boundary of the superficies; the point is the boundary of a line; unity is not quantity;* and so on. In order that all these declarations be true, they, and similar propositions, must certainly be removed from the imagination; for this reason we will not be concerned with them in what follows.

140   It should be diligently noted that in all the other propositions in which these names, while retaining the same signification, are said to be in some manner abstracted from subjects, but yet not to exclude or deny anything from which they are not really distinguished, we can and ought to use the help of the imagination: because then, although the intellect attends precisely only to that which is designated by the word, nevertheless the imagination ought to frame a genuine idea of the thing, so that the intellect can turn its attention to other conditions not expressed by the word whenever it is required to do so; for the intellect should never imprudently conclude that such conditions have been excluded. Thus if it is a question about number, let us imagine some subject that is measurable by many units. Now, it is permitted to the intellect to reflect solely on the multitude of the units in the subject before it. Nevertheless we shall beware lest afterward the intellect concludes anything in which it supposes that the things numbered have been excluded from our conception—such as those people do who ascribe astonishingly mysterious characteristics to, and say unadulterated nonsense about, numbers; for they certainly would not bestow such confidence upon these inanities unless they conceived number to be distinct from the things numbered. In like manner, if we are dealing with figure we consider ourselves to be concerned with an extended subject conceived only under this aspect, namely, that it is figured; if we are dealing with a body, we deem ourselves concerned with it as something having length, breadth, and depth; if we are dealing with a superficies, we conceive the body as having length and breadth, omitting but not denying depth; if we are dealing with a line, we consider the body as long only; if we are dealing with the point, we treat of the body omitting everything else except the fact that it is a being.

141   Even though I am here drawing out all these matters at length, nevertheless because the native wits of men are so overwhelmed

by preconceived ideas, I still fear that very few people are sufficiently well protected from all danger of mistake in these matters; and, for all its length, such people will find the explanation of my meaning too brief. For even the very arts of arithmetic and geometry, although the most certain of all, nevertheless deceive us in this matter: who is the calculator who does not believe that his numbers are abstracted from every subject, and not just by means of the intellect, but also that they must be distinguished from every subject by means of the imagination? Who is the geometer who does not obscure the evidence of his object with contradictory principles when he judges that lines lack breadth and superficies lack depth, but yet proceeds to compose some of these from others, not noticing that the line, from whose motion he conceives the superficies to be constructed, is a genuine body and, moreover, that what is lacking in breadth is nothing but a mode of body, and so on? But to avoid spending more time at listing these mistakes, it will be quicker to explain the manner in which we suppose our object must be conceived in order to demonstrate as easily as possible everything that is true in arithmetic and geometry.

Accordingly, we are here dealing with an extended object, and   142 we manifestly consider nothing else about it other than extension itself; and we intentionally refrain from talk about quantity, because some philosophers are so subtle that they have distinguished quantity even from extension; rather we suppose that all questions have been drawn out to that point where nothing else is sought but some unknown extension on the basis of a comparison to some other extension that is known. Since we do not here expect the cognition of any new entity, but merely wish to reduce proportions, however complicated, to that point where what is unknown is found equal to something known, it is certain that all differences of proportions, whatever the various subjects in which they exist, can also be found among two or more extensions; and accordingly it suffices for our project if we consider everything in that same extension which can help us in explaining differences of proportions; and only three things present themselves for this purpose: namely, *dimension, unity,* and *figure.*

By dimension we do not understand anything but the manner   143 and respect according to which any subject is considered to be measurable: so that not only are length, breadth, and depth dimensions of a body, but gravity also is a dimension, according to which subjects are weighed, celerity is a dimension of motion, and there are infinitely many others of this kind. To be sure, the division into very many equal parts, whether real or only intellectual, is itself properly a dimension according to which we number things; and that measure that makes number is properly said to be a species of dimension, although there is some difference in the signification of the name. For if we consider parts as constituting a whole, then we are said to number, whereas, on the contrary, if we regard a whole as distributed into parts, we measure it. For example, we measure centuries by years, days, hours, and moments; if, on the contrary, we number moments, hours, days, and years, we shall finally reckon a century.

144   From these things it is manifest that there can be infinitely many different dimensions in the same subject, and that these dimensions add nothing further to the things measured but should rather be understood in the same manner whether they have a real foundation in these same subjects or were devised by the decision of our mind. For the weight of a body is something real, as is the celerity of motion or the division of centuries into years and days; however, the division of a day into hours and moments is not something real. Nevertheless, all these things are on a par if they are considered only under the aspect of dimension, as must be done here and in the mathematical disciplines; for it pertains more to the physicists to determine whether their foundation is real.

145   Attention to this matter bestows a great light upon geometry, because in geometry nearly everyone erroneously conceives of three species of quantity: the line, the superficies, and the body. For it has been already said that the line and the superficies do not fall under conception as truly different from body or from each other; indeed, if they are considered simply, as abstracted by the intellect, then they are no more different species of quantity than "animal" and "living" in a man are different species of substance. In passing, it should be noted that the three dimensions of bodies—length, breadth, and depth—vary from each other only as far as the names are concerned: for whatever the solid given, nothing prohibits us from selecting any extension we please as length, another as breadth, and so on. And although these three dimensions have a real foundation in every extended thing, simply as something ex-

tended, nevertheless we pay no greater attention to them here than to the infinity of dimensions that are either devised by the intellect or have other foundations in things: thus consider a triangle—if we wish to measure it perfectly, then, from the point of view of the thing, three dimensions must be known, namely, either the three sides, or two sides and one angle, or two angles and the area, and so on; likewise, in a trapezoid five things must be known; six things in a tetrahedron, and so on; and all of these things can be said to be dimensions. However, in order to choose here those dimensions that will be of greatest help to our imagination, we will never attend to more than one or two dimensions simultaneously depicted in our fantasy, even though we understand that in the proposition with which we will be dealing any number of others exist—for art consists in distinguishing as many dimensions as possible, so that we may attend to all of them successively, but yet only to the fewest at one and the same time.

Unity is that common nature which we said above ought to be 146 participated in equally by all those things that are compared with each other. And unless something is already determined as unity by the question, we can assume as unity either one of the magnitudes already given, or any magnitude we choose, and it will be the common measure of all the others: and we will understand there to be as many dimensions in this unity as in those extremes that are to be compared among themselves; and we will consider unity either simply as something extended (by abstracting from everything else), and then it will be the same as the point of the geometers, or we will consider it to be a particular line, or a square.

As regards figures, it has already been shown how the ideas of 147 all things can be devised by means of them alone; it remains for me to state that, from among the innumerable different images of figures, we will here use only those by which all differences of relations or proportions are most easily expressed. Now, precisely two kinds of things are mutually compared—multitudes and magnitudes. And we also have two kinds of figures for displaying them to our conception: for example, the points by which the number of a triangle is designated, or the tree that explains someone's genealogy,

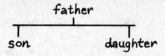

and so on, are figures for expressing a multitude; however, those figures that are continuous and undivided, such as the triangle, square, and so on,

represent magnitudes.

148   Indeed, in order to explain which of all these figures we will use here, it must be known that all relations that can obtain between entities of the same kind must be referred to two headings: namely, to order or to measure.

149   It furthermore should be known that no little effort indeed is involved in devising an order, as is evidenced by this method, which hardly teaches anything else; however, once the order is discovered, there is no further difficulty in recognizing it; rather according to the Rule VII, we can easily mentally run through the individual parts that have been ordered—because in relationships of this kind one thing is directly referred to another without requiring, as in measure, a third as intermediary. Hence we are going to treat here only of transforming relations of measure; for I recognize the order that exists between A and B without taking into consideration anything else but both extremes; however, I do not recognize the proportion of magnitude between two and three unless I consider some third thing, namely, the unity that is the common measure of both.

150   It should also be known that, thanks to the assumption of unity, continuous magnitudes can occasionally all be reduced to a multitude and can always be at least partially so reduced; moreover, the multitude of unities can afterward be placed in such an order that the difficulty that pertained to the recognition of measure finally depends upon an inspection of order alone—and it is in advancing our progress at this that art yields its greatest assistance.

151   Finally, it should be known that, from among the dimensions of

continuous magnitudes, obviously none are conceived more distinctly than length and breadth; nor should we simultaneously attend to more [dimensions] in the same figure in order to mutually compare two different [objects]*: for when a comparison is required among more than two different [objects] it is the nature of art that we run through them successively and attend to only two at one time.

From what has been pointed out, it is easily gathered that even when it is a question of the figures of which the geometers treat, propositions should no less be abstracted from them than from any other matter; and to this end no figures are to be retained except rectilinear and rectangular superficies or straight lines. Moreover, we say that straight lines are also figures, because, as said above, we no less imagine a truly extended subject by the use of straight lines than by the use of a superficies. Finally, these same figures are sometimes to be used to express continuous magnitudes and sometimes also to express a multitude or number; and nothing simpler for expressing all the differences of relations can be found by human effort. 152

Rule XV 153

It very often helps to draw these figures and to display them to the external senses so that in this manner our thinking is kept attentive.

Moreover, it is self-evident how they must be depicted so that, when displayed to our very eyes, their images are formed more distinctly in our imagination: first we will depict unity in three ways, namely, through the square, □ , if we attend to the unit as something with length and breadth, or through the line, ——— , if we consider it only as something with length, or finally through the point, ● , if we do not regard it except in the respect that a multitude is composed from it; and whatever the manner in which it is depicted and conceived, we understand that unity is always a subject extended in every way and capable of infinitely many dimensions. And so also with the terms of a proposition: if we must simultaneously attend to two of their different magnitudes, then we will represent the terms by means 154

---

* The Latin seems to require a neuter plural noun, such as *objecta*, after *duo*. But perhaps Descartes intended *duas* so that we would have "two [dimensions]" instead of "two [objects]"; cf. R 156.

of a rectangle whose two sides will be the two proposed magnitudes. Furthermore, if the magnitudes are incommensurable with unity, we will represent them in this manner, ▭ ; however, if they are commensurable with unity, we will represent them in this manner, ▦ , or this manner, ⦂⦂ ; and no other representations will be employed unless it is a question of a multitude of unities. Finally, if we attend to one of their magnitudes only, either we depict it by a rectangle, whose one side is the given magnitude and whose other side is unity, in this way, ▭ , which we do each time we must compare the given magnitude with some superficies; or we depict it through length alone, in this manner, ——— , if it is regarded only as an incommensurable length; or in this manner, ● ● ● ● ● , if it is a multitude.

155

RULE XVI

As regards those things that, although necessary for the conclusion, do not require the present attention of the mind, it is better to designate them by very brief marks than by whole figures: in this way memory will not be able to be deceived, and in the meantime thinking will not be distracted by having to retain them while busying itself with deducing others.

156   Furthermore, as we said, from among all those dimensions that can be depicted in our fantasy, no more than two different dimensions are to be contemplated in one and the same intuition, whether of the eyes or of the mind. Now, it is required that we retain all the others so that they readily present themselves each time the task requires it; and it seems that memory has been instituted by nature for this purpose. But because memory is often wavering, art has very aptly discovered the practice of writing in order that we are not forced to spend any part of our attention in reviving our memories while we are applying ourselves to other things. By relying upon the help of writing, we commit nothing further to memory; but depicting whatever will have to be retained upon paper, we abandon a free and entire fantasy to present ideas. Moreover, in writing down what must be retained, we will use very brief marks in order that, after we have distinctly inspected each according to Rule IX, we can, according to Rule XI, run through all of them with a very quick motion of thought and intuit as many of them as possible at the same time.

157   Therefore, we will designate by a single mark, chosen at will,

whatever will have to be regarded as one in respect to solving a difficulty. But for the sake of ease, we will use the characters a, b, c, and so on for magnitudes already known, and A, B, C, and so on for expressing unknowns. To these we will often prefix the marks of numbers—1, 2, 3, 4, and so on—in order to express a multitude of them. Likewise, we will subjoin these marks of numbers to them in order to express the number of relations that are to be understood in them: thus if I write $2a^3$, it will be the same as if I were to say twice the magnitude indicated by the letter a in which three relations are contained. And by this means we will not only economize on words, but what is more important, we will express the terms of the difficulty so purely and straightforwardly that, although nothing useful is omitted, we shall nevertheless never discover anything superfluous in these expressions that would uselessly occupy the capacity of our inborn wits whenever very many things will have to be embraced by our mind.

In order to understand all this more clearly, it should first be noted that the calculators have been accustomed to designate individual magnitudes through very many units or through some number; however, we here no less abstract from these very numbers than a little while ago we abstracted from geometrical figures and everything else. We do so partly to avoid the tedium of long and superfluous computations, but principally in order that the parts of the subject pertaining to the nature of the difficulty always remain distinct and not become complicated by useless numbers: thus if it is a matter of seeking for the base [*basis*] of the right triangle whose two given sides are 9 and 12, the calculator will say it is $\sqrt{225}$, or 15; we, however, will substitute a and b for 9 and 12, and shall discover the base [*basim*] to be $\sqrt{a^2 + b^2}$; and those two parts, a^2 and b^2, which when presented as numbers are confused, will remain distinct. 158

It is also to be noted that by the number of relations is to be understood the proportions that follow in a continuous order. In the common algebra others attempt to express these through very many dimensions and figures and call the first of these proportions the root; the second, the square; the third, the cube; the fourth, the biquadratic, and so on. I confess that for a long time I myself have been deceived by these very names: for beyond the line and the square, nothing seemed able to be more clearly exhibited to my imagination than the cube and other figures depicted in their likeness; and certainly I resolved no few difficulties with the aid 159 of these images. But finally, after many experiences, I realized I never discovered anything through this manner of conceiving things that I could not recognize far more easily and distinctly without it; and indeed, lest they trouble conception, such names should be altogether rejected, because according to Rule XV, the same magnitude, whether called cube or biquadratic, is never to be exhibited to the imagination other than as a line or a super-ficies. Accordingly, it is principally to be noted that the root, quadratic, cube, and so on are nothing but continuously propor-tional magnitudes, and unity in these proportions always depends upon laying out in advance those assumptions about which we have spoken above: the first proportional is related to this unity by an immediate and single relation; the second proportional is related to unity by the intermediary of the first proportional, and accordingly it is related to unity by two relations; the third pro-portional is related to unity with the first and second proportionals as intermediaries, and thus through three relations, and so on. Therefore, from here on in we shall call first proportional that magnitude which in algebra is call the root, and we shall call second proportional what in algebra is called the square, and so on with the rest.

160   Finally, it must be remarked that even though we here abstract the terms of a difficulty from given numbers in order to examine its nature, nevertheless it frequently happens that with the given numbers the difficulty can be resolved in a simpler fashion than if abstracted from them: this is due to a double use of numbers that we have already hit upon, namely, the same numbers sometimes express order and sometimes measure; and therefore, after we have sought for an expression of the difficulty in general terms, it is fitting to recast the same difficulty in terms of given numbers in order to see whether by chance they will furnish us with any simpler solution: for example, after we have seen that the base [basim] of a right triangle with the sides a and b is $\sqrt{a^2 + b^2}$, we should take 81 for a^2 and 144 for b^2, which when added is 225, whose root, or mean proportional between unity and 225, is 15. From this we will know that the base [basim] 15 is commensurable with the sides 9 and 12—but not because we know in general that such is the case with the base [basis] of any right triangle whose one side is to the other as 3 is to 4. We distinguish all these things, we who seek an evident and distinct cognition of things; however,

the calculators do not distinguish them; they are content if the sum sought after presents itself to them, even if they fail to recognize how it depends upon what is given—and yet it is in such a recognition alone that science, properly speaking, consists.

And indeed we should generally follow the practice of never 161 consigning to memory things that do not require constant attention when we can put them down in writing; otherwise superfluous memories might appropriate a portion of our native talents away from the object of present cognition; and certainly an index should be made in which we will write down the terms of the question as they will first be serially proposed; and then we will write down how these same terms are abstracted, as well as the marks through which they are designated, so that after the solution shall have been found in terms of these very marks, we will apply the same marks without any help of the memory to the particular subject that will be in question; for nothing is ever abstracted except from what is less general. Therefore I will write in this manner: the base AC is sought for in the right triangle ABC, and I abstract the difficulty as follows, namely, to find generally the magnitude of a base from the magnitudes of the sides; then for AB, which is 9, I substitute a; for BC, which is 12, I substitute b; and so forth with the rest.

It is to be noted that we shall still use these four rules in the 162 third part of this treatise; and we will use them in a wider sense than has been explained here, as will be discussed in its proper place.

RULE XVII 163

The proposed difficulty should be run through directly, abstracting from the fact that some of its terms are known and others are unknown; and we should intuit the mutual dependence of individual terms upon others by correctly viewing and reviewing these terms.

The foregoing rules have taught the manner in which determinate 164 and perfectly understood difficulties are to be abstracted from individual subjects and reduced to a point such that afterward nothing else is sought for except particular magnitudes which must be known on the basis that they are referred through this or that relation to a certain thing that is given. Now, in these five following rules we will explain how these same difficulties are to be so structured that, however many unknown magnitudes are in one proposition, they are all subordinated each to another in such a manner that, as the first will be to unity, so the second will be to the first, the third to the second, the fourth to the third, and consequently even if they are exceedingly many, they make a sum equal to some known magnitude. All this is done by a method so exceedingly certain that on the basis of it we may securely assert that human skill could not have devised any way of reducing these terms to still simpler ones.

165   For the present it must be noted that in every question that is to be resolved by deduction, whereas all other ways are more difficult and indirect, there is one way that is obvious and direct; and by means of it we can most easily pass from particular terms to others. In order to understand this, it is necessary to have remembered those things said under Rule XI, where we explained that concatenation of propositions which is such that, if individual propositions are compared with those near to them, we easily perceive the manner in which the first and the last mutually relate, even though we do not so easily deduce the intermediates from the extremes. Now, therefore, if without any interruption in the order we intuit the mutual dependence of single propositions so that on this basis we infer how the last depends upon the first, then we run through the difficulty in a direct manner; but, on the contrary, if based upon the fact that we know the first and the last are connected in a certain manner, we wished to deduce what are the intermediate propositions that join them together, we would certainly follow an order that is indirect and inverted. Since in this case we are indeed dealing only with complicated questions—namely, those in which, from known extremes, particular intermediaries must be known by means of a changed order—the entire artistry will consist in the fact that, by supposing unknowns for knowns, we can hold out to ourselves an easy and direct path of research however intricate the difficulties. Moreover, nothing will hinder such a technique; for from the beginning of this part we

have supposed ourselves to know that there is such a dependence of the unknown terms in a question upon the known terms that the unknowns are obviously determined by the knowns. Thus if we reflect upon those very terms that first present themselves, and while recognizing this determination, do what is permitted— namely, consider unknowns as knowns—so that from them we gradually, and through genuine motions of thought, also deduce all the knowns as though they were unknowns, then we fulfill everything this rule prescribes: we reserve an example of this, as of very many of those things about which we speak after this point, until Rule XXIV, because such examples can be presented more conveniently at that point.

RULE XVIII

For this, only four operations are required—addition, subtraction, multiplication, and division; of these the latter two operations are often not to be completed here, both so as not to complicate matters rashly, and also because they can be completely treated more easily later on.

166

A multitude of rules often proceeds from the inexperience of the teacher, and those that can be reduced to one general precept are less perspicuous if they are divided into many particular rules. For this reason we here reduce to only four headings all the operations that are to be used in running through questions, that is, in the deducing of particular magnitudes from others; as to why these headings suffice, one will learn from the explanation of these headings.

167

If we come to the cognition of one magnitude from the fact that we have the parts from which it is composed, that happens by addition; if we come to know the part from the fact that we have the whole and the excess of the whole over some part, that happens by subtraction; nor are there more ways in which any magnitude can be deduced from other magnitudes absolutely taken in which it is in some way contained. If indeed a particular magnitude is to be discovered from other magnitudes from which it obviously differs, and in which it is in no way contained, it is necessary that it be related to these other magnitudes in some respect: and if this relation or proportion is to be directly deter-

168

mined, then multiplication has to be used; if it is to be determined indirectly, then division has to be used.

169   In order to explain clearly these last two operations, it must be known that unity, of which we have already spoken, is here the basis and foundation of all relations, and occupies the first step in the series of continuously proportioned magnitudes; moreover, the given magnitudes are contained in the second step, and the magnitudes sought after are in the third, fourth, and remaining steps, if the proportion is direct; however, if the proportion is indirect, the magnitude sought after is contained in the second and in the other intermediate steps, and the given magnitude is in the last step.

170   For if it is said that as unity is to a or to 5, which is given, so b or 7, which is given, is to the unknown, which is ab or 35,* then a and b are in the second grade, and ab, which is produced from them, is in the third grade. Likewise, if it is said that as unity is to c or 9, so ab or 35 is to the unknown abc or 315, then abc is the fourth step, and it is generated by two multiplications with ab and c, which are in the second grade, and so forth with the rest. Likewise, as unity is to a or 5, so a^2 or 25 is to a^3 or 125; and finally as unity is to a or 5, so a^3 or 125 is to a^4, which is 625, and so on: multiplication is performed in no other way than this, whether the same magnitude is expanded by itself or by a magnitude obviously different.

171   Indeed, if it is said that as unity is to a or 5, the given divisor, so B or 7, which is unknown, is to ab or 35, the given dividend, then the order is changed and indirect: that is why B, which is unknown, cannot be found except by dividing ab, which is given, by a, which is given. It is the same if it is said that as unity is to A or 5, which is unknown, so the unknown A or 5 is to a^2 or 25, which is given; or it is the same if it is said that as unity is to A or 5, which is unknown, so a^2 or 25, which is unknown, is to a^3 or 125, which is given, and so forth with the rest. We embrace all this under the name "division," although it must be noted that these last species of division contain greater difficulties than prior cases, because one more often finds in them an unknown magnitude, which, accordingly, involves more relations. The meaning of

---

* At this point Descartes does not conform with his plan of R 157 to express unknowns by capital letters.

these examples is the same as if it were said that the square root must be extracted from a^2 or from 25, or the cube root from a^3 or from 125, and so forth with the rest, which is the fashion of speech used by the calculators. Or to explain these examples with the terms of the geometers: it is the same as if it were said that we must discover the mean proportional between that assumed magnitude we call unity and that designated by a^2, or the two mean proportionals between unity and a^3, and likewise with the others.

From these things it is easily gathered how these two operations 172 suffice for discovering whatever magnitudes are to be deduced from others because of some relationship. And with these things understood, it follows that we must explain how these operations ought to be submitted to the examination of the imagination, and even how they are to be portrayed for the eyes themselves, so that afterward we may finally explain their use or practical application.

If addition or subtraction are to be performed, we conceive the 173 subject in the manner of a line or in the manner of an extended magnitude in which length alone is to be regarded: for if the line a is to be added to the line b,

we adjoin one to the other in this way, ab,

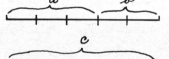

and c is produced.

If, however, the smaller is to be taken from the greater, namely, 174 b from a,

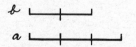

we place one above the other in this way,

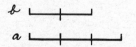

and thus we have that part of the greater line which cannot be covered by the smaller, namely,

———

175   In multiplication we also conceive the given magnitudes in the manner of lines, but we imagine a rectangle to be made from them: for if we multiply *a* by *b*,

we apply one to the other at right angles in this way,

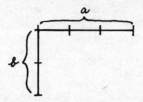

and make the rectangle:

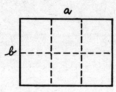

176   Next, if we wish to multiply *ab* by *c*,

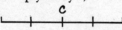

it is necessary to conceive *ab* as a line, namely, *ab*,

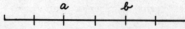

in order to yield as *abc*:

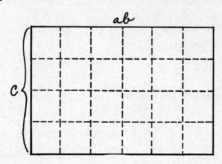

177   Finally, in division, when the divisor is given, we imagine the magnitude to be divided as a rectangle whose one side is the di-

visor and whose other side is the quotient: for example, if the rectangle *ab* is to be divided by *a*,

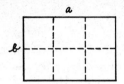

the breadth *a* is taken from it, and there remains *b* as quotient:

or, on the contrary, if the same rectangle is divided by *b*, the height *b* will be taken away and the quotient will be *a*,

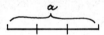

However, in those divisions in which the divisor is not given, but is designated merely by some relation, as when it is said that the square or cube root, and so on, must be extracted, then it is to be noted that the term to be divided, and all the others, are always to be conceived as lines existing in a series of continuous proportionals, the first of which proportionals is unity, and the last of which is the magnitude to be divided. Moreover, as regards the manner of discovering however many mean proportionals lie between unity and the last, we will speak about it in its place; but now it suffices to have warned that we suppose that such operations have not as yet been completely justified here, since they must be performed by an indirect and reflexive movement of the imagination, and we shall now deal only with questions that are to be run through directly. 178

As regards the other operations, their complete treatment is easiest if we follow the manner in which we said they are to be conceived. Nevertheless, it remains to be explained how their terms are to be prepared; for although when first we deal with any difficulty, we are free to conceive its terms as lines or rectangles, without ever attributing to them any other figures, as said in Rule XIV, still it frequently happens in our reasoning concerning the rectangle that, after it has been produced by multiplication of two lines, it soon afterward must be conceived as a line in order to 179 perform another operation; moreover, the same rectangle or line produced from some addition or subtraction must soon afterward be conceived as some other rectangle placed above a designated line by which it is to be divided.

180   Accordingly, it is part of our task to explain here how every rectangle can be transformed into a line, and, on the other hand, how a line or even a rectangle can be changed into another rectangle whose side is designated. This is very easy for the geometers to understand, provided they notice that each time we compare lines with some rectangle, as we do in this place, we always mean to conceive lines as rectangles, where one side of the rectangle is that length we have assumed as unity. Thus this entire difficulty reduces to such a proposition: given a rectangle, to construct another equal to it on a given side.

181   Although this matter is familiar to novices at geometry, it nevertheless pleases me to explain it, lest I appear to have omitted something.

182   RULE XIX
By this method of reasoning we must seek for just as many magnitudes expressed in two different ways as there are unknowns that we suppose as knowns when directly running through a difficulty: for in this way we will have just that many comparisons between two equal things.

183   RULE XX
When equations have been discovered, the operations that we have omitted must be completed, and we should never use multiplication whenever there will be place for division.

184   RULE XXI
If there are many equations of this kind, they are all to be reduced to one, namely, to that whose terms will occupy fewer steps in the series of continuously proportioned magnitudes according to which they must be arranged in order.

THE END*

---

* *FINIS* appears in A and H; see *Regulae, Oeuvres*, vol. X, p. 469.

II

DISCOURSE

Introduction

Descartes did not publish his earliest treatise, *Rules for the Direction of the Native Talents* (1628); and the condemnation of Galileo convinced him not to publish *The World*, which contains the foundations of his physics as developed by 1633. With the *Discourse concerning Method* (1637) and its three accompanying essays, *Dioptrics*, *Meteors*, and *Geometry*, Descartes officially, but anonymously, introduced his philosophy and science to the learned world. He was already forty-three when the *Discourse* and the three essays were published; he had been cautious, had resisted premature display, and was finally prepared to put in his first public appearance in a grand manner.

One need not read between the lines to see that the *Discourse* and the three essays are intended to be apology and manifesto. In the *Discourse* Descartes dwells on his philosophical autobiography —he wants to explain his original quest for a sound and generally applicable method of discovering truth. Moreover, he intends to provide evidence of the practical results he can achieve by means of the method he finally discovered; the three essays accompanying the *Discourse* are meant to be impressive samples of his method at work. Clearly buoyed up and confident of his method, he does not refrain from applying it to the problems of metaphysics. The *Discourse* gives every indication that Descartes is ready to rival, and will try to supplant, the comprehensive authority of Aristotle.

It is inappropriate to look for any detailed statement of Descartes's method in the *Discourse*. He outlines his method, but he explicitly advises readers to learn it by studying the three sample applications—the essays. Only in the *Rules* is there anything like a formal statement of Descartes's method, and where appropriate I shall borrow from the details of the *Rules* in pointing up some of the subtleties in the *Discourse*.

In the very important fourth part of the *Discourse* Descartes employs his method to demonstrate the nature of the human mind and the nature and existence of God. He regards these two questions as the primary questions of "First Philosophy," or metaphysics. The demonstrations of these questions as contained in the *Discourse* are less elaborate than those in the *Meditations*—and there is great advantage in studying the *Discourse* before proceeding to the *Meditations*. The *Discourse* moves more rapidly than the *Meditations*, it enables one to focus with comparative ease on the major steps in Descartes's demonstrations, and it makes less use of refined technical vocabulary. Such refined distinctions are useful in the *Meditations* because it is a response to the objections made to the *Discourse*; but the distinctions of the *Meditations* are likely to be lost on one who reads it first.

In turning to the fourth part of the *Discourse* we should first consider the general procedures of demonstration that Descartes employs; next, the order of the various arguments; and finally, each of the arguments seriatim.

Descartes does not use the word "demonstration" lightly. He means to suggest that the reasons by which he claims to prove the nature of the human mind and the nature and existence of God are absolutely conclusive. Descartes distinguishes two modes of demonstration, analysis and synthesis.

"Analysis" refers to the process of teaching someone, possibly oneself, to recognize first principles. First principles, or those a priori truths that are the starting points for all other knowledge, are clearly not proved by reference to other truths. However, we are likely to be blinded to these first principles by confusing prejudices that are psychologically more familiar than the first principles. An analysis proceeds by exposing the dubious character of more familiar beliefs in order to aid the mind to discover what is truly a first principle or an a priori. "Synthesis" refers to the process of proceeding from first principles by necessary deduction to other truths that follow from them, or are a posteriori.[1] In my opinion the *Discourse* and *Meditations* contain both analysis and synthesis, although Descartes claims to use only the analytic, or didactic, procedure in the *Meditations*.[2]

In the *Discourse* Descartes argues, first, that the nature and existence of material things can be doubted, while the nature and existence of mind can be known with absolute assurance; second, that the knowledge of oneself as a thinking thing provides one with a general criterion of truth; third, that God's nature and existence can be known; fourth, that God's existence can be proved in a second way; fifth, that all other knowledge depends on our knowledge of God.

Consonant with the reductive character of analysis, Descartes treats any belief that is not certain and indubitable as if it were false. In this way he denies to such beliefs the status of first principles and recognizes that if they are ever to be known, they must be retrieved from theoretical doubt by being deduced with necessity from the first principle or principles that emerge at the end of the process of reductive analysis.

Now, Descartes says: "And because there are men who make a mistake in reasoning even regarding the most simple matters of geometry, and form paralogisms, I, judging myself subject to error as much as any other man, rejected as false all the reasons I had previously taken as demonstrations."[3] A paralogism is a contradiction, and whatever implies a contradiction is itself contradictory. Mathematics has its starting points in simple things or natures and rules of derivation that may at first seem certain and indubitable. But no matter how certain and indubitable these simple things or natures and rules of derivation may at first seem, we cannot be sure that they are true unless we also know that no contradiction is implied by them. However, Descartes maintains that (prior to knowing God) we cannot know beyond a shadow of doubt that mathematics is not contradictory. And since geometry and arithmetic enter into our representations of the nature of material things, by doubting arithmetic and geometry we ipso facto call into doubt not merely the existence, but also the nature of material things—there is always the possibility that in representing matter by means of mathematics, we are in effect representing something that is contradictory and hence impossible.

Thus reductive analysis leads Descartes to the point where no beliefs about the once-so-familiar world remain certain and indubitable—he is left with sense qualities or images that do not reveal their causes. But then—as it were at the terminus of reductive analysis—there emerges what he takes as his first principle,

I think, therefore I am. From this he will somehow have to deduce with necessity whatever else he can know.

As stated, Descartes moves more rapidly in the *Discourse* than in the *Meditations.* The next transition is a case in point. This transition elicited objections that caused him to argue more cautiously in the *Meditations.* Let us consider what he says in the *Discourse,* explain the difficulties it posed, and see in a general way how he reformulated his arguments in the *Meditations.*

In the *Discourse* Descartes says that because the soul or mind can be known to exist without knowing whether material things exist, it thereby follows, first, that the mind is a substance whose entire essence or nature is to think and, second, that this substance is distinct from any material substance, even if such a material substance does in fact exist.

The complexities that underlie this assertion demand attention. In exploring this topic Descartes means by a substance a thing that is presupposed by the particular features that inhere in it, but that itself does not inhere in something further. The essential meaning, then, is that two substances, despite their causal relations to each other, are distinct things—that is, not identical with each other. Still, the difficulty remains. Why should Descartes say that just because one can know that the mind exists without yet knowing whether the body or anything material exists, it thereby follows that mind is a different substance from body and thus not identical with the body even if the body does exist and interact with it?

To shed some light on this we have to consider further Descartes's manner of reasoning about substances. When the human mind conceives the thing or substance in which properties have to inhere in order to exist, it conceives this thing or substance through some property essential to the thing or substance; and all other properties that presuppose the thing or substance are referred to the thing or substance through an essential property. Since the only way the human mind has of conceiving a thing or substance in which certain properties inhere or can inhere is by an essential property presupposed by inessential properties of the thing or substance, it follows that we would lose our conception or understanding of the thing or substance if we did not consider it as always bound to have its essential property. For example, we would lose our conception or understanding of a material thing or substance if we did not consider it as bound to have the essential property that enables us to conceive or understand a material thing or substance—namely, the property of extension. From this it follows that the same thing or substance cannot be conceived to have two essential properties, that is, two properties neither of which necessarily involves the other or any third common property. For to say that the same substance could have two essential properties is equivalent to saying that we could conceive the substance as not having a property that is essential to it. Thus every thing or substance can have only one essential property that is presupposed by other properties that can be in it. It therefore follows that the substance that thinks cannot be conceived as identical with the substance that is extended in space, that is, with material substance. Thinking substance and material substance are not identical because, as we have seen, we can conceive and know that thinking exists without knowing whether anything material exists and, moreover, we can conceive the nature of body—that is, extension—without attributing any thinking to it.

One can still question whether it is correct to employ a notion of substance whereby we reason about substance only on the basis of properties. Should we, perhaps, introduce a notion of substance such that no human reasoning on the basis of properties could tell us which property or properties are essential to a particular thing or substance? The introduction of such a notion of substance would certainly have the result that no matter how much it seemed to us that mind and matter were capable of distinct existence we would never know it as certain. Such a notion of substance would, however, saddle us with something we do not understand. For since we can reason only the basis of what we discern as necessarily connected or not necessarily connected, if we should proceed to say that such reasoning has no relevance to judging which things can exist one without the other, we would in effect have said that reasoning is not reasoning at all.

Indeed, in the *Meditations* Descartes will not immediately infer the distinctness of the substance of mind and the substance of matter simply because thinking can be known to exist while the existence and nature of matter is in doubt. However, neither will he hastily assume that there is but one substance in which thinking and extension could co-inhere. Rather than immediately concerning himself with the notion of substance, or with other difficult matters such as the correctness of mathematical reasoning, he will there proceed to a more primary question—namely, the grounds that human reason has for trusting any of its ideas. In the *Meditations* no doctrine about the substantial distinction of mind and matter will be asserted until after Descartes believes himself to have proved God's power, goodness, and existence.[4]

We shall soon turn to the principal proof of God's existence in the *Discourse,* but first it is necessary to consider Descartes's general criterion of truth.

Descartes says:

> And having noticed that there is nothing at all in this *I think, therefore I am* that assures me I am speaking the truth except that I see very clearly that in order to think it is necessary to exist, I judged that I could take as a general rule that things we conceive very clearly and very distinctly are all true; but there is only some difficulty to note well the things that we conceive distinctly.[5]

I believe that Descartes's reasoning is clarified by reference to his *Rules.* In the *Rules* he emphasizes that the only way the human mind can perceive necessity is by a single act of reasoning that immediately allows for a universal generalization about what is necessarily connected. Thus, if one perceives that it is true that he himself thinks, because one clearly and distinctly intuits the fact, this clarity and distinctness cannot be an absolutely sufficient guarantee of truth in that case unless it is recognized to be such in all cases. Furthermore, in the *Rules* Descartes points out that certain and evident cognition is knowledge. That is akin to saying that whatever is very clear and very distinct is knowledge. However, he distinguishes between two senses of the word "knowledge," a weaker and a stronger. Only those objects that are certain and evident, or such as can be seen into by intuition, are firm knowledge; other objects, for which we require an element of memory, because we cannot render them evident by reducing them to an intuition, are not firm cases of knowledge. Since in both the *Discourse* and *Meditations* Descartes is interested in metaphysical certitude or absolutely firm knowledge, he can rely only on certain and evident cognitions or on very clear and very distinct perceptions in seeking first principles and immediate inferences from them.

Having placed into doubt both the existence and the nature of

matter, having affirmed the truth of the *I think, therefore I am,*
and having pointed out the general rule that whatever one perceives very clearly and very distinctly is true, Descartes proceeds to
say that the existence of God—the existence of an infinite, eternal,
immutable, all-knowing, all-powerful, and all-perfect being—is
manifestly true. His assertion that God exists seems like a very
bold forward step, and I will try to explain why I think he believed himself entitled to make so sudden and bold an advance.

Whatever can be immediately known, based on the first principle, *I think, therefore I am,* must be perceived as necessarily
implied in that first principle by an immediate inference. Thus
we cannot expect Descartes to prove an immediate consequence
of the *I think, therefore I am* by first proving other things on which
it depends, for if such had to be done it would not be an immediate consequence. However, what we can expect of him—and this
he tries to do—is to remove certain prejudices that may blind us
to perceiving an immediate consequence of the *I think, therefore
I am.* To understand how Descartes tries to remove these obstacles, and thus to understand better why he says that the existence of God is an immediate consequence of the *I think, therefore I am,* we must pay close attention to the conditions of his
argument.

The problem Descartes poses is to determine whether any ideas
are true in addition to those that represent what we immediately
discern in ourselves when perceiving the *I think, therefore I am.*
It is obvious that any idea representing something about whose
nature or existence we are in doubt cannot be said to be a true
idea. Any such idea provides us with no firm basis for determining
why we have that idea in the first place—in short, it provides no
firm basis for reasoning about causality. For example, since we
can doubt the nature and existence of matter, it follows that our
idea of the nature of matter cannot persuade us that matter exists
and causes our idea of it, nor can our idea of matter tell us what
else other than matter does cause our idea of matter. Thus any
idea whose truth is in doubt provides no basis for knowing what,
if anything, exists outside ourselves as immediately known in the
I think, therefore I am. By contrast, any idea so representatively
perfect as to assure us that what it represents truly exists will also
provide us with a reliable notion of causation by reference to which
we can show that we would not have the idea unless it were caused

in us by an object such as it represents. Thus the determination of the real representative perfection of ideas, the determination of the truth of ideas, and the determination of the metaphysically valid notion of causation must be established concurrently.

Accordingly, when Descartes says that he sees no reason why those ideas that he doubts—for example, the idea of matter—may not arise from himself, he is simply emphasizing that they do not indicate with certainty and evidence that they proceed from what they represent. He is not affirming that he knows those ideas are caused by himself so much as emphasizing that he is unable, on the basis of what they represent, to determine conclusively what causes them to be in him.

However, this manner of leading each of us to focus in on our own self—because we have been unable to find familiar causes for our ideas—removes an important obstacle by intuiting the true nature of causation. It vividly reminds each of us that there is no prospect for discerning the true nature of causation except on the basis of things clear and evident to us. Since what thus far has been clear and evident is only the immediately known nature of oneself as a thinking thing, one wonders whether one might indeed cause oneself and one's ideas—and thus be self-sufficient and alone in the world.

Yet since we have doubts about our own causal self-sufficiency, we are made to realize that the most essential problem is to determine both what makes something self-sufficient be self-sufficient and what makes something dependent (or an effect) be something dependent (or an effect). Clearly, our existence, or the existence of anything whatever, has some explanation, for whatever exists either is self-sufficient or depends on the self-sufficient. Thus, by determining what makes the self-sufficient be self-sufficient and what makes an effect be an effect, we shall finally have the standard whereby we may know whether we explain our own existence or whether, by contrast, we depend on some self-sufficient thing whose nature we understand but recognize to be different from our own.

Before proceeding any further in our attempt to determine what constitutes the nature of self-sufficiency and what constitutes the nature of an effect, it is important to note that we cannot know what makes an effect be an effect without knowing what makes the self-sufficient on which the effect depends be self-sufficient. In

the language of Descartes's *Rules* cause and effect are not correlative, but the cause is absolute. To know what effects are possible it is first necessary to know what the cause is. This is so
because were it not in the nature of an effect to be necessarily
dependent on its self-sufficient cause, we could conceive everything in the nature of an effect as capable of existing without its
self-sufficient cause. If this were so, what we called an effect would
actually be represented as having a self-sufficient nature itself. Thus
we may infer that every effect is *necessarily* dependent on the self-
sufficient nature on which it depends. Moreover, it becomes clearer
that the self-sufficient nature, or cause, is at most one "thing." This
is so because the self-sufficient nature cannot be multiplied in
instances on whose individual features it would then depend. In
short, the self-sufficient nature cannot be a universal like "man"
that so depends upon the matter of particulars that various causes
can make it exist in some particulars and cease to exist in others.
If one needs an analogy for the self-sufficient nature—and it is
only an analogy—it is more like "space," which couldn't be in one
place without being everywhere and which is always of one nature
throughout.

Since one cannot know whether one is effect or self-sufficient
without understanding the nature of an effect and the nature of
self-sufficiency, and since one can know the nature of an effect only
by first recognizing the nature of self-sufficiency that is necessarily
presupposed by the nature of an effect, and since the only things
known with certainty and evidence are those things immediately
discerned in oneself as a thinking thing—the best procedure for
each of us is to consider whether he himself could be self-sufficient
by virtue of what is certain and evident about himself, namely,
thinking and willing.

Now, by analyzing this provisional possibility and by seeing if
I can reduce it to absurdity, I have the best prospect that the true
nature of self-sufficiency, and consequently the true nature of an
effect, will present itself to my intuitive grasp. What I must constantly bear in mind throughout this procedure is that that there
is no prospect of intuiting the true nature of self-sufficiency, and
consequently the true nature of an effect, among those natures I
have called into doubt—that is, among mathematical and material
natures and among any secret or obscure powers or capacities I
may fancy to lie within "regions" of the self that I do not im-

mediately know in the *I think, therefore I am.* To go to any of these dubious terrains to look for an intuition of the true nature of self-sufficiency, and hence for the true nature of an effect, would be as silly as going back to the nature of a square in order to understand it once I have already realized that it cannot be understood except by first understanding simple things on which it must somehow depend, such as lines, angles, and so on.

Hence, realizing that my self-sufficiency, if indeed I am self-sufficient, can consist only in things known to me, I in turn must realize that the nature of self-sufficiency will have to consist in intellect and will—which is what is immediately known to me in the *I think, therefore I am.* In short, self-sufficiency can be clearly and evidently thought of by me only if I represent it through intellect and will.

However, as has been said, the self-sufficient is perfect inasmuch as all else depends on it and nothing can limit it. Thus, since I can think self-sufficiency only through intellect and will, and since the self-sufficient is perfect and unlimited, the self-sufficient nature will have to be conceived as an intellect and will that is perfect and unlimited. But to be such is to be God—it is to be omnipotent and omniscient. Therefore I can only think self-sufficiency, and hence the nature of an effect, through omnipotence and omniscience. However, my doubt informs me that I myself am not omnipotent and omniscient. Hence I know that I am not the self-sufficient but that I have the nature of an effect and must depend on this self-sufficient being who is God.

The idea of the self-sufficient, by reference to which the idea of an effect must be clarified, is now seen to be the idea of God. Thus God's existence is shown to be an immediate necessary presupposition of the *I think, therefore I am* even if it did not seem so at first. Moreover, reference to God's nature must become the grounds whereby to assign the true, and not the seeming, representative value to the ideas that have been called into metaphysical doubt. In short, only by considering God's nature can one know which ideas are true and which ideas are irredeemably probable.

Since God has been discovered to be the self-sufficient cause whom all effects necessarily presuppose, and since God's sufficiency is a sufficiency as an intellect and will, it is clear that the human mind cannot completely fathom or comprehend God's nature. To do so we would have to be God; however, our doubt informs us that we are not omnipotent and omniscient. Moreover, we know that nothing can be conceived as in God that detracts from his self-sufficiency. Thus we can know that there are possibilities that the divine nature could, but need not necessarily, have created—and these possibilities extend even to essences, not simply to things with these essences.[6] An example may help to show that God determines essences.

Arithmetical and geometrical considerations themselves, such as the possibility of deducing paralogisms, are enough to show us that mathematics is not of itself metaphysically certain. Hence we cannot allow that these same mathematical ideas (no change in the evidence allowed) compel God's intellect without implying either (1) that we can know the truth of these ideas independently of knowing the infinite power and consequent goodness of the author of human reason, or (2) that these ideas are deduced necessarily from God's nature once we know his infinite power and consequent goodness. Now, as regards the first alternative, we certainly do not know these ideas independently of knowing God, for otherwise we would not have been able to sustain a metaphysical doubt about them until we discovered God. As regards the second alternative, knowledge of God provides no new mathematical reason for guaranteeing the necessity of such ideas. Rather knowledge of God's power and infinite goodness persuades us only that God would not have placed these ideas in us unless they were true—and we can well understand that with equal goodness God could have created other truths of which he had given us ideas.

I will conclude my comments on the *Discourse* by speaking breifly about Descartes's second proof of God's existence. The second proof is more traditional than the first, and it is also repeated in the *Meditations*. It is useful to note some of the major differences between the first and second proofs.

In the first proof, Descartes argues that God's existence can be discerned as immediately presupposed by the *I think, therefore I am*. In short, no chain of necessary deductions or reliance on memory is required to prove the conclusion that God exists. To be sure, we removed certain obstacles that stood in the way of our immediately intuiting that the true nature of causation, by reference to which our existence must be explained, is given in the idea of God. This we did by reminding ourselves that whatever is in metaphysical doubt is not a basis for a valid notion of cause and hence for a valid notion of effect. Nevertheless, none of those things in metaphysical doubt were premises by which we came to a conclusion about the true nature of the self-sufficient cause. Thus memory was not required for the purposes of validating our conclusion, and God's existence was a matter of certain and evident cognition.

In the second proof of God's existence, Descartes does not proceed from the existential fact of his own existence. Rather he deduces from the idea of God as a self-sufficient or infinitely perfect being that God must necessarily exist. Descartes says that this reasoning is at least as conclusive as geometrical demonstrations. Since, before knowing God's existence in the first proof, Descartes had placed mathematical reasoning into metaphysical doubt, the implication seems to be that the second proof is not as metaphysically certain and evident as the first.

However, Descartes does not make it clear exactly why the second proof is not as metaphysically certain as the first proof. Perhaps he believes that to deduce God's necessary existence from the idea of God as self-sufficient requires some reliance on memory. But perhaps he believes the second proof is weaker than the first for a reason much more basic than the reliance on memory that the second proof may require. Perhaps the weakness of the second proof vis-à-vis the first turns on the fact that in the second proof we have no metaphysical certitude that the "reasoning" used on route to the conclusion "God exists necessarily" is reasoning at all. Perhaps he means that the representative value of all that so-called reasoning may be nothing, since we have no guarantee that it does not imply paralogisms or that the ideas on which we rely in the process represent something rather than nothing.

However, if this is the weakness of the second proof vis-à-vis the first, it is necessary to show that in the first proof we need never consider ourselves to be employing any valid reasoning without already knowing God's existence. Thus it is necessary to show that in the first proof whatever reasoning occurs without knowing God can be doubted—even the *I think, therefore I am*. But to show that all such reasoning can be doubted, it will suffice to show that as soon as we assuredly consider ourselves to be reasoning, or understanding, or knowing that what is asserted in the *I think, therefore I am* is truly possible (which is presupposed if we consider ourselves to know the existential fact of our thinking), we must already know God's nature and existence.

Perhaps it is obvious that to know it is truly possible for us to think, we must recognize God's nature and existence, and for the following reason. If we were to consider it truly possible for us to think without depending on God (and obviously without depending on anything, such as matter, that is in metaphysical doubt), we would be implying that our own thinking, that is, our own intellect and will, is conceived as having a self-sufficient nature in the only way that self-sufficiency can then be thought of by us, namely, as a self-sufficiency *qua* intellect and will. In short, we would be implying that we are God. But we could understand what we are hypothesizing about ourselves only if we recognized that because of our doubt, we are not self-sufficient as intellect and will, that is, that we are not infinite or God, and that we therefore depend on the self-sufficient or God. It seems that Descartes does believe that even knowledge of the *I think, therefore I am* depends on God, for in the *Discourse* he says: "But if we do not know that everything in us that is real and true comes from a perfect and infinite being, no matter how clear and distinct our ideas would be, we would have no reason that assured us that they have the perfection of being true."[7]

SOURCE FOR THE FRENCH TEXT

The *Discourse concerning Method and the Essays* was first published without Descartes's name by Jan Maire at Leiden in 1637. That text is contained in Adam and Tannery and is the basis of my translation.*

---

* *Discours, Oeuvres,* vol. VI, p. v.

1   # Discourse concerning the Method

for Conducting His Reason Well and for Seeking the Truth in the Sciences*

2   *If this discourse seems too long to be read entirely at one sitting, it can be divided into six parts. And in the first will be found different considerations bearing upon the sciences. In the second the principal rules of the method that the author has cultivated. In the third particular rules of morality that he has extracted from this method. In the fourth the reasons by which he proves the existence of God and of the human soul—which are the foundations of his metaphysics. And in the fifth the order of questions belonging to physics that he has researched, and particularly the explanation of the movement of the heart and of some other difficulties that pertain to medicine, as well as the explanation of the difference that exists between our soul and the soul of beasts. And in the last certain things he believes required in order to advance beyond what has been accomplished in the research into nature, as well as the reasons that have persuaded him to write.*

FIRST PART

3   Good sense is the best distributed thing in the world; for everyone thinks himself so well endowed with it that even those most difficult to satisfy in every other matter do not usually desire more

---

* The translation of *sa raison* as "his reason" seems to me to be grammatically justified and consonant with the spirit of the *Discourse*; cf. D 7.

of it than they have. It is not likely that everyone is mistaken about this; it rather testifies to the fact that the ability of judging well and of distinguishing the true from the false, which is what is properly called good sense or reason, is naturally equal in all men; and thus the diversity of our opinions does not derive from the fact that some people are more reasonable than others, but only from the fact that we direct our thinking along different paths and do not consider the same things. For it is not enough to have a good wit, but the principal thing is to apply it well. The greatest souls are capable of the greatest vices as well as the greatest virtues; and if they always follow the right path, those who march only very slowly can advance further than those who run but go astray.

As for myself, I have never presumed my wit in any respect 4 more perfect than that of ordinary men; indeed, I have often wished for thought as prompt, or an imagination as precise and distinct, or a memory as ample or quick, as some other men have. And I know no qualities but these that contribute to the perfection of our wit: for, as regards reason or sense, inasmuch as it is the only thing that makes us men and distinguishes us from the beasts, I wish to believe that it exists complete and entire in each of us; and in this matter I follow the common opinion of the philosophers who say that there is no place for more or less except among the *accidents,* and certainly not among the *forms,* or natures, of *individuals* of the same *kind.*

But I shall not hesitate to say that I think I have had great luck 5 to discover myself ever since youth on particular paths that have led me to certain considerations and maxims out of which I have formed a method; and with this method it seems to me that I have a means of increasing my knowledge by degrees, and of raising it little by little to as high a point as the moderate character of my wit and the brief duration of my life will allow. Now, although in judgments about myself I try always to lean toward the side of caution rather than presumption, and although in looking at the different activities and undertakings of all men with the eye of a philosopher, I find hardly any that do not seem to me vain and useless—nevertheless I have already derived such fruits from this method that I do not fail to receive an extreme satisfaction in the progress I think I have already made in the search for truth. And I conceive such prospects for the future that, if there is any occupation solidly good and important among the occupations of men purely as men, I dare to believe it is the one I have chosen.

6   All the same, perhaps I am deceived, and possibly it is only a bit of copper and glass that I am mistaking for gold and diamonds. I know how much we are prone to fool ourselves in vital matters; and I know also how often the judgments of our friends, if those judgments run in our favor, should be held suspect. However, I will be very agreeable to showing in this discourse what paths I have followed, and to represent herein my life like a painting, so that everyone can judge it; and thus by gathering from the general response the opinions that readers shall form about this discourse, I will have a new means of instructing myself, which I shall add to those I customarily use.

7   Thus my design is not to teach here the method everyone should follow to conduct his reason well, but only to explain the manner in which I have tried to conduct my own. Those who involve themselves in laying down precepts should consider themselves abler than those to whom they give them; and such people, if they are lacking in the least thing, are blameworthy. But since I offer this essay only as an autobiography, or, if you prefer, as a fable, in which, among some examples a reader can imitate, he will perhaps find very many others he will be right not to follow, I hope that the essay will be useful to some without being harmful to anyone, and that everyone will recognize that I am inclined to be candid.

8   I was nourished on letters from my childhood, and because I was persuaded that by their means one could acquire a clear and assured knowledge of everything useful for life, I had a great desire to learn them. But as soon as I had finished the entire course of study at the end of which one is customarily received into the ranks of the learned, I changed my opinion completely. For I found myself embarrassed by so many doubts and errors that it seemed I had derived no other profit in trying to instruct myself except that I had more and more discovered my ignorance. And nevertheless I was in one of the most celebrated schools of Europe, where I thought there ought to be other knowledgeable men, if any are to be found on this earth. I had learned at school everything the others learned there; moreover, not being content with the sciences taught to us, I surveyed all the books I could

manage to lay hands upon that treat of things deemed most curious and most rare. Furthermore, I knew the evaluations others made of me; and I did not notice that they esteemed me inferior to my fellow students, although there were already some among them who were destined to fill the places of our teachers. And finally our century seemed to me as flourishing and as fertile with good wits as any preceding century had been. This made me exercise the liberty of judging on my own about all previous times and of thinking that no doctrine in the world was such as I had previously been made to expect.

I did not completely cease to esteem the exercises with which 9
one occupies oneself in the schools. I knew that the languages one learns there are necessary to understand the ancient books; that the gracefulness of the stories awakens our wits, and that when such actions are praised with discretion, they help to form the judgment; that the reading of all good books is like a conversation with the most virtuous people of past ages who have authored them, or even like a considered conversation in which they reveal to us only the best of their thoughts; that eloquence has powers and incomparable beauties; that poetry has delicacies and delights that are very ravishing; that mathematics contains very subtle discoveries that can offer a great deal, as much to content the curious as to facilitate all the arts and diminish the work of men; that the writings that treat of customs contain very many teachings and very many exhortations to virtue that are very useful; that theology teaches how to gain heaven; that philosophy provides a means of speaking with probability about everything, and of eliciting the admiration of the less learned; that jurisprudence, medicine, and the other sciences bring honors and riches to those who cultivate them; and finally that it is good to have examined all of them, even the most superstitious and most false, in order to know their just value and to guard against being deceived by them.

But I believed that I had already devoted enough time to 10
languages, and also even to the reading of ancient books and to their histories and fables. For to converse with the people of other centuries is nearly the same as to take a journey. It is good to know something about the customs of different peoples in order to judge our own more sanely and to guard against thinking that everything contrary to our own is ridiculous and irrational, such as those who have seen nothing customarily believe. Yet when

one spends too much time journeying, one finally becomes a stranger in his own country; and when one is too curious about things practiced in past centuries, one ordinarily remains very ignorant of those practiced in this century. Besides, fables make one imagine very many things to be possible that are not possible; and the most faithful histories, even if they do not change or augment the value of things to make them more worthy of praise, at least nearly always omit the most base and the least renowned circumstances: and from this it arises that the rest does not seem such as it is; and those people who direct their customs by the examples they select out are subject to fall into the extravagances of the knights-errant of our novels, and to conceive designs that surpass their powers.

11   I esteemed eloquence very much, and I was enamored of poetry; but I thought that both were gifts of wit more than the fruits of study. People who have the strongest power of reasoning, and who direct their thoughts in the best manner to render them clear and intelligible, are always best able to persuade us of what they propose, even if they speak only low Breton and have never learned rhetoric. And those with the most agreeable fancies, and who know how to explain them with the most embellishment and grace, would not fail to be the best poets, even though the art of poetry were unknown to them.

12   I was pleased most of all by the mathematical [disciplines] because of the certitude and evidence of their reasonings; but as yet I did not at all notice their true usage; and thinking they served only in the mechanical arts, I was astonished that, since their foundations were so firm and solid, nothing more dignified had been built upon them. However, on the other hand, I compared those writings of the ancient pagans that treat of customs to those very imposing and very magnificent palaces built only upon sand and mud. These writings elevate the virtues to a high degree, and they make them appear estimable in relation to all the things in the world; but they do not teach us well enough to come to recognize the virtues, and often what they call by so beautiful a name is only an insensibility, or pride, or despair, or parricide.

13   I revered our theology, and intended as much as any other person to gain heaven; but having learned, as something very assured, that the path to heaven is not less open to the most ignorant than to the most instructed person, and that the revealed truths that

lead to heaven are above our intelligence, I did not dare to submit them to the weakness of my reasonings; and I thought that to attempt to examine them and be successful at it required some extraordinary assistance from heaven, and that one be more than man.

I will say nothing about philosophy except, seeing that for many   14
centuries it has been cultivated by the most excellent wits who have lived, and yet still contains nothing that is undisputed, and as a consequence, is not doubtful, I did not have enough presumption to expect to discover more in it than others did; and considering how many different opinions touching on the same matter can exist and be maintained by learned people, even though there cannot be more than one opinion that is true, I regarded as all but false everything that was only probable.

Then, as regards the other sciences, inasmuch as they borrow   15
their principles from philosophy, I judged that one could not have built anything solid on foundations so little secure. And neither the honor nor the gain they promise were sufficient to urge me to learn them; for I did not find myself, thanks to God, in a condition that obliged me to make a profession of science in order to augment my riches. And although I did not make a profession of disdaining glory as the cynics do, I nevertheless placed little importance upon what I could only hope to acquire by false titles. And finally, as for wrong doctrines, I thought that I already sufficiently knew their worth so as to be no longer subject to deception by either the promises of an alchemist, or the predictions of an astrologer, or the impostures of a magician, or the devices or windy claims of those who make a profession of knowing what they do not know.

That is why, as soon as my age permitted me to quit the direc-   16
tion of my teachers, I entirely abandoned the study of letters. And resolving to seek no longer for any science other than that which could be found in myself, or else in the great book of the world, I employed the rest of my youth voyaging, in seeing courts and armies, in making contact with people of different temperaments and conditions, in cultivating different experiences, in testing myself in the situations fortune held out to me, and in every situation devoting such reflection to the things that presented themselves that I would be able to extract some profit from them. For it seemed to me that I should be able to encounter very much more

truth in the reasonings everyone makes about things that concern them, and whose outcome, if they judge badly, would punish them, than in those reasonings a man of letters makes in his study regarding speculations that produce no effect and involve no further consequence for him—excepting perhaps that he will derive a greater vanity the more they are removed from common sense, since he will have to employ so much more ingenuity and inventiveness to try to render them probable. And I always had an extreme desire to learn to distinguish the true from the false, in order to see clearly in my actions, and to walk with assurance in this life.

17   It is true that, while I did nothing but consider the customs of other men, I found hardly anything there to provide me with assurance; and I noticed almost as much diversity among these customs as I had previously noticed among the opinions of the philosophers. Thus the greatest profit I derived from it was, seeing very many things that, although they seem very extravagant and ridiculous to us, are nevertheless commonly received and approved by other large nations, I learned not to believe too firmly any of those things I had been persuaded of only by example and custom; and so I delivered myself, little by little, from very many errors that can obfuscate our natural light and render us less capable of listening to reason. But after I had spent a few years studying the book of the world, and in trying to acquire some experience, one day I made a resolution to also study of myself and to employ all the forces of my wits in choosing the paths I ought to follow. This succeeded for me very much more than if I had never separated myself from my country or my books.

18   SECOND PART

19   At that time I was in Germany, where I had been attracted because of the wars that are still not finished there; and as I was returning to the army from the coronation of the emperor, the beginning of winter caused me to put up in a place where, finding no conversation that diverted me, and fortunately having no cares or passions that disturbed me, I remained all day near a stove, where I had complete freedom to weigh my thoughts. Among my thoughts one of the first I undertook to consider was

that often there is not as much perfection in works composed of many parts and made by the hands of different masters as in those upon which one person has labored. Thus one sees that the buildings a single architect has undertaken and completed are ordinarily more beautiful and better ordered than those that several persons have tried to renovate by making use of old walls built for other purposes. Thus those ancient cities, initially only small market towns, that finally became large cities after periods of time, are ordinarily badly organized in comparison with the regular places an engineer lays out as suits his fancy upon a plain; for although in considering their edifices individually, one finds in them as much or more artistry, still, seeing their arrangement, with a large edifice here and a small one there, and how they cause the streets to be curved and unequal, one would say that it is more luck than the will of men employing their reason that has arranged them thus. Moreover, if one considers that, despite all this, there have always been certain officers in charge of taking care of particular buildings in order to make them serve as public ornaments, one will certainly recognize that it is difficult, in laboring only upon the works of another, to produce results that are very accomplished. And so I imagined that peoples who, having been formerly half savage and having civilized themselves little by little, thus made their laws only in proportion as the inconvenience of crimes and feuds forced them to do so, could not be so well regulated as those who, from the time they assembled, have observed the constitutions of some prudent legislator. Similarly, it is very certain that the state of true religion, whose ordinances God alone has laid down, ought to be incomparably better regulated than all others. And to speak of human affairs, I believe that if Sparta was very flourishing in former times, it was not because of the goodness of each of its laws in particular, seeing that some were very strange and contrary to good customs; rather it was because the laws, having been devised by a single person, all tended to the same end. And thus I thought that the sciences found in books—at least in those whose reasonings are only probable, and that, since they have been put together and have grown little by little from the opinions of many different persons, contain no demonstrations—are not at all so close to the truth as are the simple reasonings that a man of good sense can naturally make in regard to things that present themselves. Likewise, I thought that because we were all

children before being men, and because we had to be directed
for a long time by our appetites and teachers—who often contra-
dicted one another, and who perhaps, neither one nor the other,
always counseled us for the best—it is almost impossible that our
judgments be so pure or so solid as they would have been if we
had had the complete use of our reason from the time of our
birth, and had been led only by reason.

20   It is true that we do not find anyone completely razing all the
houses of a village solely to make them over anew in another
fashion and to render the streets more beautiful; but one certainly sees some people pulling down their own houses in order
to rebuild them; one even finds people who are forced to do so
when their houses are in danger of falling down themselves and
the foundations are not entirely firm. In imitation of this, I persuaded myself that there certainly would be no plausibility in an
individual undertaking to reform a state by changing all its foundations, and by turning them upside down to straighten them
out; I was also persuaded that one would not even undertake to
reform the body of the sciences, or the order established in the
schools for teaching them; however, as for all the opinions I had
accepted among my beliefs until this time, I was persuaded that
I could not do better than to undertake, once and for all, to reject them, in order to replace them afterward, either by better
beliefs, or perhaps even with themselves, when I had made them
conform to the standard of reason. And I firmly believed that by
this means I would succeed in conducting my life very much
better than if I built only upon old foundations and relied only
upon principles I had allowed to persuade me in my youth, without ever having examined whether they were true. For although
I noticed diverse difficulties in this undertaking, they were not,
however, such as have no remedy; nor were they comparable to
those involved in reforming even the slightest matters that have
reference to the public. These large bodies are too difficult to
build anew once they have been built; indeed, they are too difficult to hold up once they are disturbed; and their falls can only
be very violent. Moreover, as regards the imperfections of states,
if such imperfections exist—and the single fact of diversity among
states suffices to assure us that some states are imperfect—they
undoubtedly are very much tempered by customs; and custom has
even avoided or corrected in an imperceptible amount imperfec-

tions that one could not so well foresee by prudence. And finally, these imperfections are nearly always more bearable than their changes would be: just as the great paths that wander through the mountains little by little become so connected and so convenient, simply because they are used, that it is very much better to follow them than to proceed straight ahead, jumping over rocks and descending to the bottom of precipices.

This is why I cannot at all approve those persons with mischief-making and unquiet temperaments who, being called neither by birth nor fortune to the management of public affairs, do not hesitate always to conjure up some new reform in their minds. And if I thought this essay had contained anything whatever on the basis of which anyone could have suspected me of this folly, I should be very grieved to have allowed it to be published. My goal has never extended further than to try to reform my own thoughts and to build upon a foundation entirely my own. But if, because my work has pleased me so, I wish to make you see here the model for it, I do not for all that wish to counsel anyone to imitate the model. Those upon whom God has bestowed his graces more abundantly will perhaps have grander goals; but my fear is that the goals set out [in this discourse] are already too venturesome for some people. The single resolve to rid oneself of all the opinions one has hitherto accepted among one's beliefs is not an example everyone ought to follow; the world is, as it were, composed of two sorts of wits for whom such a design is not at all fitting. There are those who, believing themselves abler than they are, cannot prevent themselves from precipitously forming judgments, and lack sufficient patience for conducting their thoughts in an orderly manner: from which it follows that, if once they had taken the liberty of doubting the principles they formerly accepted and of deviating from the common path, they could never stick to the route it is necessary to take to proceed straight ahead, and they would remain astray all their lives. Then there are those who have the reason, or modesty, to judge that they are less capable of distinguishing the true from the false than are some others by whom they can be instructed—these less capable persons ought certainly to content themselves in following the opinions of these others rather than to seek to form better opinions on their own.

As for myself, I undoubtedly would have been numbered among 22 this last group had I had only one teacher, or had I never known the differences that have always existed among the opinions of the most learned. But having learned at college that one could imagine nothing so strange or so incredible that it has not been maintained by one of the philosophers; and having recognized in journeying that everyone who has sentiments contrary to our own is not on that account barbarous or savage, but that some of them use as much, or more, reason than us; and having considered how often the same man, with the same wits, in being reared from childhood among the French or Germans turns out differently than he would have had he always lived among the Chinese or the cannibals; and realizing how, even as regards the fashions in our own customs, the same thing that has pleased us for ten years, and perhaps will again please us before ten years hence, now seems to us extravagant and ridiculous: I accordingly discovered that we are persuaded very much more by custom and example than by any certain knowledge, and that, nevertheless, a plurality of voices constitutes no proof of any value in regard to truths somewhat difficult to discern, because it is certainly more probable that a single man has discovered them rather than an entire nation. And since I was unable to select anyone whose opinions seemed to me preferable to those of others, I found myself, as it were, forced to assume the direction of my own studies.

23   But like a man who walks alone and in the darkness, I resolved to proceed so slowly, and to use so much circumspection in every matter, that however small my advance, I would at least protect myself from falling. Accordingly, I did not wish to begin to reject entirely any of the opinions that formerly were able to slip into my belief without having been placed there by reason until I had first employed sufficient time to establish the design of the task I was undertaking, and to seek the true method for arriving at the knowledge of everything of which my wit would be capable.

24   When younger I had studied a little logic from among the parts of philosophy, and a little of the analysis of the geometers and a little algebra from among the parts of mathematics. It seemed to me that these three arts or sciences ought to contribute something to my goal. However, in examining them I noticed that, as regards logic, its syllogism and the greater part of its other instruc-

tions, rather than helping one learn things, serve more to explain to another the things one knows, or even, like the art of Lully,* to make one speak without judgment about things of which one is ignorant. And although logic in effect contains many very true and good precepts, there are always so many harmful or superfluous precepts mixed among them that to separate the two is nearly as difficult as to extract a Diana or a Minerva out of a block of marble upon which no design has yet been sketched. Then, as regards the analysis of the ancients and the algebra of the moderns, besides the fact that these extend only to very abstract matters that seem to have no application, the former is always so bound to the consideration of figures that it cannot exercise the understanding without very much fatiguing the imagination; and in the latter discipline one is so subjected to certain rules and notations that, instead of a science that cultivates the wits, one produces from all of it only a confused and obscure art that embarrasses one's wits. This was the reason why I thought it necessary to seek some method that would comprise the advantages of these three but be exempt from their defects. And as the multiplicity of laws often furnishes excuses for vices, so that a state is better regulated when, having only very few laws, they are observed very strictly; so also, in place of the great number of precepts composing logic, I believed that the four following rules would suffice, provided I took a firm and constant resolution not to fail even once to observe them.

The first rule was never to receive anything as true unless I knew it evidently to be such—that is to say, to avoid assiduously precipitation and obstinacy—and to include nothing among my judgments except what presented itself so clearly and so distinctly to my mind that I would have no occasion to place it in doubt.

25

---

* Raymond Lully (1235?–1315), Catalan philosopher, known in connection with the *Ars Brevis*. According to Gilson, Descartes seems not to have directly studied the *Ars Brevis*, but he discoverd from a Lullist that this art, which supposedly equips one to speak extensively on any topic, includes more than the manoeuvres of the dialecticians (*loci dialecticorum*); see *Discours de la méthode*, commentary by Étienne Gilson (Paris: Vrin, 1947), pp. 185–186. Lully attempted apologetics with this art—by combining circles he produced relations of concepts that correspond to truths of religion; see Étienne Gilson, *History of Christian Philosophy in the Middle Ages* (New York: Random House, 1955), pp. 350–353, 700–702.

26   The second rule was to divide each of the difficulties I would examine in as many parts as would be possible, and as would be required in order to solve them better.

27   The third rule was to direct my thoughts according to an order, beginning with the simplest objects, and those easiest to know, in order to lead up little by little, as by degrees, to the knowledge of the most composite objects, supposing an order even among those that have no natural precedence one over the other.

28   The last rule was in every case to make such complete enumerations and such general reviews that I would be assured of omitting nothing.

29   Those long chains of reasonings, all simple and easy, that the geometers are accustomed to use in order to arrive at their more difficult demonstrations had given me occasion to imagine that everything that can fall within the knowledge of men follows each other in that same fashion, and—provided only one abstains from accepting anything as true that is not true, and heeds the order required for deducing one thing from the others—there can be nothing so distant that one may not reach it, or nothing so hidden that one may not discover it. And it was not difficult to discover where to begin: for I already knew that it was necessary to begin with the simplest and easiest objects to know; and considering that, among those who previously sought for truth in the sciences, only the mathematicians had been able to find any demonstrations—that is to say, any certain and evident reasons—I did not doubt that they conducted their examinations by the same means; however, I hoped for no other advantage from these mathematical exercises except that they would accustom my mind to delight in truths, and not to satisfy itself at all with false reasons. But for all that, I did not set it as my goal to try to learn all the particular sciences commonly called mathematics; and seeing that although the objects of these sciences differ, all these sciences nevertheless accord in the respect that they consider only the different relations or proportions in their objects, I thought it would be more worth-while to examine these proportions only in general, and without supposing them except in subjects that serve to render knowledge of them easier for me; and I also decided not to bind these proportions in any way to such objects, in order that I could more easily apply them afterward to all the other subjects upon which they have a bearing. Then, having noted that to know

them I would sometimes need to consider each individually, and sometimes merely to retain them or comprehend them severally together, I thought that to consider them better individually I ought to suppose them in lines, because I found nothing simpler and nothing that I could more distinctly represent to my imagination and my senses; but to retain them, or to comprehend many of them together, it was necessary that I explain them by certain notations, as concise as would be possible; and thus in this way I would borrow everything good in geometrical analysis and algebra, and would correct all the faults of the one by the other. And in effect, I dare to say that the exact observance of these few precepts that I had chosen gave me such facility at disentangling all the questions to which these two sciences extend that in the two or three months I employed to examine these questions— having begun with the simplest and most general, and using each truth I discovered as a rule to serve me afterward in discovering other truths—I not only came to the resolution of many questions I formerly judged very difficult, but it also seemed to me toward the end that, even as regards unsolved questions, I could determine by what means and to what extent it was possible to resolve them. Perhaps I will not appear very vain in my claims if you consider that, since there is only one truth about each matter, whoever discovers it knows as much as one can know about it; thus, for example, a child instructed in arithmetic who has performed an addition according to arithmetical rules can be assured to have found, in regard to the sum he examined, everything the human mind can find out. For the method that teaches us to follow the true order, and to enumerate exactly all the conditions of what one seeks after, contains everything that gives certitude to the rules of arithmetic.

But what contented me the most with this method was that it assured me of using my reason in every matter, if not perfectly, at least as well as was in my power; besides, I felt that in practicing this method my mind was accustoming itself little by little to conceive its objects more plainly and distinctly; and not having restricted this method to a particular matter, I promised myself to apply it as usefully to the difficulties of the other sciences as I had applied it to those of algebra. However, I did not on that account immediately dare to undertake to examine all the difficulties that would arise; for that itself would have been contrary to the order the method prescribes. But having noticed that their principles ought all to be borrowed from philosophy, in which I as yet found nothing certain, I thought it necessary before anything else to try to establish something certain in philosophy. And yet, since this is the most important thing in the world, and the place where precipitation and obstinacy were most to be feared, I thought I ought not undertake to solve the matter until I had attained an age far more mature than twenty-three years, which was my age at that time. Likewise, I thought I could not employ too much time beforehand in preparing myself for the task, as much in uprooting from my mind the wrong opinions I had hitherto accepted as in making an accumulation of experiments that afterward would constitute the matter for my reasonings, and by constantly exercising myself in the method I had prescribed for myself in order to become more and more adept at its use.

31   THIRD PART

32   And finally, just as it does not suffice, before beginning to rebuild the house in which one dwells, to rip it down and to supply oneself with materials and architects, or to practice architecture oneself, and, indeed, to have a plan painstakingly worked out; but as it is also necessary to be provided with another house where one can be lodged comfortably during the time one will work on the new dwelling; so too, in order that I should not remain irresolute in my actions while reason would oblige me to be so in my judgments, and in order that I should not fail to live from that point on as happily as possible, I formed for myself a provisional morality consisting of only three or four maxims that I very much wish to share with you.

33   The first was to obey the laws and customs of my country, retaining constantly the religion in which God gave me the grace to be instructed since my childhood, and governing myself in every other matter according to the most reasonable and least excessive opinions commonly received in practice by the more judicious of those with whom I would have to live. For beginning from then onward to esteem my own opinions as nothing, since I wished to subject all of them to examination, I was assured I could not do better than to follow the opinions of the more judicious of people.

And although among the Persians or the Chinese there are perhaps people as judicious as among us, it seemed to me the most useful thing was to regulate myself according to those with whom I would have to live; moreover, it seemed to me that to know what their opinions really were, I was to take notice of what they practiced rather than what they said; and this, not just because in the corrupt state of our customs few wish to say everything they believe, but also because many people are not aware of their own beliefs; for the action of thought by which one believes a thing being different from that by which one knows that one believes it, these actions often occur the one without the other. And among several opinions equally received, I chose only the most moderate: I did this because such opinions are always the most convenient as regards practice, and are probably best, since all excess is customarily bad; and I did this equally so that, in case I erred, I would turn myself away from the true path to a lesser extent than if, having chosen one of the extreme opinions, it had been the other extreme that it had been necessary to follow. And, in particular, I placed among excesses all the promises by which one diminishes something of one's liberty. It was not that I disapproved of the laws that, to remedy the fickleness of feeble minds, permit one to make vows or contracts obliging one to persevere in some good design, or even, for the security of commerce, in a design that is only indifferent. But because I did not see anything in the world that always remained in the same condition, and because, as my particular goal, I promised myself to perfect my judgments more and more and not to render them worse, I would have thought myself as committing a great breach of good sense if, because I approved something up until that time, I obliged myself to consider it as good even afterward, when perhaps it would have ceased to be good or I would have ceased to deem it such.

My second maxim was to be as firm and resolute in my actions as I could be, and when once I decided on them, to follow doubtful opinions no less constantly than if they had been very assured. In this matter I would imitate those travelers who, finding themselves lost in some forest, should not wander about by heading first this way and then another way, nor still less remain in one place, but should instead always walk as straight as they can in the same direction, and certainly not change their direction for petty reasons, despite the fact that at the beginning it has perhaps been chance alone that determined them to choose that direction; for by this means, if they do not come exactly to the place they wish, they at least will arrive at the end of some part of the forest, where probably they will be better off than in the middle. And so the actions of life often permitting no delay, it is a very certain rule that when it is not in our power to discern the truest opinions, we ought to follow the most probable ones; furthermore, even if we do not notice more probability in some opinions than in others, we ought nevertheless to choose certain ones, and afterward no longer consider them as doubtful in respect to their relation to action; we ought rather to consider them as very true and very certain, because the reason that has determined us to do so is very true and very certain. And this maxim was henceforth capable of sparing me all the repentances and remorse that customarily disturb the consciences of those feeble and vacillating minds who with wavering resolution allow themselves to practice as good things they afterward judge to be bad.

35   My third maxim was to try always to control myself rather than fortune, and to change my desires rather than the order of the world; and generally to accustom myself to believe that nothing is entirely in our power except our thoughts, so that after we have done our best regarding things lying outside us, everything that fails to happen, and yet is required for success, is, from the point of view of what we can do, absolutely impossible. And this alone seemed to me sufficient to prevent me from desiring in the future anything I do not acquire, and thus to render me content. For since our will naturally inclines to desire only those things our understanding represents to it as possible, it is certain that if we consider all the goods lying outside us as equally beyond our power, we will no more regret lacking those things that seem owed to us at birth, when we shall be deprived of them by no fault of our own, than we regret not possessing the kingdoms of China or Mexico; and making, as it is said, a virtue of necessity, we will no more desire to be well when we are sick, or free when we are in prison, than we now desire to have a body made of a matter as incorruptible as diamonds, or wings to fly like the birds. But I admit it requires long practice and oft-repeated meditation to accustom oneself to view everything from this point of view; and I believe it is principally in this that the secret of those philosophers consisted who in former times were able to free

themselves from the dominion of fortune, and despite hardships and poverty, to rival their gods in happiness. For by constantly directing their attention to a consideration of the limits prescribed for them by nature, they persuaded themselves so perfectly that nothing was in their power except their thoughts that this was sufficient to prevent them from having any affection for other things; and they ordered their thoughts so absolutely that it gave them a reason to consider themselves richer, more powerful, more free, and happier than any of those other men (however much favored by nature and fortune they might be) who, not having any of this philosophy, never rank everything they desire in this manner.

Finally, as a conclusion to this morality, I took it upon myself   36 to make a review of the different occupations men hold in this life in order to choose the best; and without wishing to say anything about the occupations of others, I thought I could not do better than to continue in the same occupation I found myself engaged in, that is to say, to employ all my life to cultivate my reason, and to advance myself as much as I could in the knowledge of the truth, following the method I prescribed for myself. I had found such great satisfactions since I had begun to avail myself of this method that I did not believe one could have received sweeter or more innocent satisfactions in this life; and discovering each day by this means some truths that seemed to me sufficiently important and yet commonly unknown to other men, the satisfaction I had from it so filled my mind that everything else had no effect upon me. But very importantly, the three preceding maxims had been built only upon the plan I had of continuing to instruct myself; for since God has given each person some light by which to distinguish the true from the false, I would not have believed I ought to content myself with the opinions of another even for a moment unless I intended to employ my own judgment to examine those opinions when there should be time; and I would not have known how to relieve myself of scruples in following the opinions of others had I not hoped, for all that, to lose no opportunity to find better opinions in the event that there might have been such. And finally, I would not have known how to limit my desires or to rest content if I had not followed a single path by which I thought myself assured of acquiring not only all the knowledge of which I would be capable, but also all the true goods that would be in my power; and inasmuch as the will does not incline to pursue or avoid anything except according as our understanding represents the thing to it as good or bad, it follows that in order to do well it suffices to judge well, and in order to do one's very best, it suffices to judge the best one can—which is to say, to acquire all the virtues together with all the other goods one can acquire; and when one is certain that one has done that, one could not lack contentment.

37   After having thus assured myself of these maxims, and having placed them to one side together with truths of faith, which have always been the foremost elements of my belief, I judged that as far as all the rest of my opinions were concerned, I could freely undertake to forsake them. And seeing that I hoped to be better able to achieve my goal by conversing with other men than by remaining any longer near the stove where I had all these thoughts, I began again to journey before the winter was long gone. And throughout all the nine years that followed I did nothing but roam here and there in the world, trying to be a spectator rather than an actor in all the comedies that take place there; and particularly by giving reflection in every subject matter to what could render it suspect and provide an occasion for making a mistake, I uprooted from my mind all the errors that previously had been able to pass into it. I did not do so to imitate the skeptics, who doubt only for the sake of doubting, and who pretend always to be irresolute: for, on the contrary, my whole plan was directed only to convince myself, and to cast away the shifting earth and sand in order to find rock or clay. It seems to me that this was succeeding well enough, since in trying to discover the falsity or uncertainty of the propositions I was examining (and this I did not by weak conjectures, but by clear and assured reasonings), I did not encounter any proposition so doubtful that I would not extract some sufficiently certain conclusion from it, even if the conclusion was only that the proposition contained nothing certain. And as in pulling down an old house one ordinarily preserves its materials to use them in building a new house; so also in abolishing all my opinions that I had judged ill founded, I made various observations and acquired many experiences that have served me since in establishing more certain opinions. And furthermore, I continued to exercise myself in the method I had prescribed for myself; for beyond the fact that I had taken care generally to

direct all my thoughts according to its rules, I reserved some hours for myself from time to time that I particularly employed in applying the method to the difficulties of mathematics, and also even to some other difficulties that, by detaching them from all the principles of the other sciences that I did not find sufficiently firm, I was able to express as if similar to the difficulties of mathematics —as you will see I have done with many of the difficulties explained in this volume. And so while appearing like those who, having no occupation except to pass a calm and innocent life, study how to separate pleasures from vices, and occupy themselves with honorable amusements to enjoy their leisure without boredom, I was not remiss about pursuing my plan. And I did not fail to make advances in the knowledge of the truth—perhaps more advances than if I had only read books or associated with men of letters.

However, these nine years passed away before I had again taken any part in the difficulties customarily disputed among the learned, or had begun to seek the foundations of any philosophy more certain than the common one. And the example of many excellent minds who previously had this goal, but seemed to me not to have succeeded, made me imagine so great a difficulty in erecting a philosophy that perhaps I would still not as yet have dared to undertake to erect one had I not observed that some people were already spreading the rumor that I had succeeded. I could not say upon what they based this opinion; and if I had contributed something to it by my discussions, it was bound to have been by confessing more truthfully the things of which I was ignorant than is typical of those who have studied only a little, and perhaps also by making plain the reasons I had for doubting very many things others deem certain, rather than by flaunting any doctrine of my own. But since my heart was sincere enough not to wish that anyone mistook me for something different than I was, I thought it necessary to try by every means to make myself worthy of the reputation bestowed upon me; and it has been exactly eight years since this desire made me resolve to remove myself from every location where I could have acquaintances, and to retire here, in a country where the long duration of the war has caused such order to be established that the armies maintained here seem only to allow one to delight in the fruits of peace with so much the more security; in a country where, among the mass of a great and very active people who are more concerned with their

38

own affairs than curious about those of others, I have been able to live in as much solitude and retirement as in the most isolated desert, and yet without lacking any of the conveniences of the busiest cities.

39 FOURTH PART

40 I do not know whether I ought to share with you the first meditations I made here; for they are so metaphysical and so uncommon that perhaps they will not be to everyone's taste. And yet in order that one may judge whether the foundations I have employed are sufficiently firm, I find myself in some way constrained to speak of these first meditations. I had been aware for many years that in respect to customs it is sometimes necessary to follow opinions one knows to be very uncertain just as if they were indubitable, as has been said above; but because at that time I desired to attend only to the search for truth, I thought it necessary to do exactly the contrary, and to reject, as if absolutely false, everything in which I could imagine the least doubt, in order to see if there would not afterward remain among my beliefs something entirely indubitable. Thus because our senses sometimes deceive us, I wished to suppose there was nothing such as they make us imagine it. And because there are men who make a mistake in reasoning even regarding the most simple matters of geometry, and form paralogisms, I, judging myself subject to error as much as any other man, rejected as false all the reasons I had previously taken as demonstrations. And finally, considering that all the same thoughts we have when awake can also come to us when we are sleeping without any of them being true at that time, I resolved to suppose that all the things that had ever entered my mind were no more true than the illusions of my dreams. But immediately afterward I noticed that, while I thus wished to think that everything was false, it was necessary that I who was thinking be something. And noting that this truth, *I think, therefore I am*, was so firm and so assured that all the most extravagant suppositions of the skeptics were not capable of disturbing it, I judged that I could receive it, without scruple, as the first principle of the philosophy I was seeking.

41 Then, examining with attention what I was, and seeing that

I was able to suppose I had no body, and that there was no world nor any place where I might be; and seeing also that, for all of that, I was not able to suppose that I was not; but seeing, on the contrary, that, from the very fact that I was thinking of doubting the truth of other things, it followed very evidently and very certainly that I was; whereas had I only ceased to think, even if all the rest of what I had ever imagined had been true, I should have no reason to believe that I had been: from that I knew that I was a substance whose entire essence or nature is only to think, and which, in order to exist, has no need of a place nor depends upon any material thing. So that this I, that is to say, the soul by which I am what I am, is entirely distinct from the body, and is even easier to know than the body, and even if the body had never been, the soul would not fail to be everything that it is.

After that I considered in general what is required for a proposition to be true and certain; for since I came to find one which I knew to be such, I thought I must also know in what this certitude consists. And having noticed that there is nothing at all in this *I think, therefore I am* that assures me I am speaking the truth except that I see very clearly that in order to think it is necessary to exist, I judged that I could take it as a general rule that things we conceive very clearly and very distinctly are all true; but there is only some difficulty to note well the things that we conceive distinctly.

Following this, in reflecting upon the fact that I doubted, and that consequently my being was not completely perfect—since I saw clearly that it was a greater perfection to know than to doubt—I resolved to inquire whence I had learned to think of something more perfect than I was; and I recognized evidently that this ought to be from some nature that was in fact more perfect than myself. For as regards the thoughts I had of things outside me—such as of heaven, earth, light, heat, and a thousand other things—I was not very hard pressed to know whence they came; because, not noticing anything in them that seemed to render them superior to myself, I was able to believe that if they were true, they were dependent upon my nature inasmuch as it had some perfection; and if they were not true, that I derived them from nothingness, that is to say, they were in me because I had some defect. But it could not be the same as regards the idea of a more perfect being than my own; for to derive that idea from

nothingness was something manifestly impossible; and because for
the more perfect to be a consequence of, and dependent on, the
less perfect is no less contradictory than that nothing proceed
from something, I was not able to maintain that that idea derived
from myself. Thus it remained that that idea had been placed in
me by a nature that was truly more perfect than I was, and that
had in itself all the perfections of which I could have some idea,
that is to say, to explain myself in a word, who was God. To
which I added that, since I knew of some perfections I did not
have, I was not the only being who existed (if you please, I shall
here make free use of the words of the school), but that it followed of necessity that there was another more perfect being upon
which I was dependent, and from which I had acquired everything that I had. For if I had been alone and independent of every
other thing, in such a way that I had had from myself all this
meager amount of perfect being in which I participate, by the
same reasoning I would have been able to derive from myself all
the other perfections I recognized myself to lack, and thus to be
myself infinite, eternal, immutable, all-knowing, all-powerful, and
lastly, to have all the perfections I was able to distinguish to be
in God. For according to the reasonings I used in order to know
the nature of God, insofar as I was capable of knowing it, I had
only to consider, in respect of all things of which I found an idea
in myself, whether it was or was not a perfection to possess these
things; and I was assured that none of those things that indicated
some imperfection was in God, but that all the other things were
in him. Thus I saw that doubt, inconstancy, sadness, and similar
things could not be there, since I saw that I myself would have
been very comfortable in being rid of them. Then, besides that, I
had ideas of many sensible and corporeal things: for although I
supposed I was dreaming, and that all I saw or imagined was false,
I was nevertheless unable to deny that these ideas were truly in
my thought. But because I had already recognized very clearly in
myself that the intellectual nature is distinct from the corporeal,
and because I recognized that all composition testifies to dependency, and that dependency is manifestly a defect, I judged from
that that it couldn't be a perfection in God to be composed of
these two natures, and that, as a consequence, he was not so composed; but I judged that if there were some bodies in the world,

or even some intelligences or other natures that were not all perfect, their being ought to depend upon his power in such a way that they could not subsist without him for a single moment.

After that I wished to seek out other truths. I proposed to 44 my study the object of the geometers, which I conceived as a continuous body, or as a space indefinitely extended in length, breadth, altitude or depth, and which is divisible into different parts that could have different figures and sizes, and be moved or transported in all sorts of ways—for the geometers assume all these things in their object. I then ran through some of their most simple demonstrations. And having noticed that this great certitude that everyone attributes to the demonstrations of geometry is founded only on the fact that one conceives them evidently, following the rule I a little while ago laid down, I also noted that there was nothing at all in these demonstrations to assure me of the existence of their object. For example, I saw indeed that, in supposing a triangle, it was necessary that its three angles be equal to two right angles; but I did not on that account see anything that assured me there was any triangle in the world; whereas returning to examine the idea I had of a perfect being, I found that existence was included there in the same way as, or even still more evidently than, the equality of its three angles to two right angles is included in the idea of a triangle, or the equality of distance of all its parts from its center is included in the idea of a sphere; and therefore I concluded that it is at least as certain as any of the demonstrations of geometry could be, that God, who is this perfect being, is or exists.

But what makes many people persuade themselves there is 45 difficulty in recognizing God, and also even in recognizing what their soul is, is that they never elevate their mind above sensible things, and they are so accustomed to consider nothing except by imagining it, which is a manner of thought specifically appropriate to thinking of material things, that everything that cannot be imagined seems to them unintelligible. This is sufficiently manifest from the fact that even the philosophers in the schools espouse as a maxim that there is nothing in the understanding that has not initially been in the senses, when nevertheless it is certain that the ideas of God and of the soul have never been in the senses. And it seems to me that those who wish to use their imagination to comprehend the ideas of God and the soul act just like those who wish to use their eyes to hear sounds or smell odors: unless there is yet this difference, that the sense of sight does not assure us any less concerning the truth of its objects than the senses of smell and hearing assure us concerning theirs; whereas neither our imagination nor our senses could ever assure us of anything unless our understanding intervened.

46   Finally, if there are men who are still not sufficiently persuaded of the existence of God and their soul by the reasons brought forward, I strongly wish that they may know that every other thing of which they think themselves perhaps more assured, such as the fact that they have a body, and that there are stars and an earth and similar things, is less certain. For although one has a moral assurance of these things such that one cannot doubt them without being extravagant, nevertheless unless one is to be unreasonable when it is a question of metaphysical certitude, one cannot deny there are grounds enough for not being entirely assured of them if only one attends to the fact that while sleeping one can in the same way imagine that one has another body, that one sees other stars, another earth, without any of these things existing. For on what basis does one know that the thoughts that come during dreams are false rather than the others, having seen that often they are not less vivid and expressive? And were the best minds to study this matter as much at is pleases them to do so, I do not believe they could give any reason sufficient to banish this doubt unless they presuppose the existence of God. For in the first place what I recently took as a rule—namely, that the things we conceive very clearly and very distinctly are all true —is assured only because God is or exists and is a perfect being, and because everything in us comes from him. From which it follows that our ideas or notions, being real things and things that come from God, must be true as regards everything in which they are clear and distinct. Thus if often enough we have ideas that contain falsity, this falsity can only be in those ideas that contain something confused and obscure, because insofar as they are confused and obscure, they participate in nothingness— which is to say, they are in us in a confused manner only because we are not completely perfect. And it is evident that it is not less contradictory that falsity *qua* falsity or imperfection *qua* imper-

fection proceed from God than that truth or perfection proceed from nothingness. But if we do not know that everything in us that is real and true comes from a perfect and infinite being, no matter how clear and distinct our ideas would be, we would have no reason that assured us that they have the perfection of being true.

But, now, after the knowledge of God and of the soul has thus 47 rendered us certain of this rule, it is very easy to recognize that the reveries we imagine when asleep should not make us doubt at all the truth of the thoughts we have while awake. For if it happened even while sleeping that one had some very distinct idea, as if, for example, a geometer discovered some new demonstration, his sleeping would not prevent that demonstration from being true. And as for the most ordinary error of our dreams, which consists in that they represent various objects to us in the same fashion as do our external senses, it makes no difference that they provide us with an occasion to be distrustful of the truth of such ideas, because the senses can also trick us often enough when we are not sleeping: as when those who have jaundice always see the color yellow, or as when the stars or other very distant bodies seem very much smaller than they are. For finally, whether we are sleeping or waking, we should never allow ourselves to be persuaded except by the evidence of our reason. And it is to be noted that I say of our reason, and not of our imagination or senses. Consider the following cases. When we see the sun very clearly we ought not to judge on that account that it is only the size we see it to be; and certainly we can distinctly imagine the head of a lion placed upon the body of a goat without it being necessary to conclude that there exists a Chimera in the world—in such cases reason does not tell us that what we thus see or imagine is genuine. However, reason certainly does tell us that all our ideas or notions have to have some foundation in the truth; for it would not be possible that God, who is all-perfect and all-truthful, had placed them in us without that being so. And since our reasonings are never so evident nor so complete during sleep as during waking—although our imaginations may be equally or more vivid and expressive— reason tells us also that our thoughts cannot all be true, because we are not all-perfect, and that what truth is in them should without question be discovered in those we have while awake, rather than in our dreams.

48   FIFTH PART

49   I should be very pleased to continue and to display here the
entire chain of other truths I have deduced from these first truths.
But since to do this it would be necessary for me to speak here of
many questions that are disputed among the learned (with whom
I do not wish to enter into controversy), I believe it better to
abstain from the details and say only in general what are the
truths I have deduced, in order to leave it to the wiser to judge
whether it would be useful for the public to be more particularly
informed about them. I always lived attached to the resolve I had
taken to suppose no other principle except that which I just used
to demonstrate the existence of God and the soul, and to accept
nothing as true that did not seem to me more clear and more
certain than the demonstrations of the geometers had formerly
seemed. And nevertheless I dare to say that not only have I found
a means of satisfying myself in a short time concerning all the
principal difficulties customarily treated in philosophy; but also I
have noted certain laws that God has so established in nature, and
of which he has impressed such notions in our soul, that after having devoted sufficient reflection to them, we could not doubt that
they are exactly observed in everything that is or that happens in
the world. Then, in considering what follows from these laws, it
seems I discovered many truths more useful and more important
than everything I had previously learned or even hoped to learn.

50   But because I tried to explain the principles in a treatise that
certain considerations prevent me from publishing,* I cannot
reveal these principles any better than by saying here in summary
fashion what that treatise contains. It was my goal to include in it
everything I thought I knew before writing it concerning the
nature of material things. However, just as painters, finding themselves unable to represent on a flat board all the different sides
of a solid body, choose one of its principal sides, which is the only
one they position squarely in daylight, while they shadow the
others and so make them appear only as seen by looking at the
former: well, in this same manner, fearing myself unable to place

---

* Le Monde (Oeuvres, vol. XI, pp. 3–202).

in that discourse everything I had thought about, I undertook to explain there very amply only what I conceived to be the nature of light. I resolved to add, in their turn, something concerning the sun and the fixed stars, because light proceeds nearly completely from them; next, to treat of the heavens, because they transmit light; next, to treat of the planets, comets, and the earth, because they cause light to reflect; next, to treat particularly of all the bodies on the earth, because they are either colored, or transparent, or luminous; and finally, to treat of man, because he views light. However, to fill in these matters a little better, and to say more freely what I judged about them, without being obliged to follow or refute the opinions held among the learned, I resolved to consign this entire world to their disputes, and to speak only about what would come about in a new world if God created someplace in imaginary spaces enough matter to compose such a world, and agitated its different parts without any order so as to compose a chaos as confused as the poets could imagine, and afterward did nothing but impart his ordinary operation on nature, and allow her to act following the laws he established. Thus, first of all, I described this matter and tried to represent it such that there is nothing in the world, it seems to me, clearer or more intelligible, except what has already been said of God and of the soul: for in the same manner I expressly supposed that this matter did not have within it any of those forms or qualities disputed about in the schools, and I supposed generally that it contained nothing whose knowledge was not so natural to our souls that anyone could even feign ignorance of it. Furthermore, I made it manifest what the laws of nature were, and without resting my reasons on any other principle except the infinite perfections of God, I tried to demonstrate everything about which one could have had some doubt, and to make it clear that the laws of nature are such that, even if God had created many worlds, there could not be any in which these laws failed to be observed. After that I showed how the greatest part of the matter of this chaos ought, as a consequence of these laws, to dispose itself and arrange itself in a certain fashion that rendered it similar to our heavens; and how, meanwhile, certain of these parts of matter ought to have composed an earth and some planets and comets, and why still other parts ought to have composed a sun and fixed stars. And here, pursuing the subject of light, I explained in long detail what this light was that ought to be found in the sun and stars; and how, from these places, it traversed in an instant the immense spaces of the heavens; and how it reflected from the planets and the comets toward the earth. And there I also added many things regarding the substance, the situation, the movements, and all the different qualities of these heavens and stars, in such a way that I thought I said enough to make one recognize that one notices nothing as regards the heavens and the stars of this world that would not have, or at least could not have, appeared completely similar in those of the world I described. After that I came to speak particularly about the earth: how, even though I expressly supposed that God had not placed any weight in the matter from which it was composed, nevertheless all its parts would not fail to tend exactly toward its center; how, with water and air on the superficies of the earth, the disposition of the heavens and the stars, and principally of the moon, would cause a certain rising and ebbing on the superficies of the earth, which it seemed to me was similar in all circumstances to that which we notice upon our seas; and moreover, how this would cause a certain flow not only of water, but also of air, from east to west, such as one also notices between the tropics; how the mountains, the seas and the fountains, and the rivers were able to form naturally; and how the metals came to exist in the rivers, and the plants to grow upon the fields, and generally how all the bodies that are called mixed or composed are formed on earth. And regarding the other things, since other than the stars I knew nothing in the world that produces light except fire, I studied how to understand very clearly everything that pertains to the nature of fire: how it is made; how it nourishes itself; how there is only sometimes heat without light and sometimes light without heat; how fire can introduce different colors into different bodies as well as other different qualities; how fire can melt certain bodies and harden others; how it can nearly completely consume bodies, or change them into cinders and smoke; and finally how from these cinders, by the mere violence of its action, fire forms glass—for since this transmutation of cinders into glass seems to me to be as admirable as anything else that appears in nature, I took particular pleasure in describing it.

51   Nevertheless, I did not wish to infer from all these things that this world had been created in the fashion I proposed; for it is very much more probable that from the beginning God formed it

such as it ought to be. But it is certain, and an opinion commonly received among the theologians, that the action by which he now conserves this world is entirely the same as that by which he has created it; and this in such a way that even if God would not have bestowed upon it in the beginning any other form but that of chaos, still, provided after he established the laws of nature he imparted to this chaos his support, so as to make it operate in its customary manner, one can believe, without committing an error as regards the miracle of creation, that by this alone all the things that are purely material could have with the passage of time disposed themselves such as we see them at present. And their nature is very much easier to conceive when one sees them born little by little in this manner than when one considers them only as completely formed.

From the description of inanimate bodies and plants, I passed to the description of animals, and particularly to that of men. But because I did not as yet have enough knowledge to speak of them in the same style as of the rest—that is to say, to demonstrate the effects by causes, and to make obvious from what seeds, and in what manner, nature ought to produce them—I contented myself with assuming that God formed the body of man entirely similar to our body, as much in the exterior figure of its members as in the conformity of its interior organs; and that he composed this body only from the matter I had described, and without placing in it, in the beginning, any reasoning soul, or any other thing to serve therein as a vegetative or sensitive soul, except that he excited in its heart one of those fires without light that I had already explained and conceived as having the same nature as the fire that heats hay when one has stored it away before it was dry, or that activates new wines when one allows them to ferment over sediment. For in examining the functions that could be in this body as a result of that, I found there exactly all those functions that can be in us without our thinking of them, and consequently without our soul contributing anything to them—that is to say, without this part distinct from the body, of which it has been said above that its nature is only to think, contributing anything to them. And these functions are exactly those in which one can say the animals without reason resemble us. However, for all this, I could not find any of those functions that, being dependent upon thought, are the only ones that pertain to us insofar as we are men;

and yet I found all of them afterward, when once I supposed that God created a reasoning soul and joined it to his body in a certain manner that I described.

53   But in order that one can see in what manner I treated this matter, I wish to present here the explanation of the movement of the heart and arteries: since it is the principal and most general movement that one observes in the animals, one will easily judge from it what one ought to think of all the other movements. And in order that there may be less difficulty in understanding what I will say about it, I should wish that those who are not versed in anatomy would take the trouble before reading this to cut up in front of themselves the heart of some large animal that has lungs, because such an animal is in all respects sufficiently similar to man; and I should wish them to expose the two chambers or cavities within the heart. Firstly, there is that cavity in the right side of the heart to which correspond two very large tubes: they are, namely, the vena cava, which is the principal receptacle of the blood, and is like the trunk of a tree of which all the other veins are the branches; and the arterial vein, which has been inappropriately called by this name, because in fact it is an artery that, after taking its origin from the heart, divides into many branches that spread throughout the lungs. Secondly, there is that cavity in the left side of the heart to which in the same fashion correspond two tubes, and these are as large or larger than the preceding: they are, namely, the venous artery, which also has been badly named, since it is only a vein that comes from the lungs, where it is divided into many branches interlaced with those of the arterial vein, and with those of that passageway one calls the windpipe, through which the air enters during respiration; and then there is the grand artery, which, coming from the heart, distributes its branches throughout the entire body. I should also like one to observe carefully the eleven small skins that, acting like as many small doors, open and close the four openings in these two cavities of the heart: namely, the three small skins at the entrance of the vena cava, where they are so disposed that they can in no way prevent the blood it contains from running into the right cavity of the heart, but furthermore, perfectly prevent the blood in the heart from running out; the three small skins at the entrance to the arterial vein that, being disposed in a completely contrary manner, easily permit the blood in this cavity to

pass into the lungs, but prevent that which is in the lungs from returning into this cavity; and also the two other skins at the entrance to the venous artery that allow the blood from the lungs to flow toward the left cavity of the heart, but oppose any motion of that blood back into the cavity; and finally, the three skins at the entrance of the grand artery that permit the blood to leave the heart, but prevent it from returning. And it is not necessary to seek any other reason for the number of these skins beyond the fact that the opening of the venous artery, being oval in shape because of the conditions it encounters where it is located, can easily be closed by two skins, whereas the other openings, because they are round, are more easily closed by three skins. Furthermore, I would like one to consider that the grand artery and the arterial vein are of a composition very much harder and firmer than are the venous artery and the vena cava, and that these last two enlarge before entering the heart and form there, as it were, two sacks, called the ears of the heart, which are composed of flesh similar to the flesh of the heart; and I would like one to consider that there is always more heat in the heart than in any other place in the body, and finally that this heat is capable of bringing it about that, when some drop of blood enters into its cavities, the heart promptly inflates and dilates, just as generally all liquids do when one allows them to fall drop by drop into some very hot vessel.

After this I have no need to speak of anything else in order to explain the movement of the heart, except that when its cavities are not filled with blood, then blood necessarily flows from the vena cava into the right cavity and from the venous artery into the left cavity, and this occurs because these two vessels are always filled with blood, and their openings, which face the heart, cannot be closed when the cavities are not filled by blood; but as soon as two drops of blood enter into the heart, one into each of its cavities, these drops—which can only be very large because the openings by which they enter the cavities are very large, and the vessels from which they come are very filled with blood—rarify and dilate because of the heat they encounter there, by means of which heat they inflate all the heart and push and close the five little skins at the entrances of the two vessels from which they come, thus preventing more blood from descending into the heart; and continuing to rarify more and more, they push and open the six other small skins at the entrance of the two other vessels through which they leave, and by this means they inflate all the branches of the arterial vein and of the grand artery at about the same time as they inflate the heart; immediately afterward the heart deflates, as also do these arteries, because the blood that entered them has cooled; the six small skins of these arteries close and the five small skins of the vena cava and the venous artery open and allow passage to two other drops of blood that again make the heart and the arteries inflate in the same manner as before. And because the blood that thus enters into the heart passes through those two sacks called the ears of the heart, from this it comes about that the movement of these ears is contrary to that of the heart, and that these ears deflate when the heart inflates. Moreover, in order that those who do not know the force of mathematical demonstrations, and are unaccustomed to distinguish true reasons from probabilities, will not venture to deny this account without examining it, I wish to alert them that this movement I am explaining follows just as necessarily from the combination of, first, the disposition of the organs of the heart that one can see with the human eye; second, the heat one can feel in the heart with one's finger; and third, the nature of the blood one can know by experience—it follows just as necessarily from this combination as the movement of a clock follows from the force, situation, and figure of its counterweights and wheels.

55   But if one asks why the blood in the veins is not dissipated in thus continually flowing into the heart, and why the arteries are not too filled, since all the blood that passes through the heart collects there, I have no need to say anything different concerning this matter than what has already been said by a medical physician from England,* upon whom it is necessary to bestow praise for having broken the ice on this matter, and who is the first to have taught that there are many small passages at the extremities of the arteries by which the blood they receive from the heart enters into the small branches of the veins from where it flows to collect anew in the heart, in such a way that its motion is nothing else than a perpetual circulation. And this he proves very well, based upon the ordinary experience of surgeons who, having bound the arm moderately tightly above the place where

---

* William Harvey (1578–1657), English physician and anatomist.

they open the vein, make the blood flow out more abundantly than if they had not made the tie. But the opposite would occur if they tied the arm below, that is, between the hand and the opening in the vein, or indeed, if they tied the arm very tightly above the opening. For it is manifest that the tie moderately tightened, being able to prevent the blood already in the arm from returning toward the heart by the veins, does not, on that account, prevent the blood from always coming again by the arteries, because the arteries are situated below the veins and their skins, being harder, are less easy to compress; nor does such a tie prevent the blood that comes from the heart from tending to pass by means of the arteries toward the hand with more force than it tends to return from the hand to the heart by means of the veins. And since this blood leaves the arm by the opening in one of the veins, there ought necessarily to be some passages in the arm below the tie, that is to say, near the extremities of the arm, by which the blood can come from the arteries. He also proves very well what he said about the course of the blood by referring to certain small skins that are so disposed in different places along the veins that they do not permit the blood to pass from the middle of the body toward the extremities, but only to return from the extremities toward the heart; and furthermore he proves this by the experiment that shows that all the blood in the body can leave in a short amount of time by one artery alone when it is cut—and this is true even when the artery has been tightly tied very close to the heart, with the cut in the artery made between the heart and the tie, in such a way that there is no reason to imagine that the blood that runs out comes from some place other than the heart.

But very many other things testify to the fact that the true cause of this movement is what I have said. For, firstly, the difference one notices between the blood that leaves by the veins and that which leaves by the arteries could derive only from the fact that, being rarefied and as it were distilled in passing through the heart, the blood is subtler, more forceful, and warmer immediately after leaving the heart, that is to say, when in the arteries, than a little while before entering the heart, that is to say, when in the veins. And if one takes notice of this, one will find that this difference clearly appears only near the heart, and not in places that are farthest away. Moreover, the hardness of the skins from which the arterial vein and the grand artery are composed show sufficiently well that the blood strikes against them with more force than against the veins. Why else would the right cavity of the heart and the grand artery be wider and larger than the left cavity and the arterial vein if it is not that the blood from the venous artery, which has been only in the lungs since passing through the heart, is subtler and rarefies more forcefully and easily than that which comes immediately from the vena cava? And what can the medical physicians conclude by feeling the pulse unless they know that, according as the blood changes nature, it can be rarefied by the heat of the heart more or less forcefully and more or less quickly than beforehand? And if one examines how this heat communicates itself to the other members of the body, must not one admit that it happens by means of the blood that is reheated in passing through the heart and that spreads out from there throughout the body? From this it results that if one removes the blood from some part of the body, by the same means one also removes the heat; and although the heart were as hot as red-hot iron, it would not suffice to warm the feet and the hands as much as it does if it did not continually send new blood there. Then one also recognizes from this that the true usage of respiration is to deliver enough fresh air into the lungs to make the blood that comes there from the right cavity of the heart, where it has been rarefied and as it were changed into vapors, thicken and change into blood again before falling back into the left cavity, without which process it could not be suited to serve as nourishment for the fire that is in the left cavity of the heart. This is confirmed by the fact that one sees that animals without lungs also have only one cavity in the heart and that infants, who cannot use their lungs when they are enclosed in their mother's womb, have one opening by which the blood runs from the vena cava into the left cavity of the heart, and a passage by which the blood comes from the arterial vein into the grand artery without passing through the lungs. Then, as regards digestion, how would it take place in the stomach unless the heart sent heat there by means of the arteries, as well as some more motile parts of the blood that aid in dissolving the foods that have passed there? And as regards the action that changed the juice from these foods into blood, is it not easy to recognize what it is if one considers that this juice is distilled by passing and repassing through the heart, perhaps more than a hundred or two hundred times each day? And what need is there of anything else to explain nutrition and the production of the different humors in the body, except to say that the force with which the blood in rarifying passes from the heart to extremities of the arteries makes some of its parts stop among some of the bodily members they encounter and supplant other parts they eject; and that, according to the situation, or the figure, or the smallness of the pores they encounter, some of these parts collect in certain places rather than in others, in the same manner as each of us has seen different sieves that, when pierced in various ways, serve to separate different grains each from the other? And finally, what is most remarkable in all this is the generation of animal spirits, which are like a very subtle wind, or rather like a very pure and very lively flame that, continually rising up in great abundance from the heart into the brain, proceed from there by means of the veins into the muscles and provide movement to all the bodily members. And as to why those parts of the blood—which being the most agitated and penetrating are most fitted to compose these spirits—will gather in the brain rather than in other areas of the body, there is no need to imagine any other cause than as follows. First of all, the arteries that carry them proceed from the heart in the straightest line of all. Moreover, according to the rules of mechanics, which are the same as the rules of nature, when many parts tend together to move toward the same side, but there is not enough room for all—which is the case with the parts of the blood that in leaving the left cavity of the heart will tend toward the brain—then the weakest and least agitated parts ought to be deflected by the most forceful. Thus in this way the most forceful parts of the blood will gather together in isolation in the brain.

I sufficiently explained all these matters in the treatise I hitherto had in mind to publish. And after these matters, I showed what the structure of the nerves and muscles of the human body ought to be to allow the animal spirits, once within them, to have the force to move the bodily members—just as one sees that heads, a little while after decapitation, still move and bite the earth, although they are no longer animated. I also showed what changes ought to take place in the brain to cause the waking state, sleep, and dreams; how light, odors, tastes, heat, and all the other qualities of exterior objects can implant different ideas in the brain by means of the senses; how hunger, thirst, and the other interior passions can also send their own ideas to the brain. I showed what should be considered as the common sense where these ideas are received. And I showed what should be considered as the memory that conserves ideas and as the fantasy that can change them in diverse ways to compose new ideas and by the same means to distribute the animal spirits into the muscles so as to make the body move in as many different fashions and ways—all apropos in relation to the objects that its senses present or that come to it from the interior passions—as our bodies can move without the will directing them. This shall not seem at all strange to those who, knowing how many different automata, or moving machines, the industry of men can make by using only very few parts in comparison with the great number of bones, muscles, nerves, arteries, veins, and all the other parts in the body of each animal, will consider the body as a machine that, having been made by the hands of God, is incomparably better ordered and has in it movements more noteworthy than any of those that can be invented by men.

58   And I stopped here particularly to make it clear that, if such machines had the organs and figure of a monkey or some other animal lacking reason, we would have no means of recognizing that they were not of exactly the same nature as these animals; whereas if there were machines that had a resemblance to our bodies and imitated as many of our actions as would be morally possible, we would always have two very certain means of recognizing that they would not be, for all that, real men. Firstly, these machines could never use words or other signs to compose words as we do in order to declare our thoughts to others. For one can well conceive a machine made in such a way that it produces words, and even some words that are fitting as regards the corporeal actions that cause some change in its organs: as if, when one touched it in a particular place, it asked what one wished to say to it; and as if, when one touched it in another place, it cried out that one was hurting it, and similar things. But one could not conceive that such a machine would arrange its words in different ways to respond to the meaning of everything one shall say in its presence, as even the most primitive men can do. Secondly, although these machines would do many things as well, or perhaps even better than any of us, they would unfailingly lack in some

other things; and because of this one would discover that they act, not by means of knowledge, but only by the disposition of their organs. For whereas reason is a universal instrument that can serve in all sorts of situations, these organs require some particular disposition for each particular action; from this it follows that it is morally impossible that there be enough diversities in a machine to make it act in all the occurrences of life in the same manner as our reason makes us act.

Well, then, by these same two means one can also know the difference between men and the beasts. For it is a very remarkable thing that there are no men so primitive or so stupid, not excepting even the most insane, that they are not capable of arranging different words together and composing from them discourse by means of which they make us understand their thoughts; but, on the contrary, there is no other animal, however perfect and well born it be, who does something similar. This does not occur because they lack organs, since one observes that magpies and parrots can produce words just as we do, and nevertheless they cannot speak as we do, that is to say, by giving evidence that they think what they say. However, even men born deaf and dumb, who are as much or more deprived than the beasts of the organs that serve others for speaking, will usually invent of themselves certain signs by which they make themselves understood to those who, because they are customarily with them, have the time to learn their language. And this does not signify merely that the beasts have less reason than men, but that they have no reason at all. For one sees that only very little reason is required to learn to speak; and inasmuch as one notes the inequality between animals of the same species as well as between men, and observes that some beasts and men are easier to train than others, it is unbelievable that a monkey or a parrot considered one of the most perfect of its species has not equaled in this matter of language the most stupid of children, or at least a child with a troubled brain—unless the soul of these beasts is of a nature completely different from our own. And one should not confuse words with natural movements, which are evidence of the passions, and which can be imitated by machines as well as by other animals; nor should one think, as some ancients thought, that the beasts speak even though we do not understand their language: for if that were true, since the beasts have many organs related to ours, they should also be able to make themselves understood by us as well as by their own kind. It is also very noteworthy that, although there are many animals who give evidence of more skill in certain of their actions than we do, one nevertheless notices that the same animals do not manifest any skill whatever in very many other actions: thus what they do better than us does not prove that they have a mind; for if this tale were true they should have more of a mind than we have and should be better at everything; but rather the beasts have no mind at all, and it is nature that acts in them according to the dispositions of their organs—just as one sees that a clock, which is composed only of wheels and springs, can count the hours and measure the time more accurately than we can with all our foresight.

60   After that I described the rational soul, and I showed that it can in no way be derived from the power of matter, as could the other things of which I spoke, but that instead it must be expressly created; and I showed why it is not sufficient for it to be lodged in the human body like a pilot in his ship—unless perhaps to move the bodily members—but that it is necessary that it be joined and united more intimately with the body in order to have, beyond the ability to move the bodily members, feelings and appetites similar to ours, and thus to compose a genuine man. I have just here lingered somewhat over this subject of the soul because it is one of the most important; for after the error of those who deny God, which I think that I have sufficiently refuted above, there is nothing that more readily leads feeble minds away from the path of virtue than to imagine that the soul of beasts is of the same nature as ours, and that consequently we have nothing more to fear or hope for after this life than do the flies and ants: whereas when one knows how much the souls of beasts differ from our souls, one understands very much better the reasons that prove that our soul is of a nature entirely independent of the body, and consequently that it isn't subjected to die with the body; then, inasmuch as one doesn't see other causes that would destroy it, one is naturally inclined to judge that it is immortal.

61   SIXTH PART

62   It is now three years since I came to the end of the treatise containing all these matters, and was beginning to review it to place

it in the hands of a printer. But then I learned that certain persons, to whom I defer, and whose authority over my actions can hardly be less than that of my own reason, had disapproved of an opinion in physics published a little while beforehand by someone else.* I do not wish to say that I held this opinion, but certainly I had noticed nothing in the opinion, before their censure, that I could imagine to be prejudicial either to religion or to the state, or that consequently might have prevented me from writing it had reason persuaded me of it. And this circumstance made me fear that in just the same way there would be found among my own opinions one in which I would be mistaken, despite the great care I have always exercised to receive nothing new into my belief without very certain demonstrations, and to write nothing that could turn out to be to anyone's disadvantage. This was sufficient to oblige me to change the resolve I had had to publish those opinions. For although the reasons why I had held them beforehand were very strong, my inclination, which has always been to hate the profession of writing books, made me at once find enough other reasons to excuse myself from the task of writing. And all these reasons are such that not only have I some interest in stating them here, but perhaps it is also in the public's interest to know them.

I have never had a great opinion of the things that came from 63 my hand; and as long as I received no other fruits from the method which I was using except the satisfaction it gave me in regard to some difficulties pertaining to speculative science, or when I tried to regulate my customs by the reasons it taught me, I did not believe myself obliged to write anything about the method. For regarding customs, everybody readily and so confidently offers his opinions that one would find as many reformers as heads were it permitted to others than those whom God has either established as sovereigns over the nations, or given sufficient grace and zeal to be prophets, to undertake to change anything; and although my speculations strongly pleased me, I believed that other people also made speculations that pleased them perhaps even more. But as soon as I had acquired some general notions about physics, and began to test them in different specific prob-

---

* Galileo, condemned for the theory of the movement of the earth proposed in his *Massimi Sistemi*; see *Discours de la méthode*, commentary by Étienne Gilson (Paris: Vrin, 1947), p. 440.

lems, I noted how far these notions can take one, and how much they differ from the principles that have been used until the present time; thus I believed that I could not hide these notions without sinning greatly against the law that obliges us to procure, as much as we can, the general good of all men. For these notions have made me see that it is possible to reach various knowledge very useful to life, and that, instead of the speculative philosophy taught in the schools, one can find another practical philosophy by which we can know—as distinctly as we now know the different professions of our artisans—the force and action of fire, water, air, the stars, the heavens, and all the other bodies that surround us; and thus, in the same way that we employ artisans, we could also employ all these things for all the uses for which they are fit, thereby rendering ourselves like masters and possessors of nature. And this is to be desired not only in order to discover an infinity of devices that would allow one to enjoy without difficulty the fruits of the earth, and all the conveniences involved in that; rather it is principally to be desired to preserve health, which is without a doubt the first good, and the foundation of all the other goods of this life; for even the mind is so much dependent upon the temperament of the body and the disposition of its organs, that if any means can be found to generally render men wiser and abler than they have been until now, I believe that it ought to be sought after in medicine. It is true that the medicine now practiced contains few things whose utility is noteworthy; but without having any wish to disparage it, I am assured there is hardly anyone, not even among those whose profession is medicine, who does not admit that what is known in it is nearly nothing in comparison with what remains to be known and that one could eliminate an infinity of illnesses, both of the body and of the mind, and perhaps also the weakening that comes with old age, if one had enough knowledge of their causes, and of all the remedies nature has provided to us. Thus, since my goal was to employ all my life in the quest of so necessary a science, and since I encountered a path that, it seems, must unfailingly lead to its discovery if one pursues it and is not prevented either by the brevity of life or by the lack of experiments, I judged that there was no better remedy against these two impediments than to communicate faithfully to the public all the few things I had found, and to urge good minds to advance further, each contributing according to his inclination and abilities to the experiments it would be necessary to perform, and also communicating publicly all the things he would learn; so that, with the last researcher beginning where the preceding ones left off, thus joining together the lives and works of many, we would all progress very much further than each person working alone could do.

I even noticed, as regards experiments, that they are more necessary the more one has progressed in knowledge. For in the beginning it is preferable to use only those experiences that present themselves of their own accord to our senses—for of these we could not be ignorant provided we devote a little reflection to them—rather than to seek out the more unusual and studied experiences. The reason for this is that the more unusual experiences are often deceptive when one does not as yet know the causes of the most ordinary—for the circumstances upon which these more unusual experiences depend are nearly always so particular and detailed that it is very difficult to take note of them. The order I employed in this matter has been as follows. First, I tried to find in general the principles or first causes of everything that is or can be in the world, without considering anything for this purpose except God alone, who created the world; and I did not attempt to understand these principles except by extracting them from certain seeds of truths naturally in our souls. After that I examined what were the first and more ordinary effects one could deduce from these causes: and it seems to me that by doing this I discovered the heavens, the stars, and earth, and also on the earth, water, air, fire, minerals, and some other such things that are the most common and simplest of all, and consequently the easiest to know. Next, when I wished to descend to things more particular, so many different things presented themselves to me that I did not believe it possible for the human mind to distinguish the forms or kinds of bodies that are on the earth from an infinity of others that could be there had God willed it so; and consequently I did not think it possible to relate such things to our practice unless one proceeds to causes by way of effects and makes use of many particular experiments. In consequence of this, upon reviewing with my mind all the objects that had ever been presented to my senses, I venture to say definitely that I never noticed anything I could not explain easily enough by the principles I had found. But it is also necessary for me to admit that the power of nature is so great and vast, and these principles so simple and general, that scarcely did I notice a particular effect before I immediately recognized that it could be deduced in many different ways from these principles; and my greatest difficulty ordinarily consists in discovering the specific way in which an effect does depend upon principles. In regard to this matter I do not know any other technique but to seek afresh for certain experiments that are such that their outcome is not the same if the effect ought to be explained in one of these ways rather than in another of these ways. Moreover, I have now reached the point where it seems to me that I see well enough on what basis one ought to rely to devise the greatest part of those experiments that can serve this purpose; but I see also that these experiments are such, and so great in number, that neither my hands nor funds, although I were to have a thousand times more of them than I have, would suffice to perform all of them; so that, according as I will henceforth have the opportunity to perform more or less of these experiments, I will advance the more or the less in the knowledge of nature. This is what I promised myself to make known in the treatise I had written, and therein to manifest so clearly the utility the public can derive from such experiments, that I would oblige all those who desire the general good of men—that is to say, oblige all those who are in effect virtuous, and not by false pretense or only by opinion—both to communicate to me those experiments that they had already made, and to assist me in researching those that remain to be performed.

65 But since that time I have found other reasons that made me change my opinion and think that I ought to continue to write about all the things I judge of some importance insofar as I discover the truth about them, devoting the same care to this as if I wished to have the matter published: I chose to do this, first, to have so much the more opportunity to examine them well, since undoubtedly one always looks more closely at what one believes bound to be seen by many people than at what one prepares only for oneself, and because often things that have seemed true when I began to conceive them have seemed false when I wished to put them down on paper; second, to lose no occasion to benefit the public, if I can do so, and in order that, if my writings are worth something, those who will have them after my death can use them in whatever way will be most proper. But it was my choice that I should not at all consent to have my writings

published during my life, so that neither the oppositions and the controversies to which they would be subject during my life, nor even such reputation as I would be able to gain, would give me any occasion to lose the time I had planned to employ instructing myself. For although it is true that every man is obliged to procure, as much as he is able, the good of others, and although it is truly of no value to be useful to nobody, nevertheless it is also true that our concerns ought to extend further than the present time, and that it is good to omit things that perhaps would bring some profit to those who are alive when the goal is to produce other advantages that pertain more to our posterity. In fact, I certainly wish that everyone realize that the little bit I have learned until this time is hardly anything in comparison with that of which I am ignorant and hope to learn; for the situation of those who discover the truth little by little in the sciences is nearly the same as the situation of those who, beginning to become rich, have less difficulty making great acquisitions than they previously had when poor in making very much lesser acquisitions. Or else one can compare those in the sciences with the leaders of an army, whose forces customarily grow in proportion to their victories, and who require more leadership to maintain themselves when they have lost a battle than to take cities and provinces after they have won a battle. For it is truly to undertake battles when one tries to vanquish all the difficulties and errors that prevent us from arriving at a knowledge of the truth, and it is the same as losing a battle when one accepts some false opinion respecting a matter somewhat general and important; for afterward, to put oneself back on the same footing as before requires very much more cleverness than is required to make great progress when one already has principles that are assured. For me, if I have hitherto found some truths in the sciences (and I hope that the things contained in this volume will serve to make others judge that I have found some), I can say that these truths are only the consequences dependent upon five or six principal difficulties that I have overcome, and that I consider to be as many battles where the hour fell to my side. Moreover, I will not fear to say that I think I do not need to gain more than two or three similar battles to achieve my goals entirely; and my age is not so advanced that, according to the ordinary course of nature, I may not still have sufficient opportunity to do so. But I believe myself the more bound to manage the time remaining to me, the more I hope to be able to use it well; and without a doubt I would have many occasions to waste that time if I published the foundations of my physics. For although they are nearly all so evident that it is necessary only to understand them to believe them, and although there is not one of them of which I think myself unable to give demonstrations, nevertheless because it is impossible that they accord with all the different opinions of other men, I foresee that I would often be diverted by the oppositions to which they will give birth.

66   One can say that such oppositions would be useful to make me recognize my mistakes, and in order that, if I had something good, others might gain more knowledge by means of these oppositions; and moreover, it can be said that, since many can see more than one man alone, by beginning to make use of what is good in my work, others might also assist me with their discoveries. But although I recognize that I am extremely subject to mistake, and that I hardly ever trust the first thoughts that come to me, nevertheless the experience I have had of objections that can be made to me prevents me from expecting any profit from such objections: for I have already often tested the judgments of those whom I considered my friends, of some others to whom I thought myself to be indifferent, and also even of certain people whose ill will and envy I knew would cause them to try hard enough to discover what the good will of my friends would hide from them; but it has rarely happened that anyone has made some objection I did not foresee at all, unless it was something very far removed from my subject; thus I hardly ever encountered any critic of my opinions who did not seem to me less rigorous or less fair than myself. And furthermore, I never noticed that one discovered any truth of which he was hitherto ignorant by means of the disputes practiced in the schools; for as long as each participant aims at victory, he occupies himself much more in defending a probability than in weighing the reasons on all sides of a matter; and one who has for a long time been a good pleader is not, on that account, afterward a good judge.

67   As for the utility others would receive from the communication of my thoughts, it could not be very great inasmuch as I have not yet carried them so far that very many things need not be added before applying them in practice. And I think that I can say without vanity that if there is anyone able to add them, it is me rather

than anyone else: not that there may not be many more minds in the world incomparably better than mine; but because one cannot conceive something so well, nor make it his own, except when he invents it himself. This is so true as regards this matter that, although I have often explained some of my opinions to persons with very good minds who, while I spoke with them, seemed to understand them very distinctly, nevertheless when these people repeated them, I noticed that they had changed them nearly all the time in such a way that I could no longer admit them as my own. On this account I feel very free in here asking posterity never to believe things that others will say issue from me when I myself shall not have divulged them. And I am not at all astonished by the extravagances that are attributed to all those ancient philosophers whose writings we lack; and for all that is said about them, I do not judge that their thoughts were so unreasonable, seeing that they were the best minds of their times; I judge only that their thoughts have been badly related to us. Thus one also sees that hardly ever has any of their followers surpassed them; and I am assured that the most passionate of those who follow Aristotle would believe themselves happy if they had as much knowledge about nature as he had, even though it was on the condition that they would never have more. They are like the ivy that does not tend to rise higher than the trees that support it, and that often goes back downward if it has arrived at the summit. For it seems to me that they do go back downward—which is to say, they render themselves less knowledgeable than if they abstained from studying—when, not contented with knowing everything intelligibly explained in their author, they wish also to find the solution of many difficulties about which he says nothing and about which he perhaps never thought. Nevertheless, their manner of philosophizing is very convenient for those who have only very mediocre minds; for the obscurity of the distinctions and the principles that they use is the reason why they can speak of all things as boldly as if they knew about them, and sustain everything they say about them against subtler and abler minds without anyone having a means of convincing them. And in this respect they seem to me to be the same as a blind man who, in order to fight without disadvantage an opponent who is able to see, lures him into the depths of some very dark cave; and I can say that it is to the interest of such as these that I abstain from publishing the principles of the philosophy of which I make use; for since these principles are very simple and very evident, I would do nearly the same thing in publishing them as if I opened some windows and allowed the daylight to enter the cave where they have descended to do battle. Moreover, the best minds have no reason to wish to know these principles of mine. For if they wish to know how to speak of all things and to acquire the reputation of being learned, they will achieve their goal more easily by contenting themselves with probability. This can be found without great difficulty in all sorts of subject matters, whereas truth is discovered only little by little in a few subject matters; and when it is a question of speaking about others, it obliges one to admit frankly that one is ignorant about them. However, if the best minds do prefer the knowledge of a few truths to the vanity of seeming to be ignorant of none, which undoubtedly is preferable, and if they wish to follow a plan similar to my own, they have no need on that account that I say to them anything more than what I have already said in this discourse. For if they are capable of advancing further than I have done, it follows that they will by themselves find all that I think I have found. And, inasmuch as I have never examined anything except in an orderly manner, it is certain that what yet remains for me to discover is in itself more difficult and hidden than what I have been previously able to find, and others would have much less pleasure in learning about it from me than from themselves; besides, the habit they will acquire in first seeking easy things, and in passing little by little by degrees to things more difficult, will serve them better than could all my instructions. As for myself, I am persuaded that if I had been taught from my youth all the truths for which I have since sought the demonstrations, and if I had no difficulty in learning them, I would perhaps never have known any others and never have acquired the habit and the facility that I think myself to have in always finding new truths in proportion to the application I devote to finding them. And in a word, if there is any work in this world that cannot be so well achieved by anyone other than he who began it, it is the work at which I labor.

68   It is true that, as regards the experiments that can be of use in this project, one man alone could not perform all of them; but he also could not usefully employ any hands but his own, except those of artisans or such people as he could pay—people to whom

the prospect of payment, which is a very efficient means, would make them do exactly everything prescribed for them to do. As for volunteers, who out of curiosity or a desire to learn would perhaps offer to aid him, besides the fact that they ordinarily promise more than they perform, thus making only fine-sounding proposals whose issue is nothing, such people invariably would want to be paid by an explanation of certain difficulties, or at least by compliments and useless conversations, which would mean the loss of more of his time than he saves. And as regards the experiments others have already performed, even when they would wish to communicate them to him (which is something those people who call experiments secrets would never do), the experiments are, for the most part, dependent on so many circumstances or superfluous ingredients that it would be very difficult for him to decipher the truth; beyond this, he would find all of them so badly explained or even so false, because those who have made them have forced themselves to make them appear in conformity with their principles, that as a result, if there had been some of them that might serve his purpose, they would not be worth the time required for him to select them out. In this way, if somewhere in the world there were a person that one assuredly knew to be capable of finding out the greatest things, and things as useful to the public as is possible, and if for this reason other men would be forced to help him by every means to achieve his goals, I do not see that they could do anything for him except to furnish the moneys for the experiments he would require, and beyond this to prevent him from being deprived of his leisure by anyone's importunities. But besides the fact that I am not so presumptuous as to wish to promise anything extraordinary, nor to feed myself on thoughts so vain as to imagine that the public ought to interest itself very much in my plan, I also do not have a soul so base that I ever wished to accept from anyone any favor that one could believe I did not merit.

All these considerations joined together were the reason why 69 three years ago I did not wish to divulge the treatise I had in my hands, and why I made a resolve not to bring into light of day during my lifetime any other treatise that might be so general, or such that one could understand the foundations of my physics. But since that time I again have had two other reasons that have obliged me to present here some particular essays and to provide the public with some account of my actions and my goals. The first is that, if I failed to do so, some who have known the intention I have previously had to publish certain writings would imagine that the reasons for my abstaining would be more to my disadvantage than they are. For although I do not love excessive glory, or even, if I dare say, hate it, because I consider it contrary to leisure, which I value above everything; nevertheless I have also never tried to hide my actions like crimes, nor have I used very many precautions to keep them unknown. Not only would I have thought it wrong for me to do that, but also it would have brought me some sort of inquietude, which again might have been contrary to the perfect repose of mind for which I seek. And since being thus indifferent between exercising care that I be recognized or remain unknown, I have not been able to prevent myself from acquiring some sort of reputation, I thought I ought to do my best at least to prevent myself from developing a bad one. The other reason that has obliged me to write this is that, seeing the goal I previously had of instructing myself daily set back more and more because of an infinity of experiments I require, and realizing I cannot perform them without the aid of others, even though I do not flatter myself that the public will participate in a large degree in my interests, nevertheless I also do not wish to withdraw so much into myself as to provide to those who will follow a reason for reproaching me someday that I could have left them many very much better things had I not excessively neglected making them understand how they could contribute to my goals.

70   And I thought that it was easy to choose certain matters that, without being subject to very much controversy or obliging me to declare more of my principles than I desire, would not fail to manifest clearly enough what I can and cannot do in the sciences. In this I could not say if I have succeeded; I do not wish to anticipate the judgments of anyone when I myself am speaking of my writings; but I would be happy if others examined them; and in order that they may have more opportunity of doing so, I urge everyone who will have some objections to make to these essays to take the trouble to send them to my publisher; and when he brings them to my attention I will try to make my replies at the same time; and by this means readers, seeing together the objec-

tions and replies, will judge so much the more easily about the truth. I do not promise ever to make long responses, but only to admit my mistakes very frankly if I have recognized them, or if I cannot perceive them, to say simply what I shall believe to be required for the defense of the things I have written, without introducing an explanation of any new subject matters in order to avoid involving myself endlessly in one thing and then another.

If some of the things about which I have spoken at the beginning of the *Dioptrics* and *Meteors* displease at first glance, because I call them suppositions and do not seem to have any desire to prove them, let the reader have the patience to read through the whole with attention, and I hope he will find himself satisfied. For it seems to me that the reasons are interdependent in such a way that just as the last are demonstrated by the first, which are their causes, so these first are reciprocally demonstrated by the last, which are their effects. And one should not imagine that I commit in this matter the mistake logicians call a circle; for since experience renders the greatest part of these effects very certain, the causes from which I have deduced them do not serve so much to prove them as to explain them; indeed, the very opposite is the case, namely, the causes from which I have deduced these effects are proved by the effects. And I have called them suppositions only so that one may know that while I think I can deduce them from those first truths explained above, I have expressly chosen not to do so in order to prevent certain minds from taking the opportunity to erect some extravagant philosophy, for which I will be blamed, upon what they will believe to be my principles. I refer to those who imagine that they can know in a day everything someone else has thought throughout twenty years once they have heard two or three words about his thoughts. Such people are the more likely to go wrong and the less capable of arriving at the truth, the more they are penetrating and precipitous. But as for opinions that are truly mine, I ask no pardon for their novelty, inasmuch as if one considers thoroughly the reasons for them, I am assured they will be found so simple and consonant with common sense that they will seem less extraordinary and strange than any other opinions that can be held on the same subject matters. And also I do not flatter myself with being the first discoverer of any of them. I take this attitude not because I have ever received them from anyone—that is, neither because others have said them nor because others have not said them—but only because reason has persuaded me of them.

72   If artisans are not soon able to build the invention explained in the *Dioptrics*, I do not believe on that account one can say it is difficult: for since skill and practice are required to make and adjust the machines I have described, even if no other requirement were lacking, I would be no less astonished if artisans would hit the mark at the first try than if someone could learn to play the lute excellently in one day just because he had been given a good score. And if I write in French, which is the language of my country, rather than in Latin, which is the language of my teachers, it is because I hope that those who make use only of their pure natural reason will judge better concerning my opinions than those who believe only in ancient books. And for those who join good sense to duty, who alone I desire as my judges, I am assured that they will not be so partial to Latin as to refuse to understand my reasons because I explain them in a common language.

73   I do not wish to speak here in detail of the progress I hope to make in the sciences in the future, nor do I wish to involve myself in any promises to the public that I am not assured I will fulfill; but I shall say only that I have resolved not to employ the time that remains to me in life at any other endeavor than to try to acquire such a knowledge of nature that one can extract from it rules of medicine more assured than those that have been followed up until the present. My inclination so strongly turns me from every other sort of goal, and principally from those that could not be useful to some without being harmful to others, that if circumstances constrained me to engage myself in such activities, I do not believe that I would be capable of succeeding at them. And as far as this is concerned, I here declare that not only do I recognize that in this way I cannot serve to establish by renown throughout the world, but also that I have no desire to be renowned; and I will always hold myself more obliged to those by whose thoughtfulness I shall enjoy my leisure without impediment than to those who would offer me the most honorable offices on the earth.

THE END

III

MEDITATIONS

Introduction

Descartes's *Meditations concerning First Philosophy* was published in 1641, four years after the publication of his *Discourse concerning Method*. In the fourth part of the *Discourse* he touched on the two questions that, in his opinion, constitute the subject matter of "First Philosophy," or metaphysics, namely, the questions of God and the human mind. In the *Meditations* he again undertakes to demonstrate the nature and existence of God and the nature of the human mind. In respect to the human mind he again sets about to prove that it is a substance entirely distinct from material substance.

His procedures in the *Meditations*, to the extent they vary from those in the fourth part of the *Discourse*, seem designed to satisfy two objections that had been made to the argumentation in the *Discourse*. In the "Preface to the Reader" Descartes identifies the two objections to which he will reply in the *Meditations*. First, in the *Discourse* he seems to affirm the real or substantial distinction between mind and matter before proving God's power, goodness, and existence. In response to an objection on this point, he clearly intends a different procedure in the *Meditations*. Here the metaphysical doubt concerning the origins and capacities of human reason is so far-reaching that he affirms nothing about our ability to distinguish definitively between created substances until he proves God's infinite power, goodness, and existence.[1] Second, it was objected that in his principal argument for God's existence Descartes had not proved that his idea of God, or of a more perfect being, derived from God rather than from himself. In the

Third Meditation he more carefully restates his principal argument. In my opinion the restatement does not vary essentially from the same argument in the *Discourse*. However, in the *Meditations* he employs technical terms ("objective reality," "formal," "eminent," and so on) that allow for a more precise formulation of his proof. I have appended to the *Meditations* a section from his replies to objections to the *Meditations*. This section includes Descartes's own definitions of technical terms used particularly in the Third Meditation. I employ these definitions in commenting on the *Meditations*.

Limitations of space, however, require great selectivity in my comments, and I have covered much of the material in introducing the *Discourse*. I will confine my remarks to a few of the matters that seem to me to involve some expansion, or interesting rephrasing, of doctrines contained in the *Discourse:* some features of the formulation of metaphysical doubt in the First Meditation; the significance of the wax experiment in the Second Meditation; the reworked version of the principal proof of God's existence in the Third Meditation; and the argument that God is good in the Fourth Meditation.

FIRST MEDITATION: FORMULATION OF METAPHYSICAL DOUBT

As explained in conjunction with the *Discourse*, Descartes recognizes two aspects of demonstrative procedures, analysis and synthesis. "Analysis" is reductive; it pinpoints the questions that have to be answered first in order to answer a proposed question. Thus analysis directs us to the simple objects of intuition, or first principles from which all further knowledge must be established by necessary deductions. "Synthesis" refers to the deduction of consequences from first principles. Since first principles are most often psychologically remote while complexities are all too familiar, analysis certainly precedes synthesis in the order of genuine and true learning.[2]

In the *Meditations*, which Descartes says contains only analysis, he first proceeds to discard familiar beliefs or prejudices because they are not completely certain and indubitable.[3] Next, he isolates his own existence and the existence of God. From the nature and existence of God as a first principle he then proceeds, in what seems to me a synthetic manner, to distinguish those beliefs that can be retrieved from metaphysical doubt and established with certainty from those that must remain matters of probability.

In the First Meditation Descartes applies a maxim that reason prescribes for anyone who chooses to seek for a certainty higher than that afforded by the provisional probabilities on which he shall act during the quest for metaphysical certitude. Descartes says: ". . . reason persuades me that assent ought to be withheld no less carefully from things not manifestly certain and indubitable than from things obviously false. . . . "⁴ This maxim is constantly applied throughout the *Meditations*. It is a formulation of the principle that governs reductive analysis and synthesis—that is, the maxim reminds us that there is no prospect of knowing a particular belief to be true, or of knowing any beliefs erected on it, unless the belief is itself self-evident or retrieved from uncertainty through necessary deduction from self-evident truths.

In respect to sense experience, Descartes notices that even so-called waking sense experiences do not guarantee the existence of matter. Thus he advises that we act as though we are in a dream. Acting in this manner is simply reason's way of reminding itself of its original maxim, namely, that assent should be withheld from all beliefs not certain and indubitable. But similar to his strategy in the *Discourse*, Descartes goes so far as to question even pure mathematics, thus calling into doubt not just the existence but also the very nature of matter.

In the *Discourse* Descartes doubts arithmetic and geometry because there is no proof that mathematical reasoning does not imply paralogisms, or contradictions. Hence the nature of matter, which is conceived through such mathematical reasoning, may itself be contradictory—that is, there is no metaphysical assurance that matter is possible. In addition to this mathematical reason for doubting mathematics and the nature of matter, Descartes emphasizes another reason for doubt in the *Meditations*. His argument is likely to have been taken from the ancient Skeptics, who applied it to claims to knowledge based on the senses.⁵ Descartes argues that mathematics can be doubted inasmuch as it has not yet been shown that a very powerful and deceiving God is impossible or nonexistent. Since Descartes himself remembers, or seems to remember, being deceived at mathematical reasoning, the suggestion is that until such a God is shown to be impossible or non-existent, there is no proof that such a God is not constantly bent on tricking him into assenting to ideas, such as mathematical ideas, that despite appearing true, might nonetheless be false. Moreover, Descartes stresses that if no design, intelligence, or providence—that is, if no good and powerful God—is at the origin of human reason, it seems that the probability only increases that the human mind is not fabricated in such a way as to attain to knowledge. Cicero too had warned against presuming that design enters into the fabrication of human "intelligence."[6]

Thus what Descartes must ultimately seek to discover is some idea, manifestly true in a way that even the reasonings of mathematics have been shown not to be, that, by revealing the origins of human reason, discloses the capacities of human reason for attaining to truth by means of the various ideas that have been thrown into metaphysical doubt. In concluding the First Meditation Descartes reminds himself of the maxim that prescribes a withholding of assent from all ideas not manisfestly certain and indubitable. He reminds himself of that maxim by pretending there is a cunning and powerful deceiver always ready to trick him into accepting what scrutiny would show is not absolutely certain and indubitable. Moreover, Descartes emphasizes that his search for the metaphysically certain and indubitable comes at what promises to be the end of the dream in which he has for so long lived, accepting the dubious and uncertain as if it were known to be true. He emphasizes that although it is tempting to do so, to return to the familiar "light" of dubious opinions would be knowingly to choose dreaming to waking. Reason is awake only when it regards, and continues to regard, the dubious as a dream.

SECOND MEDITATION: SIGNIFICANCE OF THE WAX EXPERIMENT

In the Second Meditation Descartes claims an immediate or intuitive knowledge of himself as one thing that reasons, affirms, withholds assent, imagines, and senses. He is most concerned to show that sense qualities or images, such as colors, flavors, smells, and so on, by no means exhaust the self as immediately known.

He wants to show that in addition to sense qualities, we are immediately apprised of a nonsensuous reason, intellect, or mind in which ideas, properly so-called, inhere. In order to make it clear that reasoning does not consist in sense qualities or images, but requires a nonsensuous aspect of mind, Descartes designs a wax experiment.

To appreciate the wax experiment and to learn what Descartes means by an idea in the intellect, it is useful to understand first what the wax experiment is not intended to show. Descartes does not deny that we require sense qualities, indeed complicated patterns of them, to acquire and preserve our concepts of ordinary objects, such as apples, clocks, wax, candles, and so on. It is clear that blindness or an abnormality of the nervous system would diminish or deprive us of such ordinary concepts. However, Descartes wishes to show that the human mind's ability to apply geometrical and metaphysical concepts to its sense qualities—for example, the concept of an incommensurable or the concept of mode—presupposes a nonsensuous reason or intellect with nonsensuous ideas.

Descartes points out that to understand the sensible wax as an extended or material thing, it is necessary to understand that the sensible wax would remain the same extended thing even if it were to assume innumerable other shapes. Moreover, he points out that our understanding of these innumerable other shapes could not consist in an ability to imagine them. Some of these shapes, which reason understands and distinguishes from each other, are so complicated that they cannot be perspicuously distinguished from each other on the basis of the imagination. To try to do so would be an impediment to reason—it would be a misuse of what in the *Rules* Descartes refers to as the inborn wit (*ingenium*). Since the senses do not provide a basis for distinguishing the complicated figures that reason does distinguish, it is clear that the ideas by which reason distinguishes such figures are not sense qualities or images but rather are nonsensuous.

Furthermore, in many places Descartes points out that even the simplest elements of geometrical reasoning can be understood only by nonsensuous ideas. I will work with a single example. It is easy to display to the senses a geometrical nature such as the line. However, if our understanding of the line, that is, if our idea of the line, were identical with the image that displays the line to the imagination, then we would have to have such an image every time we understand a line. But to conceive any line at all, we must understand that that line is such that it may enter into or be an element—for example, a side—of many figures. However, when the figure is of many sides, it is clear that we still understand the figure and all the lines that make it up, although we cannot distinguish or portray the lines that make it up in our imagination. Thus our idea of any line can never be identified with, and thus restricted by, an image.

Moreover, to understand geometrical reasoning, or indeed any reasoning, we have to understand what is contradictory or impossible. But if images were the same as ideas, we could never represent impossibility (for example, the impossibility of a square circle), because whatever is, strictly speaking, "portrayed" in the imagination is possible—otherwise it could not be there. It should also be clear that our ideas of numbers cannot be reduced to images. Such reduction is impossible not only because the unit is indivisible, whereas no image seems indivisible, but also because larger numbers would have to be associated with complex figures—and as has been said, our ideas of complex figures cannot be understood as combinations of images. Indeed, if what has been said is correct, no geometrical idea, however simple, could be a sense image.

Descartes's purpose in the wax experiment is only to clarify what he takes as immediately, or intuitively, obvious about the self—namely, that ideas exist in the nonsensuous reason or intellect and that it is the intellect that "perceives" the nature of anything about which we think. He designed the wax experiment only to remove the obstacle an excessive reliance on the imagination poses to the intuition of the self. It should be noted that throughout the Second Meditation Descartes preserves his metaphysical doubts concerning arithmetic and geometry. The wax experiment seems intended to go some distance in proving a view of mind he held as early as his *Rules*. But as I explained in connection with the *Discourse*, the argument whereby the substantial distinction between mind and body is established involves further complexities.[7]

THIRD MEDITATION: DESCARTES'S PRINCIPAL ARGUMENT FOR GOD'S EXISTENCE

I shall first explain the technical terminology Descartes imports into the Third Meditation. Using this terminology, I shall then very briefly recapitulate the interpretation of the argument I gave in commenting on the *Discourse*. I shall first explain the terms "idea," "materially," "objective reality," "formal," "eminent," and "formal reality."

The term "idea" has to be understood by reference to what was said about the Second Meditation. Ideas are not sense qualities or images, but they exist in nonsensuous reason or intellect. There are two ways of referring to ideas in the intellect. First, we may refer to them "materially"—which simply means we refer to them in respect to their status as operations of the intellect or of reasoning. In this sense all ideas are the same. For example, our ideas of a line, point, God, and so on, are all operations of the intellect. Second, we may refer to ideas from the point of view of their "objective realities." In this sense all ideas are not the same, because insofar as one idea represents something different from what another idea represents, we say that the ideas have different objective realities.

When we consider ideas from the point of view of their objective realities, we can say, generally, that some ideas represent an object as belonging to another object in a "literal" way. For example, we have an idea that represents an object, namely, spatiality, as attaching in a literal way to another object, namely, a triangle. We mean that the triangle is itself spatial or extended. When an object is assigned to another in this literal way, we say that it is assigned to the other "formally." By contrast, some ideas represent an object as attaching to another object, not so much in a literal way, but rather in such a way as to indicate that the one object derives from, but is not literally in, the other object. An example may help. Consider the idea that represents a material object as hot. When we say a material object is hot, we are likely to mean, at least on reflection, *not* that heat as a sense quality is in matter, but rather that something in matter causes heat to be experienced by a mind. When an object is assigned to another in this "nonliteral" way, we may say that it is assigned to the other object "eminently," implying that it proceeds from, or is caused by, something in the object but yet is not itself in the object. Thus heat, for example, which is eminently predicated of matter, would itself be formally predicated of mind, since a thinking thing is affected by feeling. Often we eminently predicate one thing of another, for example, heat of matter, without knowing exactly what is in the one thing, such as in matter, to cause the second thing, such as heat, to be formally in some third thing, such as in our mind.

Since ideas alone contain objective realities—that is, represent things—ideas alone are said to have "objective existence." Whatever is not an idea can be said to have a formal reality, although we may be in doubt about what in truth has formal reality. Yet even within the thinking thing as immediately known, the will and intellect surely have formal reality, as do sensible images. Moreover, I think it is clear that ideas, insofar as they are operations of the intellect containing specific objective realities—that is, insofar as they are taken "materially"—have a formal reality; however, Descartes prefers to single out the existence of ideas with the special term "objective existence."

By the time he reaches the Third Meditation, Descartes knows only a few things. The only objective realities he knows to be true are those that represent what has been immediately discerned in himself as a thinking thing—namely, that he has formally within him a will, senses, imagination, and an intellect in which inheres the ideas containing the objective realities that represent not only what he knows to be formally within him but many other things, such as arithmetical and geometrical natures, about which he is in doubt.

Now, to the extent that the objective realities in ideas seem to represent something, we may say they seem to have some degree of representative perfection, value, or artifice. In other words, since it is in the nature of an idea to seem to represent something, or to have an objective reality or content, it is in the nature of an idea to claim to some perfection in informing us about the truth of things. Among our various ideas, it is clear that some seem to have more objective reality, or more representative value, or more perfection, or more artifice, than do others. Some ideas seem to have more objective reality, and so forth, either because they seem to us better than other ideas or because they seem more fundamental than other ideas. For example, the idea that represents heat or cold as formally in matter is likely to seem to us to have very little objective reality, representative value, or perfection—for we are probably persuaded that matter itself is but formally extended, so that at most it can cause sense qualities in a mind, but not itself be sensuous. Or to take another example, the idea that represents a substance would seem to have more objective reality, or representative value, or perfection, than the idea that represents a mode because a mode is possible only by presupposing a substance.

Thus the ranking of our ideas in terms of the degree of their objective reality, perfection, or value indicates what we assume to be the fundamental nature of reality. For example, if the idea of substance is assigned more representative perfection than the idea of mode, it implies that we conceive reality in such a way that a mode necessarily presupposes substance. However, by the time of the Third Meditation Descartes has pushed his metaphysical doubts so far, and has launched such a critique of customary ideas, that the objective perfection, value, or artifice in the most fundamental ideas—for example, in the ideas of mathematics and of finite substance—has been questioned. In short, since the truth of these ideas is in doubt, and consequently the truth of ideas that depend on them, it seems as though the objective reality in all familiar ideas may be nothing. In any case, since these ideas are in doubt, they obviously provide no indication of why they objectively exist in the intellect. Certainly a dubious idea, such as the idea of matter, does not inform us that it is in the intellect as an objective reality because what is represents, for example, matter, in fact exists; moreover, a dubious idea, such as the idea of matter, does not reveal to us that it must or does come from something other than what it represents.

Descartes never denies that he himself and the objective realities in his ideas require some cause. Indeed, he claims that whatever exists either explains its own existence or depends on something else that, if it is not itself self-sufficient, has ultimately to depend on something self-sufficient. However, Descartes realizes that the objective reality in any dubious idea provides no basis for determining why the idea of that objective reality is in him in the first place—no basis for determining what is the nature of a cause. Thus, until Descartes can intuit the true nature of causation—

that is, until he finds the true idea or true objective reality representing the nature of causation—he provisionally assumes that he might cause himself, or be self-sufficient. Since Descartes does not immediately recognize anything about himself by virtue of which he is self-sufficient, he provisionally acts as though there might be an as yet unknown part of the self that is self-sufficient from which eminently proceeds everything he recognizes as formally in himself—that is, will, intellect, ideas, images, and sensations. Thus, if ever Descartes is to establish that he is not alone in the world, he must find an idea representing the nature of self-sufficiency in so perfect and true a way—that is, with such great objective reality—that by reference to it he can determine conclusively, first, that what it represents as self-sufficient is indeed self-sufficient; and second, that whatever exists in him, either as he already knows himself or in those respects in which he as yet does not know himself, could not meet the requirements of self-sufficiency as laid down in that true idea of self-sufficiency.

I will now briefly recount the interpretation that I offered of Descartes's' principal argument for God's existence in my comments on the *Discourse*.[8]

Descartes proceeds to investigate what is required by the nature of self-sufficiency. He takes it as obvious that whatever exists is either self-sufficient or dependent. Following a doctrine of absolutes and relatives found in the *Rules*, he argues that we cannot understand what makes an effect be an effect without understanding the nature of the self-sufficient, or cause. This assertion is tantamount to saying that the effect derives its reality from the cause and that the less perfect depends on the more perfect. Descartes also argues that we cannot understand more than one self-sufficient nature. Perhaps the following will help to clarify why there can be only one such nature. The "self-sufficient" nature is "a" nature, or is "one" nature, just as "man" is "a" nature or is "one" nature. However, the self-sufficient nature does not depend on anything else. There is nothing beyond the self-sufficient nature by reference to which it could be thought of as individuated or multiplied in different particulars. "Man" is dependent on matter; therefore, unless there is matter there cannot be a man, and by means of matter there can be more than one man. The same is not true of the self-sufficient nature because there is nothing outside itself on which its existence could depend. It depends on nothing in the sense that all dependency is on *it*. Furthermore, since the possibility of an effect can be known only by reference to the self-sufficient nature, it follows that as soon as we can *know* our own existence as possible, we must be apprised of the self-sufficient nature. Therefore, in claiming to know our own existence as thinking things, we must be knowing what the nature of self-sufficiency is that makes that existence as a thinking thing possible. Accordingly, the only way we can be thinking the nature of self-sufficiency at that time is through something known to us at that time, not through things in doubt, such as matter or a "secret" part of the self. Now the only things we know at that time are intellect and will. But self-sufficiency as intellect and will is omnipotence and omniscience, which our doubts inform us do not pertain to us. Thus it is only by reference to the idea of God—that is, by reference to the objective reality that represents God as the self-sufficient being *qua* intellect and will—that we can know the possibility and hence the fact of our own existence.

As I explained in commenting on the *Discourse*, this way of interpreting Descartes's argument captures his suggestion that all knowledge, even knowledge of ourself as a thinking thing, depends on knowledge of God.[9] Indeed, in the Third Meditation, just before discussing the proof outlined above, Descartes expresses a metaphysical doubt that seems to extend even to the claim to know oneself as a thinking thing—a doubt the proof of God was designed to remove.

FOURTH MEDITATION: GOD IS NOT A DECEIVER

The proof of God's omnipotence and omniscience removes the provisional probability that no design or intelligence is at the origin of human reason. Moreover, at the end of the Third Meditation Descartes claims that all fraud and deception are necessarily excluded from God's nature because they testify to some weakness. Nevertheless, in the Fourth Meditation Descartes tries to allay a doubt raised as early as the First Meditation—namely, if God is all-powerful and all-good, why does he allow us to be occasionally deceived?

Now, those mistakes that led us to assume the posture of metaphysical doubt were obviously positive instruments in initiating

the inquiry that led to the recognition of God's nature and existence. Had not such mistakes occurred, and had not there ensued
the metaphysical inquiry into God's primacy in the order of being
and knowledge, we would have remained more radically "deceived"
about the true nature of things. Thus mistakes per se seem to be
tokens of God's concern that we know what is most important to
know. They testify to no malice in God—unless it can be shown
that God ought to have given us a more immediate intuition of
himself.

Here Descartes pursues a line of argument reminiscent of Saint
Augustine. Descartes insists that there is no argument to prove
that God ought to have created a man more perfect than the man
that has been created. The nature of God excludes a creation as
excellent as God himself; and there is no validity to taking a single
creation, a single finite intelligence, noticing its imperfections
vis-à-vis what we conceive as more perfect an intelligence, and
then arguing that the existence of the less perfect testifies to
malice in God—for the obvious possibility remains that God may
have created a plenitude of finite intelligences varying in degree.
The existence of the more perfect would not take away the perfection in the less perfect, and thus the complaint of a single man
would be nothing more than hubris.

Moreover, Descartes argues that error does not arise from a
special faculty bestowed on man for that purpose. Error arises
from a misuse of the liberty of deciding (of the *libertas arbitrii*)—a
misuse that consists in affirming what our limited intellects do not
represent with clarity and distinctness. Granted that God does not
owe man a more perfect intelligence (and remembering too that
the error with which Descartes is concerned is theoretical error,
which is not forced on us by the exigencies of practice), any charge
against God to the effect that he ought to have made us immune
from theoretical error reduces to the claim that he ought not to
have given us the freedom to decide about matters in which the
evidence of our intellect is insufficient to guarantee their truth. But
then it would seem that that charge against God must finally
amount to the charge that he ought not to have given us the
freedom to judge about any proposition before we come to know
him—for a true knowledge of any proposition can be had only by
knowing God inasmuch as all created essences can be understood
as truly and not just provisionally possible only by knowing him.

In other words, the charge seems to amount to the claim that God ought to have given us a direct and most immediate intuition of himself rather than prompting us to seek for such an intuition by means of those mistakes that induce us to question beliefs based on received provisional probabilities. However, as was said earlier, God does not owe us such an immediate intuition of himself. Moreover, once the idea of God is recognized after a metaphysical search, it is the most clear and distinct idea, and we experience no indifference in affirming it. In short, God has not made us to be indifferent about that idea which is the sine qua non of any true knowledge of finite essences.

SOURCE FOR THE LATIN TEXT

The *Meditations,* together with "Objections and Replies," was originally published at Paris by Michel Soly in 1641. A second edition, also with "Objections and Replies," was published at Amsterdam by Louis Elzevir in 1642. Adam and Tannery base their Latin text on the 1642 edition, and my translation is based on their presentation. Adam and Tannery, like the editors of the 1641 and 1642 editions, have had to decide on a punctuation for the text.* A French translation of the *Meditations* by the Duc de Luynes and a French translation by Clerselier of certain of the objections and replies were seen and approved by Descartes.†

---

* *Meditationes, Oeuvres,* vol. VII, pp. v–xviii, 607–608.
† *Meditations* (French trans.), *Oeuvres,* vol. IX–1, pp. v–x.

Meditations concerning First Philosophy

To Those Most Wise and Very Distinguished Men of the Faculty of Sacred Theology at Paris

To the Dean and the Doctors

René Descartes

2 The motive that persuades me to present this treatise to you is so worthy—and I am confident that after you have understood the rationale of my undertaking you too will have so worthy a motive for undertaking its defense—that I can do nothing better here to procure your favor for the treatise than to state briefly what I have sought to ascertain in it.

3 I have always considered that two questions, namely, those of God and the soul, are the foremost of all those that ought to be demonstrated by philosophy rather than by theology: for although it suffices for us faithful ones to believe by faith that the human soul does not perish with the body and that God exists, certainly it seems that those without faith cannot be persuaded of any religion, nor usually even of any moral virtue, unless these two things are proved to them beforehand by natural reason: and since often in this life greater rewards are offered for vices than for virtues, few persons would prefer what is right to what is useful if they did not fear God or expect another life. And although it is indeed true that the existence of God ought to be believed

because it is taught in the sacred Scriptures, and vice versa, that the sacred Scriptures are to be believed because we receive them from God—the reason being that, since faith is a gift of God, the same God who gives grace for believing other things can also give the grace that we may believe in His existence—nevertheless this cannot be proposed to those without faith, because they would judge it a circle. And certainly, not only have I noticed that all of you and other theologians affirm that the existence of God can be proved by natural reason, but also I have noticed that we can infer from sacred Scripture that a knowledge of God is easier than knowledge of the many things we know about created things, and indeed so easy that those who do not have it are blameworthy. This is evident from these words in Wisdom, 13: *Neither should they be pardoned. For if they could know so much as to be able to render a judgment about the world, how is it that they did not more easily discover its lord?* And in Romans, chapter 1, it is said that they are *not to be excused.* And again, in the same place, through these words, *What is known of God is manifest in them,* we seem to be admonished that everything that can be known about God can be made manifest from reasons drawn from no other source but our very own mind. Accordingly, I did not think it outside my prerogative to inquire how to do this, and into the manner in which God is known more easily and certainly than the things of the world.

And as regards the soul, although many have judged that it is   4 not easy to investigate its nature, and some have even dared to say that human reasonings persuade us that it perishes at the same time as the body, and that the contrary is held only on the basis of faith, nevertheless because the Lateran Council, held under Leo X, session 8, condemns such people, and expressly orders Christian philosophers to destroy their arguments and to show the truth to be stronger, I did not hesitate to attempt this also.

Moreover, I know that very many of the impious do not believe   5 in God, and in the distinction of the human mind from the body, for no other reason than because they say that up until the present nobody has been able to demonstrate these two things: although I in no way agree with them, but, on the contrary, think that nearly all the reasonings that have been brought forth by great men concerning these two questions have the force of demonstrations when properly understood; and although I am persuaded that hardly any other reasonings can be given that have not been discovered previously by others; nevertheless I believe that nothing can prove more useful in philosophy than for once studiously to seek after the best of all these arguments, and to explain them so accurately and perspicuously that afterward they are received by everyone as demonstrations. And finally, I am entreated to consider it of the greatest importance that I undertake to do this. This entreaty comes from people to whom it is known that I have cultivated a particular method for resolving certain difficulties in the sciences, not indeed that this method is new, since nothing is older than the truth, but they have often seen me use it with fortunate results in other subject matters. Accordingly, I thought it my obligation to attempt something in this matter.

6 Whatever I have been able to achieve is completely contained in this treatise. Not that I have attempted to gather here all those different reasonings that can be brought forward to prove these same matters, for that seems required only in those undertakings where there are no sufficiently certain reasonings; rather I have pursued only the primary and principal reasonings in such a way that I now dare to propose them as most certain and most evident demonstrations. And I may also add that they are such that I think there is no way open to human wits by which better reasonings can ever be discovered: for the gravity of the subject, and the glory of God, to which all this relates, compel me to speak here somewhat more freely of myself than I am ordinarily inclined to do. But notwithstanding the fact that I think these reasonings certain and evident, I am nevertheless not on that account persuaded that they are suited to everyone's grasp: but just as there are many demonstrations in geometry laid down by Archimedes, Apollonius, Pappus,* and other writers, which, although they are considered by everyone as also evident and certain, because they manifestly contain nothing that individually considered is not easily known and nothing in which what follows does not accurately cohere with the antecedents, nevertheless they are not understood except by very few persons because they are lengthy and demand a truly attentive reader: and so too, although I judge

---

* Apollonius, a geometrician of Perga in Pamphylia who lived about 240 B.C. Pappus, mathematician of Alexandria during the reign of Theodosius I (379–395).

those reasonings I use here to equal or even to surpass geometrical reasonings in certainty and evidence, nevertheless I fear they cannot be sufficiently perceived by many people, both because they are long and depend the ones upon the others, but also and principally because they require a mind clearly free from prejudices and a mind that leads itself away from any dependence upon the senses. And to be sure, one cannot find more people suited to metaphysical than to geometrical studies. And besides, there is this difference: that in geometry, since everyone is persuaded nothing is ordinarily written for which there is no certain demonstration, the inexperienced more ofter err by accepting falsities, which they wish to seem to understand, than by refuting the truth; in philosophy the situation is indeed the opposite—because it is believed there is nothing that cannot be argued either way in philosophy, few investigate the truth, and many more people, by daring to challenge every very good truth, strive to make themselves renowned for their wits.

Accordingly, whatever the quality of my reasonings, nevertheless because they pertain to philosophy, I do not hope to effect a great reception for my work by sheer force of these reasonings alone, unless you help me by your protection. For there is fixed so high a regard in everyone's mind for your faculty, and the name of SORBONNE is of such great authority that, not only in matters of faith has no other society, except the Sacred Councils, been as trusted as yours, but also, as regards human philosophy, there is nowhere else thought to be greater perspicuity and solidity, nor greater integrity and wisdom, in making judgments. And thus I have no doubt that if you deign to undertake such concern for this treatise as, *firstly*, to correct it—for mindful not only of my humanity but most especially of my ignorance, I do not affirm that it is free of errors; and *secondly*, to see to it that either you yourselves, or I, after being admonished by you, add, complete, or elucidate whatever is lacking to it, or insufficiently complete in it, or requiring of greater explanation; and *finally*, if after the reasons contained in it, which prove that God exists and that the mind is something other than the body, shall have been rendered so perspicuous that they ought to be received as most accurate demonstrations, as I am confident can be accomplished—if then you would wish to declare this fact and publicly testify to it, I say to you, I have no doubts that, if you do this, all the error that ever existed concerning these questions would, in a brief period of time, be removed from the minds of men. For the truth itself will bring it about that other men of native talent and learning will subscribe to your opinion; and this authority will bring it about that the atheists, who are ordinarily sophomoric rather than natively talented or learned, will leave off their spirit of contradiction, and perhaps even defend reasonings that they will know are accepted as demonstrations by all those endowed with native wit, lest they themselves seem not to understand them. And finally, everyone else will easily believe such numbers of witnesses that there will be no one left in the world who dares to call into doubt either the existence of God or the real distinction of the human soul from the body. How useful this would be, you yourselves, in your singular wisdom, can judge best of all; nor would it be fitting for me to commend further the cause of God and of religion to you, who have always been the greatest support of the Catholic Church.

8   PREFACE TO THE READER

9 I have previously touched on a few matters concerning the questions of God and the human mind in *The Discourse concerning the Method of correctly conducting reason and of investigating truth in the sciences*, published in French in the year 1637. Indeed, I did not intend to treat these questions thoroughly in that work, but only to lay down the beginnings, and to learn from the judgments of readers the way in which they ought to be treated afterward. These questions seemed to me of such importance that I judged they should be treated in more than one place; and the path I follow to explain them is so little traveled, and so remote from the common practice, that I have decided it would not be useful to set forth the more detailed explanation in a French treatise that might be read at random by everyone, lest even people of weaker talents be led to believe this path is intended for them.

10   However, although I there asked everyone to whom anything in my writings appeared deserving of rebuttal please to advise me of it, only two objections were worthy of note as regards what I said touching on these questions [of God and the mind]. I will

here respond to these objections in a few words before entering upon a complete explanation of them.

The first objection is that from the fact that the human mind 11 in turning its attention toward itself does not perceive itself to be something other than a thinking thing, it does not follow that its nature or *essence* consists *only* in the fact that it is a thinking thing; thus the word *only* excludes everything else that perhaps can also be said to pertain to the nature of the soul. To this objection I respond that at that place [in the *Discourse*] I did not wish to exclude those other things as far as the order that pertains to the very truth about the thing is concerned, for I was not dealing with this at that place; rather I merely wished to exclude those other things as far as the order of my perception was concerned, and thus my meaning was that there was nothing I plainly recognized to pertain to my essence except the fact that I was a thinking thing, or a thing having in itself the faculty of thinking. However, in what is to follow I will show the manner in which, from the fact that I know nothing else to pertain to my essence, it also follows that in reality nothing else does pertain to it.

The other objection is that, from the fact that I have in me 12 the idea of a more perfect thing, it does not follow that this idea is more perfect than myself, and much less does it follow that what is represented by this idea exists. But I here respond that an equivocation is concealed in the word "idea": for it can be understood either materially, as an operation of the intellect, in which meaning it cannot be said to be more perfect than myself; or it can be understood objectively, that is, for the thing represented through this very operation—which thing, even though it is not assumed to exist outside my intellect, can nevertheless be more perfect than myself by reason of its essence. To be sure, it will be explained at length in the present treatise how, from the mere fact that there is in me the idea of a thing more perfect than me, it follows that the thing truly exists.

Moreover, I did indeed also see two rather lengthy works that 13 were less attacks on my reasonings than on my conclusions concerning these matters; and they were based on arguments commonly employed by the atheists. Since arguments of this kind can have no force among those who understand my reasonings, and because the judgments of many men are so disordered and feeble that they are persuaded more by the opinions they have first accepted than by true and firm opinions heard later on, I do not wish to respond to these arguments here by way of refuting them, lest I have to first relate them. I will only say generally that everything ordinarily hurled forth by the atheists to attack the existence of God always assumes either that human affections are ascribed to God or that such a great power and wisdom may be arrogated to our minds that we may attempt to determine and to comprehend what God can and ought to do; thus these matters will occasion no difficulty for us, provided only we are mindful that our minds must be considered as finite, whereas God is incomprehensible and infinite.

14   Now, indeed, having once freely tested the judgments of other men, I here again enter into the same two questions of God and the human mind, and at the same time treat of the beginnings of first philosophy; however, I do so expecting no praise from the vulgar nor a great number of readers; rather I am an author suited only to those who will read this treatise to meditate in earnest along with me, and who are able and willing to lead the mind away from the senses and at the same time away from all prejudices. I know well enough that only a very few readers of this kind are to be found. However, as for those who, taking no care to comprehend the order and connection of my reasonings, will study them to dispute isolated parts of them, as is the custom among many, they will not derive much fruit from reading this treatise; and although they may accidentally discover opportunity for caviling on many points, nevertheless it will not be easy for them to make any objection that is urgent or worthy of response.

15   Because I cannot indeed promise to satisfy others in all details on first showing, and because I am not so presumptuous as to believe that I can foresee everything that will seem difficult to anyone, I will first explain in the Meditations those very thoughts by means of which I believe myself to have arrived at certain and evident knowledge of the truth, so that I may test whether perhaps I can also persuade others by those same reasons by which I have been persuaded. Afterward, I will respond to the objections of several men of surpassing native talent and learning to whom these Meditations have been sent for examination before being consigned to print. Their objections have been sufficiently many and varied that I dare to hope it is not easy for any objection, at least of any importance, to come to the minds of others that these men have not

already touched upon. And accordingly, I also ask the readers not to render a judgment about the Meditations until they have read through these objections and all the solutions to them.

A SYNOPSIS OF THE
SIX FOLLOWING MEDITATIONS

16

In the First Meditation, the reasons are explained why we can doubt all things, especially material things—that is, until we have other foundations for the sciences than those we had up to that time. However, although the usefulness of this large doubt is not obvious on first appearance, nevertheless it is very great—for it frees us from all prejudices and opens up a very easy path for leading the mind away from the senses; and it brings it about that we can finally no longer doubt those things we shall afterward accurately ascertain to be true.

17

In the Second Meditation, the mind, using its proper liberty, supposes that nothing exists about whose existence it can doubt in the least degree; and it notices that it is impossible but that it exists. This also is of the greatest usefulness, because in this manner the mind easily distinguishes between what pertains to itself, that is, to its intellectual nature, and what pertains to the body. But since at this point some will perhaps expect to find reasonings about the immortality of the soul, I warn them right now that I view myself as inclined to write down nothing I have not accurately demonstrated; and accordingly I have been able to follow no order except that used by geometers—that is, I would set out in advance all those things on which the proposition I wished to prove depends before drawing any conclusion concerning the proposition. But now, the first and principal thing prerequisite to knowing the immortality of the soul is for us to form as perspicuous a conception of it as possible, and one manifestly distinct from every conception of body; and this has been done here. Furthermore, we must certainly also know that everything clearly and distinctly understood by us is true in the very same way in which we understand it, which could not be established before the Fourth Meditation; and moreover, we must have a distinct conception of corporeal nature, which is formed partially in this Second Meditation and also partially in the Fifth and Sixth Medi-

18

tations; and from all the foregoing it should be concluded that everything clearly and distinctly conceived to be different substances, just as mind and body are conceived to be, are in truth substances really distinct from one another; and this I concluded in the Sixth Meditation. This same conclusion is also confirmed in the Sixth Meditation by the fact that we understand no body unless it is divisible, whereas, on the contrary, we understand no mind unless it is indivisible: for we cannot conceive a half part of any mind as we can of any body however small; thus, in the same manner, the natures of mind and body are recognized as not merely different, but even as in a certain way contrary. However, I have dealt no further with this matter in this treatise; not only because what I have said suffices to show that the perishing of the mind does not follow from the corruption of the body, and thus to provide mortals with a hope for another life; but also because the premises from which this immortality of the mind can be concluded depend upon the explanation of all of physics: for, first, it would have to be made known that all substances generally— that is, things that must be created by God in order to exist—are incorruptible from their nature and can never cease to exist unless they are reduced to nothing by that same God refusing them his support; and next, it would have to be noted that certainly body considered in general is a substance, and accordingly also never perishes. However, the human body differs from other bodies only insofar as it is constituted from a specific configuration of members and other accidents of this kind; but indeed the human mind is not in this way constituted from any accidents; rather it is a pure substance, because even if all its accidents are changed, so that it understands other things, wills other things, senses other things, and so on, this very mind does not, on that account, become something else; yet the human body does become something else from the mere fact that the figure of some part of it is changed: from all this it follows that the body indeed perishes very easily, but, on the contrary, the mind is immortal from its very nature.

19   In the Third Meditation, it seems to me I explained at sufficient length my principal argument for proving the existence of God. Nevertheless, since I have chosen not to employ there any comparisons drawn from material things, in order to lead the minds of the readers as far as possible away from the senses, perhaps

many obscurities have remained that I hope are afterward, however, completely removed in the responses to the objections; as, among others, how the idea of a most perfect entity—which idea is in us—has so much objective reality that it cannot fail to be from a most perfect cause; and this I illustrate in this same Third Meditation by a comparison to an exceedingly perfect machine, the idea of which is in the mind of some artisan; for as the objective inventiveness of this idea must have some cause, namely, the knowledge of this artisan or of someone else from whom he received the idea, so also the idea of God, which is in us, can only have God Himself as its cause.

In the Fourth Meditation, it is proved that everything is true   20
that we perceive clearly and distinctly, and at the same time the cause in which falsity consists is explained: these things must necessarily be known, as much to strengthen what preceded as to understand what remains. (But nevertheless, it must be noted that in this Fourth Meditation I in no way treat of sin, or of the error that is committed in pursuing good and evil; rather I treat only of such errors as occur in judgment about the true and the false. Neither am I concerned with matters pertaining to faith nor with matters related to the conduct of our lives, but only with speculative truths known solely by means of the natural light.)

In the Fifth Meditation, beyond an explanation of corporeal   21
nature generally considered, the existence of God is demonstrated by a new argument; but here again perhaps some difficulties occur that will be resolved in the responses to the objections; and finally, I show the manner in which it is true that the certainty of the very demonstrations of geometry depends upon the knowledge of God.

Lastly, in the Sixth Meditation, the intellect is distinguished   22
from the imagination; the signs of the distinctions are described; the mind is proved to be really distinguished from the body; nonetheless, it is shown that the mind is so intimately joined to the body that it forms the body into a single thing with itself; all the errors that are wont to arise from the senses are examined; the ways in which they can be avoided are explained; and finally, all the reasons are set forth by which the existence of material things can be concluded. I set them forth not because I deemed them very useful for proving what they do prove, namely, that there is in truth some world, that men have bodies, and similar things concerning which no one of healthy mind ever seriously doubted;

but because, by considering them, one recognizes that these reasons are not so firm nor perspicuous as those by which we arrive at a knowledge of our mind and of God; hence our mind and God are the most certain and most evident things that can be known by means of our native talents. The proof of this one thing is what I proposed for myself as the goal in these Meditations. Accordingly, I do not here enumerate other questions that it is also out of place to consider in these Meditations.

Of the Meditations concerning First Philosophy

In Which the Existence of God and the Distinction of the Soul from the Body Are Demonstrated

THE FIRST

Concerning those things that can be called back into doubt

It is now some years since I noticed that, starting from the beginning of life, I had embraced very many falsities for truths, and that whatever I afterward erected upon them is equally dubious; accordingly I noticed that were I at any time to wish to establish something firm and lasting in the sciences, then once in my life everything would have to be overturned right from the bottom and built up anew from the first foundations. However, the task seemed monumental, and I looked forward to a time of life so mature that none would follow it more suited to the goal because of my accumulation of learning. Wherefore have I delayed so long that hereafter I would be guilty were I to consume in deliberation the time that remains to me for action. Fortunately therefore, I have today released my mind from all cares and arranged an untroubled leisure for myself. I withdraw alone, and at last I shall freely and earnestly devote myself to this completely general overthrowing of my opinions.

However, to accomplish this it will not be necessary to show all these opinions false, which perhaps I can never do; rather, since even now reason persuades me that assent ought to be withheld no less carefully from things not manifestly certain and indubitable than from things obviously false, it will suffice to reject all my opinions if I might find some reason for doubting each of them. And to do this it is likewise unnecessary to run through them individually, which would be an infinite task; rather, since once the foundations are undermined, whatever has been built upon them will automatically collapse, I shall immediately consider the very principles upon which everything I formerly believed depended.

27   Indeed, whatever I accepted as most true up until this time, I accepted either from the senses or on the basis of the senses; however, I have discerned that they occasionally deceive, and it is prudent never to quite trust things that have deceived us even once.

28   But although the senses occasionally deceive us concerning certain small objects or those farther away, perhaps there are very many other things about which it is manifestly impossible to doubt even though they are drawn from the senses: for example, that I am now here, seated in this place, clothed in a winter garment, holding this sheet of paper in my hands, and similar things. Indeed, by what reasoning could it be denied that these very hands and this entire body exist? unless, perhaps, I were comparing myself to some insane people whose brains are injured by so exceedingly unyielding a vapor from the black bile that they constantly maintain that they are kings when they are very poor, or that they are clothed in purple when they are naked, or that they have a head of clay, or are completely pumpkins, or composed of glass—but such people are out of their minds, nor would I seem any less demented were I to apply to myself an example drawn from them.

29   All this seems magnificently sane, just as though I were not a man who is accustomed to sleep at night and to undergo in dreams all those same things, or even on occasion things less probable than what these insane people undergo while awake. How often indeed does the quiet of night persuade me of these ordinary things—that I am here, dressed in a garment, seated in this place —when I am nevertheless lying nude between the bed covers. But, on the contrary, I am now certainly intuiting this paper with

waking eyes, this head I move to and fro is not lulled to sleep, it is adroitly and knowingly that I extend and sense this hand; things so distinct would not occur to one who is sleeping. As though I do not remember having been deluded even by similar thoughts at other times; in dwelling on these matters more attentively, I so manifestly see that waking can never be distinguished from sleeping by signs that are certain that I become bewildered—and this very stupor is nearly enough to confirm me in the opinion that I am sleeping.

Therefore, let us act as though we are dreaming and none of these particulars are true: that we open our eyes, move our head, extend our hands, or perhaps even that we have hands or an entire body that are such [as they seem]. Nevertheless it must indeed be acknowledged that appearances occurring in sleep are, as it were, certain painted pictures that could only have been fashioned in the likeness of true things. Accordingly at least these general things—eyes, head, hands, the entire body—are not imaginary, but truly exist. For, to be sure, painters themselves, even when they strive to fashion Sirens and Satyrs with the most extraordinary forms, cannot assign them natures new in every detail; rather they merely intermingle the members of different animals; or if perchance they do think up something so new that nothing at all similar to it shall have been seen, nevertheless at least the colors out of which they form it must certainly be true. By similar reasoning, even if these general things—eyes, head, hands, and so on —could also be imaginary, it is at least necessary that some other still more simple and universal things be acknowledged as true, which, like true colors, are the sources from which are fashioned all these images of things, whether true or false, that exist in our thinking.

Corporeal nature in general and its extension seem to be of this simple and universal kind; and so also does the shape of extended things; and so also does quantity, which is the magnitude and number of extended things; and so also do place, in which extended things exist, time, throughout which they endure, and the like.

For this reason perhaps, from what has been said above, we shall not unreasonably conclude that physics, astronomy, medicine and all the other disciplines that depend upon a consideration of composite things are indeed dubious, whereas there is something

certain and indubitable in arithmetic, geometry, and other disciplines of this kind that treat only of very simple and most general
things, and are not particularly concerned whether or not they
exist in nature. For whether I am awake or asleep, 2 and 3 joined
together is 5, the square does not have more than four sides; nor
does it seem possible that truths so perspicuous may incur any
suspicion of falsity.

33   Nevertheless, there is a certain age-old opinion ingrained in my
mind that a God exists who is able to do everything, by whom I,
with such a nature as I presently exist, have been created. But
now how do I know he has not arranged things such that there
is definitely no earth, no heaven, no extended thing, no figure, no
magnitude, no place, and nevertheless all these things appear to
me to exist just as at present? In fact, the same way I judge
that other people occasionally err about things they think they
know most perfectly, may it not happen that I am deceived each
time I add 2 and 3 together, or number the sides of a square, or
anything else, if anything easier can be thought? On the other
hand, perhaps God has not wished to deceive me, for he is said
to be exceedingly good; but were it inconsistent with his goodness
to have created me such that I am always deceived, by the same
reasoning it would also appear inconsistent with his nature to
allow me to be occasionally deceived; but it cannot be said that he
does not allow me to be occasionally deceived.

34   Perhaps indeed there are some people who, rather than believe
everything else uncertain, would prefer to deny the existence of so
powerful a God. But let us not contradict them, and let us grant
them that everything said about God is fictitious; then, in whatever way they suppose that I have become what I presently am—
be it by some fate, chance, or a continuous series of events, or in
any other manner—still, because to be deceived and to err seems
to constitute some imperfection, it will be more probable that I
am so imperfect as always to err, the less perfect the author they
assign to my origins. And to these arguments I indeed have nothing I may use in reply, but at last I am forced to confess that
nothing I formerly believed true is such that one cannot doubt it
for strong and well-thought-out reasons, and not just because of
lack of consideration or flippancy; accordingly if I wish to discover
anything that is certain, my assent must hereafter be carefully

withheld from all these former beliefs no less than from what is manifestly false.

But it does not yet suffice to have noticed this; care must be 35 taken to remember it. My customary opinions still relentlessly recur, and almost as though I invite them, they lay hold upon my belief. Because, as it were, of a long-time use of them and the right of familiarity, my beliefs have become resistant to change. I will never disaccustom myself to assenting to them and to placing trust in them as long as I shall suppose them of the sort they really are—namely, in some way dubious indeed, as has already been shown, but nevertheless exceedingly probable, such that it is much more consonant with reason to believe them than to deny them. Accordingly, it is my opinion that I shall not act improperly if, with a will turned completely toward the opposite, I shall deceive my own self and shall pretend for some period of time that these beliefs are altogether false and imaginary, until finally, because, as it were, of the equal weights of the prejudices on both sides, my perverse habit will no longer divert my judgment from the right perception of things. I know that by acting in this way no danger or error will arise in the meanwhile, and that it is no longer possible for me calmly to give way to diffidence, since I am not turning my attention toward doing things but only toward understanding them.

Accordingly, I will suppose not that God, who is most good 36 and the fountain of truth, but rather that some evil genius, at once very powerful and cunning, has bent all his efforts to deceive me. I will suppose heaven, air, earth, colors, shapes, sounds and everything external are nothing but the delusions of dreams that he has contrived to lure me into belief. I will consider myself not to have hands, eyes, flesh, blood, or any senses, but as falsely thinking myself to have all these things. I will remain obstinately attached to this point of view, and thus, if indeed it is not in my power to know anything of the truth, still, in virtue of a power I certainly do have, I will resolutely guard against assenting to falsities and against whatever this deceiver can employ to trick me. But this project is laborious and a certain slothfulness draws me back to my customary manner of life. I am like a prisoner who by chance was enjoying an imaginary liberty in his dreams, and at the very moment when he later on begins to suspect that he is sleeping, fears being awakened, and persistently fails to notice his agreeable illusions for what they are: thus I spontaneously relapse into my old opinions, and fear to be awakened lest the labors of that waking life that follow on this calm repose have to be spent, not amidst the light, but among the labyrinthine obscurities of those constantly elusive difficulties already discussed.

37

MEDITATION II
On the nature of the human mind:
that it is better known than the body

38 I have been thrown into such great doubts by yesterday's meditation that I can no longer forget them; nor do I see by what argument they are to be resolved. Rather, just as though I fell unexpectedly into a whirlpool, I have been so battered about that I cannot get a foothold on the bottom or swim up and out of it. Nevertheless, I shall rally my energies and again try the same path I had entered upon yesterday, namely, removing everything that admits of the slightest doubt, just as if I had learned it to be altogether false; and I will proceed onward until at length I shall know something certain, or if nothing else, at least know this for certain, namely, that nothing is certain. To move the earth from its place, Archimedes asked for nothing but one small spot that should be firm and stable; similarly, great things are to be hoped for if I shall find at least one thing that is certain and unshaken.

39 I suppose therefore that everything I see is false; I believe that nothing that my deceptive memory represents has existed; I manifestly have no senses; body, shape, extension, motion, and place are chimerical. What then will be true? Perhaps this one thing, that nothing is certain.

40 But on what basis do I know there is not something—different from everything I have just now enumerated—about which there is not even the slightest occasion for doubting? Is there not some God, or by whatever other name I may call him, who sends me these very thoughts? Yet on what grounds may I assuredly believe this, since perhaps I myself can be their author? Therefore am I at least not something? But I have already denied I have any senses and any body. Nevertheless, I stick to this point; for what follows from the fact that I have already denied I have any

senses and any body? Am I so bound to the body and senses that I cannot exist without them? I have persuaded myself that there is manifestly nothing in the world—no heaven, no earth, no minds, no bodies. Does it not accordingly follow that I also do not exist? On the contrary, I certainly existed if I persuaded myself of something. But there is that deceiver—I know not exactly who—who is very powerful and very cunning and always purposefully deceives me. Beyond a doubt therefore I also exist if he deceives me; and let him deceive as much as he can, nevertheless he will never bring it about that I am nothing as long as I shall think myself to be something. Accordingly, with everything above having been sufficiently thought out, it must finally be concluded that this axiom, *I am, I exist*, every time it is pronounced by me, or mentally conceived, necessarily is true.

However I do not yet sufficiently understand what it is that I 41 may be, I who now necessarily am; and next, care must be taken lest by chance I imprudently take something else in place of myself and thus go astray even as regards that cognition which I contend is the most certain and most evident of all. For this reason I will now ponder anew what I formerly believed myself to be before I had launched on these reflections. Afterward I will remove from this whatever can have been weakened, even in the least degree, by the arguments that have been brought forth; thus, finally, there will remain only what is certain and unshaken.

Accordingly, what did I formerly consider myself to be? Namely 42 this—a man. But what is a man? Shall I say a rational animal? No, because afterward it should have to be determined what "animal" is, what "rational" is, and thus from one question I would have slipped into many others more difficult; moreover, I do not now have so much leisure as to wish to waste it upon subtleties of this kind. Rather I will here direct attention to what formerly occurred spontaneously to my thought each time I considered what I was. First, that I have a face, hands, arms, and this entire contrivance of members such as is discerned in a corpse: and this I called by the name of "body." Furthermore, that I am nourished, that I walk, sense, and think: which actions I indeed referred to the soul. But either I did not notice what this soul was, or I vaguely imagined it as something subtle—resembling wind, fire, or ether—diffused through my more solid parts. As far as the body is concerned, I certainly did not doubt about it, but thought I knew its nature distinctly—a nature that, had perchance I tried to describe it such as I considered it in my mind, I would have explained as follows: by "body" I understand everything capable of being bounded by some shape, circumscribed in some place, and filling a space in such a way as to exclude from it every other body; moreover, it is capable of being perceived by touch, sight, hearing, taste, or smell, and of being moved in many ways, not indeed by itself, but by some other body by which it is touched at any place; for I judged that to have the force of moving itself, and likewise of sensing or thinking, in no way pertains to the nature of body; to be sure I was rather astonished that such faculties are found in certain bodies.

43   What, however, do I now think myself to be, since I am supposing some very powerful—and if it is not impious to say so—evil deceiver has employed every effort in his power in order to delude me? Can I affirm I have even the least of those things I already said pertain to the nature of body? I consider this matter, think about it, and go over it again—but nothing qualifies. Which of those things I attributed to the soul can I now truly affirm to belong to me? To be nourished or to walk? Since indeed I do not now have a body, these too are only figments [of my imagination]. To sense? To be sure even this does not exist without a body, and I seemed to sense very many things in dreams that I afterward noticed I had not sensed. To think? Here I hit upon it: it is thinking; this alone cannot be separated from me. I am, I exist: it is certain. For how long however? Well, for as long as I think; for perhaps it could even happen that, were I to stop all thinking, I would with that completely cease to be. Now, I admit nothing but what necessarily is true; I am, accordingly, precisely only a thinking thing, that is, a mind, or soul, or intellect, or reason—words whose signification was previously unknown to me. I am however a true thing, and truly existing; but what sort of thing? I have said so—a thinking thing.

44   What else am I? I will imagine: I am not that network of members called the human body; I am not even some subtle air dispersed through these members, not a wind, nor a fire, nor a vapor, nor an exhalation, nor anything I imagine to myself—for I have supposed all these to be nothing. The situation remains, however, I am nonetheless something. Indeed, perhaps it is the case that all these things that I suppose are nothing because they are un-

known to me nevertheless do not really differ from that which I have come to acknowledge as myself. This I do not know, and I am not now disputing about this matter; I can make a judgment only about those things that are known to me. I have come to acknowledge that I exist; I seek to learn what I am—this "I" that I have acknowledged. It is most certain that thus precisely taken, the notion of this "I" does not depend on those things I have not yet recognized to exist; and accordingly it does not depend on any of these things I portray in the imagination. And these words, "I portray," warn me of my error: for I would truly be portraying myself were I to imagine myself to be something, since to imagine is nothing else than to contemplate the shape or image of some bodily thing. However, I now certainly know that I exist and at the same time know it possible that all these images, and generally whatever is related to the nature of body, may be nothing more than dreams. Having noticed all this, I seem no less foolish in saying: I will use my imagination in order to recognize more distinctly what I am, than if I should say: I am now indeed awake and see something of the truth, but because I do not yet see it sufficiently evidently, I will purposefully fall asleep so that dreams may represent it to me more truly and evidently. And so I know that none of those things I can comprehend by the use of the imagination pertain to that notion I have of myself, and I know that my mind must most carefully be called back from those things in order that it may perceive its own nature as distinctly as possible.

But what then am I? A thinking thing. What is that? It is some- 45 thing doubting, understanding, affirming, denying, wishing for, wishing not, imagining as well, and sensing. To be sure, these are not just a few things, if they all pertain to me. But for what reason should they not pertain to me? Am I not the very one who now doubts about nearly everything, who nevertheless understands some things, who affirms this one thing to be true, who denies other things, desires to know many others, is unwilling to be deceived, and who also notices many things as if coming from the senses? Even though I may always be sleeping, or even though he who created me deludes me as much as he can, which of these things is not just as true as that I exist? Which of these things is such as may be distinguished from my thinking? Which of these things is such as can be said to be separated from myself? For that I am the one who doubts, understands, and wills is so manifest that nothing could happen by which it may be explained more evidently. And indeed I am also the same one who imagines; for although perhaps, as I have supposed, none of the things imagined by me are true, nevertheless this very force of imagining truly exists and constitutes a part of my thinking. Finally, I am the same one who senses or notices corporeal things, as it were, through the senses. For it is manifest that I now see light, hear noise, feel heat. Yet these are false, for I am sleeping. But on the other hand, I certainly seem to see, hear, grow warm. This cannot be false; this is what in me is properly called "to sense"; and this, thus precisely taken, is nothing but to think.

46   From these things I certainly begin to recognize a little better what I am; but it still nevertheless seems, nor can I keep from believing, that corporeal things, whose images are formed in thinking, and which these very senses explore, are much more distinctly recognized than this something I know not what of me that does not come under the imagination: but this would indeed be truly marvelous if things that I recognize are unknown and foreign to myself are comprehended by me more distinctly than what is true, known, or in a few words, more distinctly than my very self. But I see what the problem is: my mind likes to wander and as yet refuses to allow itself to be restrained within the limits of the truth. Very well, let us continue to give it once and for all very free rein, so that somewhat later, having pulled back those reins at the opportune time, the mind will allow itself to be governed more easily.

47   Let us consider those things ordinarily thought the most distinctly comprehended of all, namely, the bodies we touch and see; not indeed bodies in general, because these general perceptions are usually somewhat more confused, but one body in particular. Let us take as an example this wax: it has been very recently taken from the honeycombs; it has not yet entirely lost the taste of its honey; it retains something of the odor of the flowers from which it has been collected; its color, figure, magnitude, are manifest; it is hard, cold, easily touched, and if you strike it with a finger, it will emit a sound; in short, it has everything that seems required for a particular body to be very distinctly known. But behold, while I am speaking, this wax is moved toward the fire: what remains of its flavor is lost, its odor ceases, its color is changed,

its shape is taken away, its size increases, it becomes liquified, hot, scarcely capable of being touched, and now, if you hit upon it, it will not emit a sound. Does not the same wax still remain? It must be admitted that it does remain; nobody denies it, nobody thinks otherwise. Therefore what in the wax was so distinctly comprehended? Certainly none of those things with which I came in contact by the senses; for whatever came under taste, or odor, or sight, or touch has by this time been changed: yet the wax remains.

Perhaps this wax was what I now think: namely, this same wax 48 was never that sweetness of honey, nor that fragrance of flowers, nor that whiteness, nor shape, nor sound; rather it is a body that appeared to me a little beforehand quite obviously in those ways and now appears to me in different ways. However, what exactly is this body that I thus imagine. Let us attend, and having removed those things that do not pertain to the wax, let us see what remains: namely, nothing other than an extended something, flexible, changeable. What truly is this being flexible and changeable? Is it that I imagine this wax can be changed from a round shape into a square shape, or from a square into a triangle? In no way; for I comprehend that this wax is capable of innumerable changes of this kind, and nevertheless I am unable to run through them by imagining them; therefore this comprehension is not entirely carried out by the faculty of imagining. And what is something extended? Isn't its very extension likewise unknown? For in the liquefying wax its extension becomes greater, greater again in the burning wax, and yet still greater if the heat is augmented; and I would not judge correctly what this wax is unless I would think it admits of even more differences in extension than I have ever encompassed by imagining them. Therefore it remains for me to concede that I do not at all imagine what this wax is, but perceive what it is by the mind alone; I speak of this wax in particular; as for wax in general it is even clearer. And what in truth is this wax perceived only by the mind? It is without a doubt the same wax as I see, touch, imagine, and lastly, the same as I thought it to be from the beginning. However, what must be noticed is that the perception of it is not a seeing, tasting, or imagining, and never has been, although previously it seemed so; rather it is an inspection of the mind alone, which can be either imperfect and confused as previously, or clear and distinct as it now is, depending upon whether I attend less or more to those things from which it is composed.

49   I am truly astonished how, despite all' this, my mind is prone toward errors; for although I was silently considering this to myself and without words, I am nevertheless saddled by these very words I am using, and almost deceived by this very manner of speaking. For we say we see this very wax when it is present; we do not say we judge it to be present from its color or shape. Because of this I would have forthwith concluded that therefore the wax is known by the vision of the eye rather than by an inspection of the mind alone—except that by chance I had then turned and glanced from my window upon men passing in the square, men whom it is just as customary for mc to say I see as to say I see wax. But neverthe- less, what do I see except hats and coats under which there could be automata? But I judge them to be men. And thus what I was supposing I saw with the eyes, I comprehend with the faculty of judging alone, which is in my mind.

50   But it is shameful that one who aspires to a discernment higher than that of ordinary people has rested his reason for doubt on the forms of speech common people have fallen into. So let us proceed onward in an orderly fashion. Did I more perfectly and evidently perceive what wax is when, in first seeing it, I believed myself to know it either by the external sense of sight, or at least by what they call common sense—that is, by the power of imagin- ing? Or, indeed, is it rather the case that I now perceive more perfectly and evidently what wax is, after I have more diligently investigated both what it is and the manner in which it is known? Certainly it would be silly to hesitate about this matter. For what was distinct in the first perception of the wax? What was included there that, it would have seemed, cannot be had by any animal? On the other hand, indeed, when I distinguish the wax from ex- ternal forms, and so to speak, by stripping off its garments, con- sider it naked, that is, as it truly is—when I do this, although there can still be an error in my judgment, nevertheless I cannot per- ceive it without a human mind.

51   Now, what shall we say of this very mind, that is, of me myself? For at present I am admitting nothing in me except the mind. What, I ask, am I who seem to perceive this wax so distinctly? Do I not know myself not only much more truly, much more

certainly, but also much more distinctly and evidently? For if I judge that wax exists from the fact that I see this, certainly, from the very fact that I see this, it is much more evidently proved that I myself also exist. For it can be that what I am seeing is not truly wax; indeed, it can be that I have no eyes with which to see anything; but it manifestly cannot be that, when I see, or (what I do not now distinguish) when I think I see, this very thinking "I" is not something. By similar reasoning, if I judge that wax exists from the fact that I touch this, it likewise will again be proved that manifestly I exist. If I judge that wax exists from the fact that I imagine it, or from whatever other cause, manifestly the same conclusion follows. And the same thing I notice concerning the wax can also be applied to all the remaining things posited outside me. But furthermore, if the perception of the wax has seemed more distinct after it became known to me, not only by sight or touch alone, but by many other causes, it must be conceded how much more distinctly I myself am now known by myself, since no reasons can assist my perception of the wax, or of any other body, without all these same reasons better proving the nature of my mind! But there are so many other things besides in this very mind from which the notion of it can be rendered more distinct that those things that come to it from the body seem hardly worth enumerating.

And behold, I have finally spontaneously come back to where 52 I wished to be; for since it is now manifest to me that even bodies are not properly perceived by the senses or by the faculty of imagining but by the intellect alone, and since bodies are not perceived because they are touched or seen, but only because they are understood, I manifestly know that I can perceive nothing more easily or evidently than my mind. Yet because the inclination to an old opinion cannot be so readily cast off, it is fitting to halt at this point so that by prolonged meditation this new knowledge may be more deeply ingrained on my memory.

MEDITATION III
Concerning God, that he exists

53

I will now close my eyes, stop my ears, call back my senses, and 54 even extinguish from my thinking all images of corporeal things, or because this is hardly possible to do, I will consider these images as empty and false things of no value; and by addressing myself alone, and by examining myself from my most inward depths, I will try to render myself gradually more known and familiar to myself. I am a thinking thing: that is, I am a thing that is doubting, affirming, denying, understanding a few matters, ignorant of many things, wishing for and wishing not, and even imagining and sensing; for as I noted before, although those things I sense or imagine outside me are perhaps nothing, I am nevertheless certain that those modes of thinking I call senses and imaginations are in me insofar as they are only particular modes of thinking.

55   In these few remarks I have recounted everything I truly know, or at least everything I have thus far noticed that I know. Now I will more diligently seek to find whether there are still other things in me to which I have not as yet attended. I am certain that I am a thinking thing. Do I not therefore also know what is required in order to be certain of something? Undoubtedly in this first cognition it is nothing but the particular clear and distinct perception of what I affirm; but this indeed would not suffice to make me certain of the truth of the matter if it could ever occur that anything I were to perceive just as clearly and distinctly would be false; and accordingly I now seem able to lay down as a general rule that everything is true that I perceive very clearly and distinctly.

56   But yet I formerly admitted many things as altogether certain and manifest that afterward I nevertheless recognized as doubtful. Well, then, what sorts of things were they? The earth, the heaven, the constellations of stars, and all the other things I appropriated from the senses. What, however, did I clearly perceive about them? That the very ideas of these things, or the thoughts of them, are noticed by my mind. But indeed I do not now deny that these ideas are in me. However, I affirmed something else that, because of my habits of belief, I likewise believed I clearly perceived, although I did not truly perceive it—namely, that certain things exist outside me from which these very ideas proceed, and to which they are similar. And in this either I was deceived, or if I did judge truly, it certainly did not result from the force of my perception.

57   What then do I perceive to be true? When I considered any-

thing exceedingly simple and easy in regard to arithmetical and geometrical matters, such as that 2 and 3 joined together is 5, or similar things, didn't I at least intuit those things perspicuously enough to affirm them true? Indeed, I afterward judged they should be doubted only because the thought came to my mind that perhaps some God has been able to make my nature such that I would be deceived even about those things that seem most manifest. Every time this preconceived opinion about the very great power of God occurs to me, I cannot but confess that, if he wishes, it is easy for him to bring it about that I err even in the things I consider myself to intuit as evidently as possible with the eyes of the mind. Similarly, every time I turn my attention to those things themselves that I think I perceive very clearly, I am so obviously persuaded by them that I spontaneously break forth saying: let him deceive me who can, nevertheless he will never bring it about that I am nothing as long as I shall think myself to be something; neither will he ever bring it about hereafter that I have never been, since it is now true that I exist; also, he will never bring about that 2 and 3 joined together is more or less than 5, or any similar things—that is, things in which I recognize a manifest contradiction. And certainly, since I have no occasion for thinking there is some deceiving God, and indeed, since I do not as yet well enough know whether there is any God at all, the reason for doubting that depends only on this opinion is certainly tenuous, and such as I may call metaphysical. However, in order now to remove even this reason for doubting, as soon as the first opportunity arises I ought to examine whether there is a God, and if there is one, whether he can be a deceiver; for as long as this is unknown, I seem unable ever to be manifestly certain about any other thing.

Now, indeed, order seems to require that I shall first distribute   58 all my thoughts into certain kinds and inquire in which of these kinds truth or falsity resides. Certain of these thoughts are, as it were, images of things, and to these alone the name of "idea" accurately applies: as when I think of a man, or of a Chimera, or heaven, or an angel, or of God. To be sure, other thoughts have particular forms beyond this: thus when I will, fear, affirm, deny, I always do indeed apprehend something as the subject of my thinking, but I also include in my thinking something more than the similitude of this very subject; and as regards these other things included in such thinking, some of them are named volitions or affections; others, however, are called judgments.

59   Now, as far as ideas are concerned, if they are regarded alone and in themselves, and if I do not refer them to anything else, they cannot properly [speaking] be false; for whether I imagine a she goat or a Chimera, it is no less true that I imagine the one rather than the other. Also, falsity is not to be feared in willing itself or in the affections; for although I can wish for bad things, and even for things that never exist, it is nevertheless still true that I wish for them. And accordingly only judgments remain, and in these care must be taken so that I am not deceived. Moreover, the principal and most frequent error that can be found in them consists in the fact that I judge the ideas in me are similar to, or conform to, certain things situated outside me; for certainly were I to consider these very ideas only as particular modes of my thinking, and not refer them to any other thing, they could scarcely provide any matter for error.

60   Furthermore, among these ideas some seem innate, some seem adventitious, and some seem made by me myself: for I seem to obtain my understanding of what a thing is, what truth is, and what thinking is from no other source than my very nature; moreover, until this time I have judged that the noise I now hear, the sun I see, the fire I feel, proceed from particular things situated outside me; finally, until this time I judged that Sirens, Hippogriffs, and similar things are formed by me. I am able to suspect that perhaps these ideas are all adventitious, or all innate, or all made by me: for I have not yet clearly seen through to their true origin.

61   But here I must principally inquire what particular reason leads me to suppose that the ideas I consider taken from things existing outside me are similar to those things. Certainly, nature seems to teach me so. And besides, I experience that they do not depend upon my willing, and thus not upon my own self; for often these ideas are present when unwanted—just as now, whether I will it or will the opposite, I still feel heat and therefore suspect that this feeling, or the idea of heat, comes to me from something different from myself, namely, from the heat of the fire near which I am sitting. And nothing is more obvious than for me to judge that this thing sends into me its likeness rather than something else.

I will now see whether these reasonings are sufficiently firm.   62
When just above I say I am taught so by nature, I understand
only that I feel moved to believe this by some spontaneous impulse, not that some natural light shows me it is true. These two
things greatly differ; for whatever the natural light shows me—
for example, that from the fact that I doubt, it follows that I exist,
and similar things—can in no way be dubious; for there is no
other faculty so trustworthy as this natural light that can teach
me that the things shown me by it are not true; but as for natural
impulses, I have already often judged that I was pushed by them
in the worse direction when it was a question of choosing the
good, and I do not see why I may place more trust in them as
regards any other matter.

Next, although these ideas do not depend upon my willing, it   63
is not therefore established that they necessarily proceed from
things situated outside me: for those impulses about which I was
just speaking, although they are in me, nevertheless seem different
from my will; so too, perhaps some other faculty, not yet sufficiently known, is also in me and produces these ideas, in the same
way as up until this time it has always seemed that while I sleep
ideas are formed in me without any need of external things.

And lastly, even if they were to proceed from things different   64
from myself, it does not thereby follow that they must be similar
to those things. On the contrary, I seem to have often noticed a
great crucial difference in many cases. For example, I find in myself two different ideas of the sun: one idea has, as it were, been
drawn from the senses, and I judge that it must by all means be
included among those ideas that are adventitious, and through it
the sun appears to me to be very small; the other idea is certainly
derived from the reasonings of astronomy—that is, elicited from
certain notions innate in me or made in some other way—and
through it the sun is represented to be several times larger than
the earth. Undoubtedly both these ideas cannot be similar to the
same sun existing outside me, and reason persuades me that the
former idea, which seems to have most closely originated from
the sun, is most dissimilar to it.

All these things sufficiently demonstrate that up until now it   65
has not been out of a judgment that is certain, but merely from
some blind impulse, that I believed in the existence of particular

things different from myself that send me into their ideas, or images, through the organs of the senses or by whatever other means it be.

66   But it occurs to me there is yet another particular way of inquiring whether any of those things whose ideas are in me exist outside me. To be sure, inasmuch as these ideas are only particular modes of thinking, I recognize no inequality among them, and they all seem to proceed from me in the same manner; but insofar as one idea represents one thing and another idea represents something else, it is manifest that they are indeed different from each other. Beyond a doubt, those ideas that represent substances to me are something greater, and as I may say, contain in themselves more objective reality than those representing only modes or accidents; and furthermore that idea through which I understand a supreme God—eternal, infinite, omniscient, omnipotent, and creator of all things other than himself—certainly has in it more objective reality than those through which finite substances are represented.

67   Now, it is truly manifest by the natural light that at least as much [reality] must be in the efficient and total cause as is in the effect of this same cause. For, I ask, whence could the effect receive its reality if not from the cause? And how could the cause give this reality to the effect unless it has it? Moreover, from this it follows that it is impossible both that anything come from nothing and also that what is more perfect—that is, what contains more reality in itself—come from what contains less reality in itself. And this is not only perspicuously true of those effects whose reality is actual or formal, but also of ideas in which objective reality only is considered. To take some examples, not only is it impossible for a stone that had not previously existed to now begin to exist, unless it is produced by something in which there exists either formally or eminently everything posited in the stone; or for heat to be produced in a subject previously not warm; and so forth; but furthermore, it is also impossible that the idea of heat or the idea of a stone exist in me, unless it is placed in me by some cause in which there is at least as much reality as I conceive in heat or a stone. For although that particular cause transfers nothing of its actual or formal reality into my idea, I should not on that account suppose it is a less real cause, but only that the nature of this idea is such that of itself it requires no other formal reality

beyond that which it borrows from my thinking, of which it is a mode. But now, the fact that an idea contains this or that objective reality rather than some other must indeed be due to some cause in which there is at least as much of formal reality as the idea itself has of objective reality. For if we suppose that anything is to be discovered in the idea that did not exist in the cause of the idea, this thing accordingly derives from nothing; but now, however imperfect this manner of being by which a thing is objectively in the intellect by means of an idea, it nevertheless indeed is manifestly not nothing. Also, I should not suspect that, because the reality I consider in my ideas is only objective, this same reality need not exist formally in the causes of these ideas, but that it suffices if it is also objectively in them. For just as this objective mode of being belongs to ideas from their own nature, so also the formal mode of being belongs to the causes of ideas from their very nature, or at least to the first and principal causes. And although perhaps one idea can be born from another, nevertheless an infinite regress is not allowed here; rather I must finally come to some first idea whose cause is like an archetype, which contains formally all the reality that is in the idea only objectively. Thus it is perspicuous to me by the natural light that the ideas in me are, as it were, particular images, which can indeed easily fall short of the perfection of the things from which they are taken, but cannot, however, contain anything at all that is greater or more perfect. ·

The longer and more painstakingly I examine all these things, 68 so much the more clearly and more distinctly do I know that they are true. But what then should I finally conclude from them? Namely this: if the objective reality of some one of my ideas is so great that I am certain the same reality is not in me either formally or eminently, and consequently that it is impossible that I myself am the cause of this idea, then it necessarily follows that I do not exist alone in the world but that some other thing, which is the cause of this particular idea, also exists. If indeed no such idea shall be found within me, then I will manifestly have no argument that renders me certain concerning the existence of anything different from myself; for I have most diligently inquired into every other kind of argument, and until this day have been unable to find any other.

Now, of my ideas, beyond that which represents my own self 69 to me—about which there can be no difficulty here—one idea represents God, others represent things corporeal and inanimate, others represent angels, others represent animals, and finally, others represent men similar to myself.

70   And as for ideas representing other men, or animals, or angels, I easily understand that they can be composed from those I have of my own self and corporeal things—even if there were no other men but me, nor animals, nor angels, in the world.

71   Moreover, as regards the ideas of corporeal things, nothing occurs in them so great that it seems it could not have originated from my own self. For if I consider them more thoroughly and examine them individually in the way I examined the idea of the wax yesterday, I notice there are but very few things in them that I perceive clearly and distinctly: namely, magnitude, or extension in length, breadth, and depth; shape, which arises from the fixing of a boundary of this same extension; position, which the diversely shaped bodies possess in relation to one another; and motion, or the change of this position; to which can be added substance, duration, and number. The other things, such as light and colors, sounds, odors, flavors, heat, and cold, as well as the other tactile qualities, are thought of by me only very confusedly and obscurely, so that I also do not know whether they are true or false, that is, whether the ideas I have of them are ideas of particular things or not ideas of things. For as I noted a little way back, although falsity properly so-called—that is, formal falsity—can be found only in judgments, nevertheless there is indeed a certain other material falsity in ideas when they represent what is not a thing as though it is a thing: thus the ideas I have of heat and cold are so little clear and distinct that I cannot say regarding them whether cold is only a privation of heat, or whether it is a real quality, or neither. And since there can be no ideas unless they are, as it were, of things, if it be true that cold is nothing other than the privation of heat, the idea that represents it to me as something real and positive is not unreasonably called false, and so too with the other ideas—that is, the ideas of light, colors, sounds, and so on.

72   With these things established, I need not assign these ideas of heat, light, colors, and so on, any author different from myself: for if they are indeed false, that is, if they represent no things, it is known to me by the natural light that they proceed from nothing —that is, they are in me only because something is lacking in my

nature or because my nature is not manifestly perfect; if, however, they are true, nevertheless, since they display to me so little reality that I cannot distinguish that little amount of reality from what is not a thing, I do not see why they cannot be from my own self.

To be sure, as regards those things that are clear and distinct   73
in the ideas of corporeal things, I seem able to have borrowed certain of them from the idea of my own self, namely, the ideas of substance, duration, number, and whatever else is of this sort: for when I think that a stone is a substance, or a thing suited to exist through itself, and when I likewise think that I am a substance—despite the fact that I conceive myself as a thinking and nonextended thing, and certainly conceive a stone as an extended and nonthinking thing, so that the greatest diversity is conceived between both of them—both nevertheless seem to accord as regards the aspect of substance; and in a corresponding way, when I perceive that I exist now and recall that I have also existed for some period of time beforehand, and when I have various thoughts whose number I understand, I acquire the ideas of duration and number, which I can then transfer from this source to various and sundry things. However, all the other things from which the ideas of corporeal things are composed—namely, extension, shape, position, and motion—are certainly not contained in me formally, since I am nothing but a thinking thing; yet because they are only particular modes of a substance, and I also am a substance, they seem able to be contained in me eminently.

And so the idea of God alone remains, and I must consider   74
whether there is anything in it that could not have proceeded from my very self. By the name of God I understand a particular infinite, independent, omniscient, omnipotent substance by whom not only I myself, but also every other thing of whatever sort, if any other thing does exist, is created. Undoubtedly, all these things are such that, the more diligently I consider them, the less they seem able to originate from me alone. Accordingly, from what has been said above it must be concluded that God necessarily exists.

Indeed, although the idea of a substance is in me from this   75
very fact that I am a substance, nevertheless, since I am finite, the idea of an infinite substance would not therefore have been

in me unless it proceeded from some substance that really is infinite.

76   I should not suppose that I do not perceive infinity by a true idea, but merely by negation of the finite, in the way that I perceive rest and darkness by the negation of motion and of light; for, on the contrary, I manifestly understand that there is more reality in infinite substance than in finite substance, and hence that the perception of the infinite is somehow prior in me to that of the finite—that is, the perception of God is in some way prior to the perception of my very self. For by what standard would I understand that I doubt, that I desire—that is, that something is lacking to me and that I am not altogether perfect—unless there were in me the idea of a more perfect being by comparison with which I recognized my defects?

77   Neither can it be said that this idea is perhaps materially false, and therefore can be from nothing, as I noted a little way back in regard to the ideas of heat and cold; for, on the contrary, since this idea is the most clear and distinct, and since it contains more objective reality than any other idea, no idea is in itself more true or less suspect of falsity. I say that this idea of the most perfect and infinite being is most true; for although it can perhaps be supposed that such a being does not exist, nevertheless it cannot be supposed that the idea of it diplays nothing real to me, as I previously said concerning the idea of cold. For it is most clear and distinct; indeed, whatever I clearly and distinctly perceive, because it is real and true, and because it involves some perfection, is totally contained in it. None of this is impugned either by the fact that I do not comprehend infinity or because there are innumerable other things in God that I can in no way comprehend, or perhaps even approach by thinking; for it is the character of infinity that it is not comprehended by me who am finite; and it suffices that I understand this very fact and judge that all those things that I clearly perceive and know to involve some perfections, and also perhaps innumerable other things of which I am ignorant, are either in God formally or eminently, so that the idea I have of him is the most true, and most clear and distinct, of all the ideas in me.

78   But perhaps I am something greater than I myself understand, and perhaps all those perfections I attribute to God are in a certain manner in me by means of a power, even if they do not as

yet reveal themselves or are not as yet reduced to act. For I now experience that my knowledge is gradually increased; neither do I see anything to prevent my knowledge, starting from less, from thus being more and more increased to infinity; nor do I see any reason why, with my thinking thus increased, I could not by means of it reach all the remaining perfections of God; finally, I do not see why the power for such perfections, if it is already in me, may not suffice to produce the idea of those perfections.

But, on the contrary, none of these things is possible. Firstly,   79 although it is true that my knowledge is gradually increased and that many things are in me potentially that are not yet in act, nevertheless none of these things pertains to the idea of God, in which, namely, nothing at all is potential; for this very fact— that my knowledge is gradually increased—is a very certain proof of my imperfection. Furthermore, even if my knowledge is always more and more increased, nonetheless I understand that it will never therefore be infinite in act, because it will never arrive at a point such that it is not still capable of an increment; however, I judge God to be infinite in act in such a way that nothing can be added to his perfection. And finally, I perceive that the objective being of an idea cannot be produced from a mere potential being, which, properly speaking, is nothing, but only by an actual or formal being.

There is certainly nothing in all this that is not manifest by   80 the natural light to one exercising diligent attention; but because when I am less attentive and the images of sensible things blind the sharp vision of my mind, it is not so easy for me to recall why the idea of an entity more perfect than myself necessarily proceeds from some being that really is more perfect, it is desirable to inquire further whether I myself could exist having this idea if no such being were to exist.

Indeed, where would I be from? Undoubtedly, either from   81 myself, or from parents, or from sundry other things less perfect than God; for it is impossible to think of anything more perfect than God, or even equally perfect.

And yet were I to be from myself, I would neither doubt nor   82 desire, nor would anything at all be lacking to me. I would also have given myself all the perfections of which I had any idea, and so I myself would be God. Neither ought I to suppose that perhaps those perfections that are lacking to me can be acquired with more difficulty than those already in me; for, on the contrary, it is manifest that it would have been far more difficult for me, that is, for a thinking thing or substance, to emerge from nothing than to acquire the cognitions of many things of which I am now ignorant—cognitions that are only accidents of this substance. And certainly, if of my own accord I might have what is greater, I would not have denied myself what is more easily had, and moreover, I would not in the least have denied myself any of those other things I perceive to be contained in the idea of God; and this is so because none of them seems to me more difficult to bring about; and were they more difficult to bring about, then assuming I were to have the perfections I do have from myself, they certainly would also seem so to me—for then I would experience my power to be limited by them.

83   Neither do I escape the force of these reasonings if I suppose that perhaps I have always been as I now am, as though it would follow from that that no author of my existence need be sought after. For since all the time of my life can be divided into innumerable parts, each of which in no way depends on the others, from the fact that I had existed a little beforehand, it does not follow that I must now exist, unless some cause creates me, as it were, anew at this moment—that is, unless some cause conserves me. For it is perspicuous to one who is attending to the nature of time that manifestly the same force and action is required to conserve any particular thing whatever in the single moments in which it lasts as would be required to create that thing de novo were it not yet to exist; thus one of the things manifest by the natural light is that conservation differs from creation only as regards our viewpoint.

84   Accordingly, I should now inquire as regards my own self, whether I have some force by which I can bring it about that this "I" who now exists will also exist a little afterward in the future: for since I am nothing but a thinking thing, or at least since I am now concerned only with precisely that part of myself that is a thinking thing, were such a force in me, I would undoubtedly be conscious of it. But I experience no such force, and from this very fact I know most evidently that I depend upon another entity different from myself.

85   Perhaps this being is not God, and I am produced either from parents or some other cause less perfect than God. On the contrary,

as I already said before, it is perspicuous that there ought to be at least as much [reality] in the cause as in the effect; and therefore, since I am a thinking thing having in me a particular idea of God, whatever the cause finally assigned to me, it must be admitted that it too is a thinking thing having an idea of all the perfections I attribute to God. It is again possible to investigate whether that cause is from itself or from another. For if it is from itself, it is manifest from what has been said that it is God, because since it has a force of existing through itself, it undoubtedly also has a force of possessing in act all the perfections of which it has an idea in itself—that is, all the perfections I conceive to be in God. If, however, it is from another, in the same way it again may be asked of this latter whether it is from itself or from another, until finally the ultimate cause, which will be God, is reached.

For it is sufficiently apparent that there can be no progressing   86
to infinity in this matter, particularly since I am here concerned not only with the cause that formerly produced me, but most especially also with the cause that conserves me at the present time.

Neither can it be supposed that many partial causes have come   87
together with the result of producing me, and that I have received from one of these causes the idea of one of the perfections I attribute to God, and from another the idea of another perfection attributed to God, so that all the perfections are indeed found somewhere in the universe, but are not all joined together in any one thing that is God. On the contrary, the unity, simplicity, or inseparability of all the perfections in God is one of the principal perfections I understand to be in him. And certainly the idea of the unity of all of these perfections of his could not be placed in me by any cause from which I did not also have the ideas of the other perfections: for no cause could have brought it about that I would understand them to be joined together and inseparable unless it at the same time brought it about that I would recognize which perfections they were.

Finally, as regards my parents, if everything I ever thought   88
about them were true, nevertheless they certainly do not conserve me, nor have they in any way produced me insofar as I am a thinking thing; rather they have merely placed arrangements in that matter to which I—that is, the mind, which I now alone accept as myself—have judged myself to belong. Accordingly, there can be no difficulty here concerning them; rather it is by all

means to be concluded that, from the mere fact that I exist and that the idea of a most perfect being, that is, of God, is in me, God's existence is also most evidently demonstrated.

89   It remains only for me to examine the way in which I received this idea of God; for I have not drawn it from the senses, nor does it ever come to me when I am not seeking for it, as the ideas of sensible things are wont to do when these things are present to the external organs of the senses, or seem present; also, neither has this idea of God been put together by me, for I am manifestly unable to take anything away from it or to add anything to it; consequently, it remains that the idea of God is innate in me, in the manner in which the idea of my own self is also innate in me.

90   And truly it is not astonishing that God, in creating me, has placed that idea in me, so that it would be, as it were, the sign of the craftsman impressed upon his work. And neither is it necessary that this sign be something different from his very work. Rather, from the mere fact that God created me, it is exceedingly credible that I have been made in some way to his image and likeness, and that this likeness to God, which involves the fact that I have the idea of him, is perceived by me through the same faculty through which I myself am perceived by myself: that is, when I turn the sharp vision of my mind upon my own self, I do not merely understand that I am an incomplete thing who is dependent upon another and who indefinitely aspires to greater and greater or better and better things; but also, at the same time I understand that he upon whom I depend has in himself all those greater perfections, not indefinitely and merely potentially, but rather has each perfection infinitely and thus is God. And the entire force of the argument lies here: I recognize that it is not possible for me to exist constituted of such a nature as I have, namely, having the idea of God in me, unless there also exists in reality the God whose idea is in me—that is, God manifestly subject to no defects, and having all those perfections that I am not able to comprehend, but can only to some extent approach by thinking. From these perfections of God it is sufficiently manifest that he cannot be deceitful; for it is manifest by the natural light that all fraud and deception depends on some defect.

91   But before I examine this more diligently and at the same time inquire into other truths that can be gathered from it, it is edify-

ing to rest here for some time in the contemplation of this God, to ponder his attributes, and as far as the vision of my dull wits permits me to endure, to intuit, admire, and adore the beauty of his immense light. For as we believe by faith that the greatest happiness of the next life consists solely in the contemplation of the divine majesty, so even now, although much less perfectly, we experience that in this same contemplation can be perceived the greatest delight of which we are capable in this life.

MEDITATION IV
On the true and the false

92

During these days I have so accustomed myself to leading my mind away from the senses, and I have so carefully noticed that very little is truly perceived concerning material things, and that much more is known concerning the human mind, and more still concerning God, that now, without any difficulty, I turn my thought from imaginable to solely intelligible things separated from all matter. And indeed I have an idea of the human mind insofar as it is a thinking thing not extended in length, breadth, and depth, nor having anything else that pertains to body; and this idea is much more distinct than my ideas of any corporeal thing. And when I consider that I doubt, or that I am an incomplete and dependent thing, so much the more clear and distinct an idea of an independent and complete entity, that is, of God, also presents itself to me; and from this one thing, that such an idea is in me, or that I exist having that idea, I so much the more manifestly conclude that God also exists, and that my entire existence depends on him at every moment, that I am firmly assured that nothing more evident, nothing more certain, can be known by human wits. And already I seem to see another way through which, by contemplating the true God in whom lies hidden all the treasures of the sciences and of wisdom, to reach a cognition of other things.

93

First, to be sure, I recognize that it is impossible for him ever to deceive me; for in all deceit or deception some imperfection is found; and although to be able to deceive seems some proof of shrewdness or power, undoubtedly to wish to deceive attests to either ill will or weakness, and hence does not accord with God.

94

95   Next I experience that there is in me a particular faculty of judging, which I certainly received from God, just as I received from him everything else that is in me; and since he does not wish to deceive me, he assuredly bestowed this faculty upon me in such a way that when I use it rightly I can never err.

96   Nothing doubtful would remain regarding this matter if it did not seem that as a consequence I could never err; for if everything in me is from God, and he has not given me any faculty of erring, it seems I can never err. And so, in short, as long as I think only of God and totally turn my attention to him alone, I discover no cause of error or falsity; but afterward, having turned my attention back upon myself, I experience that I am nevertheless subject to innumerable errors. Inquiring into the cause of these errors, I notice that there is present to me not only the real and positive idea of God, or of a most perfect being, but also a certain negative idea, as I may say, of nothing, or of that which is furthest removed from all perfection. Moreover, I notice that I am placed, as it were, as something between God and nothing, or between the greatest being and nonbeing; so that, to the extent that I am created by the greatest being, there is indeed nothing in me through which I will be deceived or led into error; but inasmuch as I participate in some manner in nothingness or in nonbeing, that is, inasmuch as I am not this same highest being, and so very many things are lacking to me, it is not so astonishing that I will be deceived. And thus I certainly understand that error, inasmuch as it is error, is not something real that depends upon God but is rather only a defect; accordingly my errors do not require any faculty given by God for that purpose; rather I err because the faculty of judging the truth that I have from God is not infinite in me.

97   Nonetheless, this is not yet entirely satisfactory; for error is not a pure negation, but rather a privation or the absence of such cognitions as ought in some manner to have been in me; and to one attending to the nature of God, it does not seem possible that he has placed any faculty in me that is not perfect in its kind or that is deprived of any perfection owed to it. For if the more expert the artisan, the more perfect the works produced by him, what can that most great builder of all things make that is not perfect at every level? There is no doubt that God was able to create me such that I would never err; moreover, there is no doubt

that he always wishes what is best. Is it therefore better that I am deceived rather than not?

While I ponder this matter more attentively, it occurs to me 98 that first of all it is not astonishing if God had certain reasons that I do not understand; thus, because I will perhaps find some other things that I do not comprehend as to why or how God has made them, God's existence must not therefore be doubted. I already know my nature is very weak and limited, and that by contrast the nature of God is immense, incomprehensible, infinite; moreover, from this very fact I also sufficiently well know that God can do innumerable things, the causes of which I am ignorant; and because of this single reason, I consider that the entire genus of causes customarily taken from the end have no use in the matters of physics; for it would be rash of me to think I can investigate the ends of God.

It also occurs to me that we should regard not any one creature 99 separately, but the entire universe of things, each time we inquire whether the works of God are perfect; for a single creature, were it alone in the universe, thus holding the place of the most perfect thing in the world, would perhaps quite justifiably seem exceedingly imperfect; and although, from the fact that I wished to doubt everything, I have as yet come to know the existence of nothing except myself and God, nevertheless, from the fact that I have noticed the immense power of God, I cannot deny that many other things have been made by him, or at least can be made by him, so that I hold but the place of a part in a universe of things.

Next, focusing in upon myself more particularly, and investi- 100 gating the character of my errors (which alone provide evidence of any imperfection in me), I notice that these errors depend upon the simultaneous concurrence of two causes, namely, upon the faculty of knowing that is in me, and upon the faculty of willing, or the liberty of deciding—that is, upon the intellect together with the will. To be sure, through the intellect itself I perceive only ideas concerning which I can make a judgment, and when the intellect is precisely regarded in this way, no error can be found in it: for although perhaps innumerable things exist of which there are no ideas in me, nevertheless I am not properly called deprived of them, but rather it ought to be said, in the sense of negation only, that I am without them. This is because I can bring forward no reason by which I may prove that God ought to have given me a greater faculty of knowing than he has given me; and although I understand the craftsman is accomplished, I nevertheless do not on that account think he ought to have placed in each of his works all the perfections he can place in the others. Indeed, I also cannot question why the will, or liberty of deciding, that I received from God is not sufficiently ample and perfect; for I certainly experience that it is circumscribed within no limits. Moreover, what seems to me should very much be noted is that none of the other things in me are so perfect or great that I do not understand that there can exist the still more perfect or the greater. As an example, if I consider the faculty of understanding, I immediately recognize that in me it is very small and exceedingly finite, and at the same time I form the idea of some other much greater faculty of understanding, which by all means is the greatest and infinite; and from this very fact that I can form the idea of it, I perceive that it pertains to the nature of God. By the same reasoning, if I examine the faculty of remembering or imagining or any other, I manifestly discover none that I do not understand to be weak and circumscribed in me but immense in God. It is the will alone, or the liberty of deciding, that I experience to be so great in me that I do not apprehend an idea of any greater faculty of its kind; and so it is principally as regards will that I understand that I am an image and likeness of God. For although the will is greater beyond comparison in God than in me, both because of the knowledge and power joined to it, thus rendering it more firm and efficacious, and also because of its object, since God's will extends itself to more things; nevertheless, in itself, and formally and precisely regarded, God's will does not seem greater than mine; for the will consists only in the fact that we can either do or not do the same thing (that is, we can affirm or deny, pursue or avoid), or better still, the will consists only in that we bear ourselves in such a way toward whatever our intellect proposes ought to be affirmed or denied, or pursued or avoided, that we do not feel determined to it by any external force. Moreover, in order to be free, it is not necessary that I can bear myself to either alternative; on the contrary, the more I am inclined toward one alternative, either because I evidently understand the basis of truth and good in it, or because God so disposes the inmost asspects of my thinking toward it, so much the more freely do I choose that alternative. For assuredly divine grace and natural cognition never diminish liberty, but rather augment and strengthen it. On the contrary, that indifference I experience when no reason urges me toward one alternative more than another is the lowest grade of liberty and testifies to no perfection in the will, but merely to a defect in knowledge or some negation thereof; for were I always to see clearly what is true and good, I would never deliberate concerning what ought to be judged or chosen, and so, although I manifestly would be free, nevertheless I could never be indifferent.

Now, from these things I perceive, firstly, that the force of 101 willing that I have from God, regarded in itself, is not the cause of my errors, for it is most ample and perfect in its kind; secondly, that the force of understanding, regarded in itself, is not the cause of my errors, for whatever I understand, my understanding of it derives from God, so that, beyond any doubt, I rightly understand it, and it is impossible that I am deceived about it. Whence then do my errors take their birth? From this one thing, that since the will extends more widely than the intellect, I do not contain the will within the limits of the intellect, but also extend it to those things I do not understand; since the will is indifferent in respect to these latter things, it easily turns aside from the true and the good, and so I make mistakes and I sin.

For example, when I examined during these days whether any- 102 thing existed in the world and noticed that, from the very fact I was examining this, it evidently followed that I myself exist, I was indeed unable not to judge as true what I was so clearly understanding; not because I had been forced to judge this by any external force, but because, in conformity with the great light in the intellect, there arose a great propensity in the will; hence the less I was indifferent about this, the more spontaneously and freely I believed it. Now, however, not merely do I know that I exist insofar as I am a thinking thing, but furthermore the idea of a certain corporeal nature is presented to me, and it happens that I doubt whether the thinking nature that is in me, or better, that I myself am, is different from this very corporeal nature, or whether both are the same; and I suppose that no reason as yet presents itself to my intellect that persuades me of the one more than the other. Certainly, from this very fact I am indifferent as to which of the two ought to be affirmed or denied, or even as to whether nothing ought to be judged concerning the matter.

103   Also, this indifference extends not only to those things about which the intellect knows nothing manifestly, but to all those things that are not known by the intellect with sufficient perspicuity at the very time at which the will deliberates about them: for however probable the conjectures that draw me to one alternative, the mere cognition that they are only conjectures, but not certain and indubitable reasons, suffices to urge my assent toward the contrary. This I have experienced well enough during these days, when, because of the single fact that I had discerned they can in some way be doubted, I supposed false all those things I previously believed most true.

104   Moreover, if I do indeed abstain from casting a judgment when I do not perceive the truth sufficiently clearly and distinctly, it is clear that I act rightly, and am not deceived. But if I affirm or deny, then I do not correctly use the liberty of deciding; and if I turn myself toward that alternative which is false, I obviously will be deceived; if, however, I embrace the other alternative, I will as a matter of chance fall upon the truth, but I shall not therefore avoid blame, because it is manifest by the natural light that the perception of the intellect should always precede the determination of the will. It is in this incorrect use of the liberty of deciding that there arises that privation which constitutes the form of error: I say the privation arises from this operation insofar as the operation proceeds from me, but not that the privation inheres in the faculty that I have received from God, nor even in the operation insofar as the operation depends on him.

105   Moreover, I have no reason to complain that God bestowed upon me a will that extends more widely than my intellect; for since the will consists in one thing only—and is, as it were, indivisible—its nature does not seem to allow that anything can be removed from it; and to be sure, the more ample it is, so much the more ought I to give thanks to him who has bestowed it upon me.

106   Finally, neither ought I to complain that God concurs with me in bringing forth those acts of the will or those judgments in which I am deceived: for those acts are altogether true and good insofar as they depend upon God, and it is somehow a greater perfection in me that I can bring them forth than if I could not

do so. Moreover, this privation in which the formal reason of falsity and blame alone consists does not need the concurrence of God, because it is not a thing, and it should not be said to be related to God as to its cause; rather it should be said to be only a negation. For, to be sure, it is not an imperfection in God that he has given me the liberty of assenting or of not assenting to particular things of which he has not placed in my intellect a clear and distinct perception; but undoubtedly it is an imperfection in me if I do not use this very liberty well, and cast a judgment about things I do not rightly understand. Nevertheless, I see that God could easily have arranged things so that even though I remained free and of limited knowledge I would never err; he could have arranged it so that I would never come to deliberate about any matter concerning which he had not endowed my intellect with a clear and distinct perception, or he might simply have impressed on my memory, in a way I could not forget it, that I should make no judgment about anything I do not clearly and distinctly perceive. And I easily understand that, had God made me in this way, then, considering myself as the whole, I would have come to be more perfect than I now am. But I cannot on that account deny that there is greater perfection in a universe of things when, rather than having all its parts manifestly similar, some of them are pervious to error, and others not at all. And I have no right to complain because God wished me to bear a role in the world that is neither the foremost nor most perfect.

And furthermore, although I am as yet unable to avoid errors 107 in that first way, which requires an evident perception of all those things about which deliberation ought to take place, I can nevertheless avoid errors in the other way, which requires only that I remember that judgment is to be withheld each time the truth of a matter does not shine forth; for although I experience that I am so weak as not always to be able to remain fixed upon one and the same cognition, nevertheless I can bring it about, by an attentive and more frequently repeated meditation, that I will remember this rule each time practice demands it, and thus I will acquire a definite habit of avoiding error.

And as the greatest and foremost perfection of man consists in 108 avoiding error, I consider today's meditation of no little worth, since I was searching for the cause of error and falsity. And certainly, that cause can be nothing else but what I have explained; for every time I so restrain my will in casting judgments that it extends itself only to those things clearly and distinctly displayed to it by the intellect, it is manifestly impossible for me to err, because every clear and distinct perception is undoubtedly something, and accordingly cannot be from nothing, but rather necessarily has God as its author—God, I say, who is most perfect and whose nature it contradicts to be a deceiver; hence every clear and distinct perception is true. Moreover, I did not learn today only what I must avoid in order never to be deceived, but at the same time I also learned what must be done in order for me to arrive at truth; for I will undoubtedly arrive at truth if only I will sufficiently attend to all those things I perfectly understand, and separate them from the remaining things that I apprehend with more confusion and obscurity. And I shall diligently devote my efforts to this tomorrow.

109

MEDITATION V
On the essence of material things;
and for a second time, of God, that he exists

110 Many things remain for me to investigate concerning the attributes of God and concerning my own self, or the nature of my mind. Perhaps I will take these matters up at another time. But since I have already noticed what I must guard against and what I have to do in order to reach the truth, nothing seems more urgent now than to attempt to emerge from the doubts I have fallen into during the past days and to see whether anything certain can be established about material things.

111 And indeed before inquiring whether any material things exist outside me, I should attend to the ideas of them insofar as they are in my thinking, and I should see just which of them are distinct and which confused.

112 Certainly I distinctly imagine the quantity the philosophers commonly call continuous, or the extension in length, breadth, and depth of this quantity—or better still, of the thing having the quantity. I number various parts in it. I assign arbitrary magnitudes, shapes, positions, and local motions to these parts. And to these motions I assign arbitrary durations.

These things are not only manifestly known by me and perspicu- 113
ous to me when they are thus generally regarded, but furthermore,
in giving my attention to them, I perceive innumerable particulars
regarding shapes, number, motion, and similar things, the truth
of which is so obvious and so consonant with my nature that, although I am unveiling them for the first time, I do not so much
seem to be learning anything new as to be remembering things
I previously knew; or I seem for the first time to be taking notice
of things that indeed were formerly in me, although I had not
previously turned the gaze of my mind toward them.

What I think deserves the greatest consideration at this point 114
is the following: namely, I find in myself innumerable ideas of
particular things that, even if they perhaps exist nowhere outside
me, nevertheless cannot be said to be nothing; and although in
a certain manner they are thought of by me at my deciding,
nevertheless they are not fashioned by me, but rather have their
true and immutable natures. So that when, for example, I imagine a triangle, even if perhaps no such figure exists anywhere
outside anyone's mind, nor ever will, there nevertheless undoubtedly exists its particular nature, or essence, or immutable and
eternal form, which is not fashioned by me or dependent upon
my mind. This is manifest as follows: various properties of this
same triangle can be demonstrated—for example, its three angles
are equal to two right angles, its largest side is subtended by its
greatest angle; moreover, whether I wish it or not, I now clearly
recognize these properties even though I had not in any way
previously thought of them when I imagined the triangle. Therefore they have not been fashioned by me.

This conclusion is not affected if I say that, since I have occa- 115
sionally seen bodies having a triangular shape, this idea of the triangle has perhaps come to me from external things through the
organs of the senses; for I can also come to think of innumerable
other shapes about which there can be no suspicion that they have
entered into me through the senses, and nevertheless I can demonstrate various properties of them no less than of the triangle.
And these indeed are all true, since they are certainly clearly
known by me; accordingly, they are something, and not merely
nothing: for it is manifest that everything that is true is something, and I have already demonstrated at length that everything is
true that I know clearly. And even if I had not demonstrated it,

nonetheless it certainly is the nature of my mind that I could not withhold assent from these things, at least as long as I perceive them clearly; and I recall that even before now, when I was attached as much as possible to the objects of the senses, I had always received truths of this kind—that is, truths that I recognized evidently concerning shapes, numbers, or other things pertaining to arithmetic, or geometry, or generally, to pure and abstract mathematics—as the most certain of all truths.

116   And indeed, if from the mere fact that I can draw forth the idea of anything from my thinking, it follows that all those things that I clearly and distinctly perceive to pertain to that thing truly do pertain to it, can I not also establish on that basis an argument by which God's existence may be proved? And it is certain that, no less than the ideas of various figures or numbers, I also find in myself the idea of God, that is, the idea of the most perfect being; and moreover, I no less clearly perceive that it pertains to God's nature always to exist than that whatever I demonstrate concerning some figure or number also pertains to the nature of that figure or number; and accordingly, even if not everything I have thought out during these past days were true, still the existence of God should hold at least the same degree of certainty with me as had mathematical truths up until this time.

117   To be sure, on first appearance this is not altogether perspicuous, but it bears a certain likeness to sophisms. For since I am accustomed to distinguish essence from existence in other things, I easily persuade myself that existence can also be disjoined from the essence of God, and thus that God can be thought of as not existing. But, to one attending more diligently, it nevertheless becomes manifest that existence can no more be separated from the essence of God than the equality of its three angles to two right angles from the essence of some triangle, or the idea of a valley from the idea of a mountain: and so it becomes manifest that it is no less contradictory to think of God (that is, the most perfect being) lacking existence (that is lacking some perfection) than to think of a mountain that lacks a valley.

118   Nonetheless, even granting that I indeed cannot think of God except as existing, just as I cannot think of a mountain that has no valley, still it certainly does not follow that any mountain exists in the world because I think of one as having a valley, and so it likewise does not seem that God exists because of the fact

that I am thinking of him as existing: for my thinking imposes no necessity on things; and in the same way as it is allowable to imagine a winged horse—although no horse has wings—so perhaps I can assign existence to God although no God exists.

On the contrary, that is where the sophism lies. For from the   119
fact that I cannot think of a mountain that has no valley, it does not follow that a mountain or a valley exist anywhere, but merely that a mountain or a valley, whether existing or not, cannot be disjoined from one another. However, on the other hand, from the fact that I cannot think of God except as existing, it follows that existence is inseparable from God, and therefore that he truly exists: it is not that my thinking brings his existence about or imposes necessity on anything, but, on the contrary, it is because the necessity of the thing itself, namely, of the existence of God, determines me in thinking this: for I am not at liberty to think of God without existence (that is, of the most perfect being lacking the greatest perfection) as I am at liberty to imagine a horse with or without wings.

Moreover, it should not be said here that, once I have posited   120
that God has all perfections, then, since existence is one of them, I must indeed posit an existing God, but yet that it was not necessary for me to posit what I first posited—just as it is not necessary for me to suppose that all four-sided figures can be inscribed in a circle, but yet having posited that I may suppose this, it will then be necessary for me to agree that a rhombus can be inscribed in a circle, which nevertheless is manifestly false. For although it is not necessary that I ever make my way so far as to do any thinking about God, nevertheless every time I do think of the first and greatest being, and as it were, draw the idea of him from the treasure house of my mind, it is necessary that I attribute to him every perfection, although I do not then enumerate them or attend to them singly; moreover, this necessity manifestly suffices so that afterward, when I notice that existence is a perfection, I correctly conclude that the first and greatest being exists: just as it is not necessary for me to ever imagine any triangle, but yet every time I do wish to consider a rectilinear figure having only three angles, it is necessary for me to attribute to it those things on the basis of which it may be inferred that its three angles are not greater than two right angles, even though I am not then noticing this same consequence. However, when

I examine the particular figures inscribed in a circle, it is in no way necessary that all four-sided figures are included in their number; on the contrary, I can even suppose that it is not at all the case so long as I wish to admit nothing except what I clearly and distinctly understand; and accordingly there is a great difference between false postulations and true ideas that are inborn, of which the first and foremost is the idea of God. For I assuredly understand in many ways that the idea of God is not something fictitious depending upon my thinking, but that it is the image of a true and immutable nature: first, because I cannot think of any other thing, except God alone, to whose essence existence pertains; next, because I cannot understand two or more gods of this kind, and because, having posited that the one God now exists, I manifestly see that it is necessary that he has existed beforehand from eternity and will remain in existence for eternity; and last, because I perceive many other things in God that can neither be removed nor altered by me.

121   And so indeed, whatever reasoning I ultimately use in testing anything, I am always led back to the fact that only those things persuade me that I perceive clearly and distinctly. And although some of those things that I clearly and distinctly perceive are truly obvious to everyone, others are disclosed only by those who look more closely into them and track them down; yet once these are detected, they are considered no less certain than the former things. Thus, although in a right triangle the equality between the square of its base [basis] and the squares of its sides does not so easily become apparent as does the fact that this same base [basim] is subtended by the largest angle of the triangle, it is nevertheless no less believed—at least after it is once thoroughly seen through. Moreover, as for what pertains to God, if I were not overwhelmed by prejudices, and if the images of sensible things were not to besiege my mind at every turn, then I certainly would recognize nothing sooner or more easily than God; for what is more obvious in itself than that the greatest being or God, in whom alone existence pertains to essence, exists?

122   And despite the fact that attentive consideration was required for me to perceive this very thing, nevertheless I am now not only equally certain of God's existence and all other things that seem very certain, but I furthermore also notice that the certainty of the

other things so depends on this very thing that without it nothing can ever be perfectly known.

For although I am of such a nature that as long as I am perceiving something very clearly and distinctly I can only believe that it is true, nevertheless since I am also of such a nature that I cannot always fasten the gaze of my mind on that same thing in order to perceive it clearly, and since the memory of judgments previously made often recurs when I am no longer attending to the reasons why I made them, if I were ignorant of God other reasons could be brought forth that would turn me away from my opinion, and so I would never have true and certain knowledge of anything but only vague and changeable opinions. Take an example: I am considering the nature of the triangle, and since I am instructed in the principles of geometry, it indeed appears very evidently to me that its three angles are equal to two right angles, and I cannot fail to believe that this is true while I am attending to its demonstration. But now, it is suddenly the time immediately thereafter! I have turned the gaze of my mind away from the demonstration, although I still remember that I had most clearly seen through it. Despite this memory, if I do not know God, it can indeed easily happen that I doubt whether the demonstration is true. For I can persuade myself that nature made me in such a way as to be occasionally deceived in those things I deem myself to perceive very evidently—since I especially remember that I had often accepted many things as true and certain that afterward, when moved by other reasons, I judged to be false. 123

But by now I have already perceived that God does exist, and at the same time at which I perceived his existence I also understood that everything else depends upon him, and that he is not a deceiver; moreover, I have gathered from all this that everything I clearly and distinctly perceive necessarily is true; thus, although I am no longer attending to the reasons why I judged it true that the three angles of a triangle are equal to two right angles, provided only that I remember having clearly and distinctly perceived it, I have a true and certain knowledge of it, and no contrary reasoning can be brought forth that would move me to doubt it. This does not apply merely to that one truth about the triangle, but is applicable to all the other truths I recall having 124 demonstrated in the past, such as in geometry and in similar disciplines. For what objections may be made to me now? That I have been made in such a way as to be frequently deceived? But I now know that I cannot be deceived as regards those things I perspicuously understand. That I have accepted many other things as true and certain that I afterward discerned to be false? But even granting that, still, I had not perceived any of them clearly and distinctly; and being ignorant of this rule of truth, I had perhaps believed them for other reasons that I afterward detected to be less firm. What therefore can be said in opposition to me? Will it be said (as I not so long ago objected to myself) that perhaps I am sleeping, or that all those things I am now thinking are no more true than things that present themselves to one who is sleeping? But indeed, even that would change nothing; for certainly, even though I were dreaming, if anything is evident to my intellect, it is by all means true.

125   And thus I plainly see that the certainty and truth of every science depends solely upon the cognition of the true God, so that until I came to know him I could know nothing perfectly about anything else. But now, indeed, innumerable things concerning not only God himself and other intellectual things, but also concerning that entire corporeal nature that is an object of pure mathematics, can be manifestly known by me and certain for me.

126   MEDITATION VI
Concerning the existence of material things and
concerning the real distinction of the mind from the body

127   It remains for me to examine whether material things exist. And I now at least know that material things, insofar as they are the object of pure mathematics, can exist, because I perceive them clearly and distinctly. For there is no doubt that God can bring about everything I am able to perceive clearly and distinctly; and I have never judged that God could not do something except for the reason that for me to distinctly perceive it would involve a contradiction. Furthermore, on the basis of the faculty of imagining, which I experience myself to use in dealing with these material things, it seems to follow that they exist; for to one

more attentively considering what the imagination is, it appears to be nothing but a particular application of the faculty of knowing to a body that is intimately present to it, and that, accordingly, is existent.

But to make this manifest, I first examine the difference that 128 exists between the imagination and pure intellection. Thus, as an example, when I imagine a triangle, I do not merely understand that it is a figure enclosed by three lines, but at the same time, with the gaze of my mind, I also intuit these three lines as if they were present; and this is what I name "to imagine." If, however, I wish to think of a chiliagon, I equally well understand that it is a figure consisting of a thousand sides just as I understand that a triangle is a figure consisting of three sides; yet I do not in the same way imagine those thousand sides or intuit them as if they were presented to me. And despite the fact that now—because of my habit of always imagining something or other whenever I think of a corporeal thing—I may perhaps be confusingly representing some figure to myself, nevertheless it is manifest that it is not a chiliagon, because it in no way differs from the figure I would represent were I thinking of a myriagon or any other figure of very many sides; moreover, the figure I am representing does not help me at all in recognizing those properties by which the chiliagon differs from other polygons. But even if it is a question of the pentagon, I can indeed understand its figure, just as I understand the figure of the chiliagon, without the activity of the imagination; however, I am also able to imagine the figure of the pentagon—that is, by applying the gaze of my mind to its five sides, and at the same time to the area contained within these five sides; and by this example of the pentagon I manifestly notice that to imagine I require some peculiar effort of the mind that I do not use for understanding; this additional effort of the mind clearly shows the difference between the imagination and the pure understanding.

In consequence of this I shall carefully speculate that the very 129 force of imagining that is in me, according as it differs from the force of understanding, is not required for my own essence, that is, for the essence of my mind; for even if the force of imagining were to cease, undoubtedly I would nonetheless stay that same one who I now am; from which it seems to follow that the force of imagining depends upon something different from myself. And

I easily understand that if some body exists with which the mind is so conjoined that the mind, at its own decision, can direct itself to, as it were, look searchingly upon that body, then it is possible that I imagine corporeal things by this means; thus this mode of thinking would differ from pure understanding only in that the mind, when it understands, in a certain way turns itself inward toward its own self and considers one of the ideas that are within it; however, when the mind imagines, it turns itself to the body, and it intuits something in the body conformable to an idea that the intellect has perceived either from itself or from the senses. I say I easily understand that imagination can be carried out this way, if indeed the body does exist; and since no other equally suitable manner of explaining imagination presents itself, from that I conclude as probable, and as probable only, that body does exist. And even though I thoroughly trace out all arguments, I nevertheless do not as yet see that any argument that proves necessarily that body exists can be derived from the distinct idea of corporeal nature I discover in my imagination.

130   In addition to that corporeal nature which is the object of pure mathematics, I am certainly accustomed to imagine many other things, although not so distinctly, such as colors, sounds, flavors, pain, and the like. Moreover, I perceive these things better by the sense through which, with the help of memory, they seem to have come to the imagination. Hence a more suitable treatment of them requires that at the same time I also consider sense, and see whether any certain argument for the existence of corporeal things can be derived from any of those things perceived by that mode of thinking I name sense.

131   Firstly, I will here recall those particular things I previously considered true in the manner perceived by sense, and I shall also recount the reasons why I thought this; next, I will set down the reasons why I afterward called them into doubt; and finally, I will consider what I should now believe about them.

132   Well, then, I first sensed that I had a head, hands, feet, and the other members of which this body consists—a body I regarded as if it were part of me, or even perhaps the whole of me; moreover, I sensed that this body is placed among many other bodies by which it can be variously affected, either advantageously or disadvantageously, and I measured these advantages by a certain sense of pleasure and the disadvantages by a sense of pain. And

beyond pleasure and pain, I also sensed hunger, thirst, and other appetites of this kind within me; I likewise sensed certain propensities to gaiety, to sadness, to anger, as well as other similar affections. As regards the things outside me, beyond the extension, shapes, and motions of bodies, I also sensed hardness, heat, and other tactile qualities in these bodies; and furthermore I sensed light, colors, flavors, and sounds, and out of their variety I distinguished heaven, earth, the seas, and the remaining bodies from one another. Furthermore, based upon the ideas of all those qualities presented to my thinking (which ideas, properly speaking, I immediately and exclusively discerned by sense), I concluded that I also sense certain things manifestly different from my thinking, namely, the corporeal bodies from which these very ideas proceeded. Indeed, I did not draw this conclusion without reason. For I experienced that those ideas came to me without any consent of mine, in such a way that I could not sense any object, even though I wished to do so, unless it were present to the organ of sense, and could not fail to sense an object if it were present. And because the ideas perceived by sense were much more vivid and expressive, and also in their own way more distinct, than any of those ideas that I—who am practiced at and aware of my purposes in reflecting— could form, it did not seem possible that they proceeded from my own self; and accordingly, there remained the conclusion that they came to me from some other things. Since I had no notion of those things from which I concluded my ideas proceeded except the notion I had derived on the basis of the ideas themselves, the only conclusion that could enter my mind was that they are similar to the ideas. Moreover, because I recalled that I had first used the senses rather than reason, and because I saw that the ideas I myself formed were less expressive than those perceived by sense, and in very large measure composed from them, I easily persuaded myself that I manifestly have nothing in the intellect that I have not formerly had in sense. Moreover, not without reason did I decide that the particular body, that with a certain special justification I called my own, pertains more to me than does any other body; for I could never be separated from it as I could from the other bodies; I sensed in it, and in proportion to its condition, all the appetites and affections; and finally, I recognized pain and the titillation of pleasure in its parts, not, however, in the other bodies situated outside it. Yet, as to why a certain sadness of the soul follows upon that enigmatic sense of pain, or why that puzzling twitching of the stomach I call hunger puts me in mind of consuming food, or dryness in mind of drink, and so forth—indeed, I had no other explanation except that I was shown so by nature. For at least as far as I understand it, there is no manifest affinity between that twitching and the desire of consuming food, or between the sensation of the thing producing the pain and the thought of sorrow that arises from this sensation; rather I seemed to have learned from nature these and all the remaining things I judged about the objects of the senses—indeed, I had even persuaded myself of the truth of everything I judged about them before I had evaluated any reasons by which that might be proved.

133   Later on, numerous experiences certainly shook all the confidence I had had in the senses; for occasionally towers, which from afar had been of round appearance, appeared square from nearby, and very large statues standing at their pinnacles did not appear large to one looking up at them from the ground—in these and in innumerable other such cases I recognized that my judgments about the objects of the external senses were mistaken. I also recognized the same thing as regards my judgments concerning the internal senses; for what can be more within us than pain? Yet nevertheless, I had at one time heard from people whose leg or arm had been cut off that they still occasionally seem to themselves to feel pain in that part of the body they lack; and likewise, even as regards myself, it did not seem manifestly certain that a particular part of my body was paining me even if, on the basis of my feelings, I would be led to think the pain was in that part. To these reasons for doubting, I have also recently added two other very general grounds for doubt. The first was that while awake I never believed myself to sense anything I could not also sometimes think I sensed while sleeping; and since I do not believe that the things I seem to myself to sense in dreams come from things situated outside me, I did see why I ought to have believed this any more the case as regards the things I seem to myself to sense while awake. The other reason was that, since I still did not know the author of my origins, I saw nothing to prevent myself being so constituted by nature as to be deceived even in those things that appeared to me to be very true. And as for the reasons by which I had formerly persuaded myself concerning the truth of sensible things, I did not find it difficult to respond to them. For since I seemed to be

urged on by nature to many things from which reason dissuaded me, I did not think that much confidence should be placed in the things taught by nature. And although the perceptions of the senses did not depend upon my willing, I did not therefore think it should be concluded that they proceed from things different from myself, since there perhaps could be some other faculty in me, even if as yet unknown by me, that produces them.

Now, however, after I begin to know better my own self and   134
the author of my origin, I indeed do not think that everything I seem to be told by the senses ought to be rashly accepted, but neither do I think that everything ought to be placed into doubt.

And first, because I know that God can make all the things I   135
clearly and distinctly understand in that manner in which I understand them, it suffices that I can clearly and distinctly understand one thing without another for me to be certain that the one thing is different from the other, since it can be set up separately from the other at least by God; moreover, to conclude that two things are different, I need not be concerned with that power by which God may separate them; and accordingly, from this very fact that I know that I exist and in the meanwhile recognize manifestly nothing else to pertain to my nature or essence except this alone, namely, that I am a thinking thing, I correctly conclude that my essence consists in this one thing, that I am a thinking thing. And although I perhaps have a body (or rather, as I shall later on say for certain, do have a body) that is very intimately conjoined with me, nevertheless because on the one hand I have a clear and distinct idea of my own self insofar as I am only a thinking and nonextended thing, and because on the other hand I have a distinct idea of body insofar as it is only an extended and nonthinking thing, it is certain that I am truly distinct from my body and can exist without it.

Furthermore, I discover in me faculties for certain special modes   136
of thinking, to wit, the faculties of imagining and sensing, without which I can clearly and distinctly understand myself to be a whole, but which, on the contrary, I cannot understand without me, that is, without an intelligent substance in which they inhere: for they include some intellection in their formal concept, from which I perceive that they are distinguished from me as modes from a thing. I also recognize certain other faculties, such as the faculties of changing place, of assuming various postures, and the like.

These faculties, no more than the preceding ones, can be understood without some substance in which they inhere—and accordingly they cannot be understood as existing without a substance. But it is manifest that, if indeed they exist, then they must inhere in a corporeal or extended substance, and not, however, in an intelligent substance—for contained in the clear and distinct conception of them is some extension, but manifestly no intellection. Now, there is indeed in me a certain passive faculty of sensing, or of receiving and recognizing the ideas of sensible things; but I could make no use of it unless there existed either in myself or in something else a certain active faculty of producing or bringing about these ideas of sensible things. And this active faculty cannot reasonably be thought to be in my very self, since it manifestly presupposes no intellection and because these ideas of sensible things are produced without my coöperation, and often despite my wish: therefore it remains that this active faculty is in some substance different from me. As I already pointed out above, this substance must contain either formally or eminently all the reality that is objectively in the ideas produced by this faculty. Either this substance is body, or corporeal nature, containing formally everything that is objectively in the ideas produced by this faculty; or this substance is God or another creature more noble than the body, in which everything that is objectively in the ideas produced by this faculty is contained eminently. But since God is not a deceiver, it is altogether manifest that he does not directly of himself send these ideas of sensible things into me; it is also altogether manifest that he does not send them into me by means of any creature in which the objective reality of these ideas is only eminently, but not formally, contained. For since God gave me no faculty for recognizing this, but, on the contrary, has bestowed upon me a great inclination toward believing that these ideas of sensible things come from corporeal things, I do not seen any argument by which He could be understood not to be a deceiver if these ideas were to come from something other than corporeal things. And consequently, corporeal things do exist. Nevertheless, perhaps they do not altogether exist in such a way as I comprehend them by sense, because this comprehension of the senses is in many respects very obscure and confused. But at least all those things exist in corporeal things that I clearly and distinctly understand in them—

that is, all those things, generally regarded, that are comprehended in the object of pure mathematics.

The remaining things are all very dubious and uncertain. They 137 are either merely particular, such as that the sun has a certain size or figure, and so on; or they are less clearly understood, such as light, sound, color, and the like. But although all these things are very dubious and uncertain, nevertheless the very fact that God is not deceiving, and that, accordingly, no falsity can be found among my thoughts unless there is also in me some faculty bestowed by God for correcting it, holds out to me an assured hope of obtaining truth even as regards these things. And indeed there is no doubt that everything I am taught by nature contains something of the truth: for through nature, generally regarded, I understand nothing other than either God himself, or the co-ordination of created things instituted by God; moreover, by my nature in particular I do not understand anything other than the combination of all those things that have been bestowed upon me by God.

Moreover, there is nothing this nature of mine teaches me more 138 expressly than that I have a body that is in an improper condi-tion when I feel pain, that lacks food or drink when I undergo hunger or thirst, and the like; and accordingly I should not doubt that there is something of the truth in this.

Nature also teaches by means of these senses of pain, hunger, 139 thirst, and so on, that I am not merely present in my body as a sailor is present in his ship; rather I am very closely conjoined with it—and, as it were, intermingled with it—so that together with it I compose one thing. For otherwise when the body is in-jured, I, who am nothing other than a thinking thing, would not therefore feel pain, but would perceive this injury by the pure intellect, as a sailor perceives by sight that a part of his ship is broken. For certainly these senses of thirst, hunger, and so on, are nothing other than certain confused modes of thinking that arise from the union and, as it were, intermingling of the mind with the body.

Furthermore, I am also taught by nature that various other 140 bodies exist round and about my own, and that I should pursue some of them and avoid others. And certainly, from the fact that I sense exceedingly differing colors, sounds, odors, flavors, degrees of warmth and hardness, and the like, I correctly conclude that these various perceptions of the senses come from correspondingly various things in bodies, even if the latter are perhaps not similar to the former; and from the fact that certain of these perceptions are agreeable to me and others disagreeable, it is manifestly certain that my body, or better said, that I as a whole, insofar as I am composed from a body and a mind, can be affected with various advantages and disadvantages by the bodies round and about me.

141   But there are many other things that, although I seem to be taught them by nature, I nevertheless have not really received from nature. Rather I have approved them because of my habit of judging precipitously, and consequently it may easily occur that they are false: for example, that every space is empty in which there is nothing manifestly present to make an effect on my senses; or that in a warm body there is something manifestly similar to the idea of heat in me; that in a white or a green body there is the same whiteness or greenness I sense; that in a bitter or sweet body there is the same flavor I sense, and so on; or that stars and towers and any other distant bodies have only that size and shape they display to my senses; and all other things of this kind. But in order to avoid an insufficiently distinct perception of this matter, I should define more completely for myself what I understand when I say that I am taught something by nature. And so I here use nature more strictly than for the combination of all those things bestowed upon me by God. For in this combination are contained many things that pertain to the mind alone—for example, that I perceive that what has been done cannot be undone, and all the remaining things known by the natural light, which do not concern me here. Similarly, there are also many things in this combination that regard the body alone, which also do not concern me here—for example, that the body stretches upward and downward, and so on. Hence I here use nature only in respect to those things God has bestowed upon me as a composite of mind and body. And accordingly, this nature indeed teaches us to flee from those things that bring a feeling of pain and to seek those that bring a feeling of pleasure, and the like; however, it does not appear that nature further teaches us to conclude, without a previous examination by the intellect, that any such perceptions of the senses are located in things outside us, because to know the truth about the things outside us seems to pertain to the mind alone, but not, however, to the

combination of mind and body. Thus, although a star no more affects my eye than does the flame of a small torch, nevertheless that involves no real or positive inclination on my part to believe that the star is no larger than the flame; rather I have judged this without a reason from my earliest years. Again, although in approaching fire I feel warmth, and in approaching even closer feel pain, certainly no reasoning persuades me that there is something in the fire similar either to the heat or pain; rather reasoning persuades me only that there is something in the fire, whatever that thing might itself precisely be, that produces in us the aforesaid sensations of heat or pain. Again, although there is nothing in some space that moves sense, it does not therefore follow that there is no body in that space. Accordingly, I see that as regards the foregoing, and very many other things, I am accustomed to reverse abusively the order of nature. Thus the perceptions of the sense have been given by nature only to signify to the mind particular things that are advantageous or disadvantageous to the composite of which the mind is a part; and for that purpose they are sufficiently clear and distinct. However, I misuse them by considering them as if they are certain rules for immediately discerning what the particular essence is of bodies situated outside us, although they signify nothing about that except very obscurely and confusingly.

Now, I have already sufficiently examined by what reasoning, 142 despite the goodness of God, it may happen that my judgments are false. But here a new difficulty presents itself concerning those things that nature displays to me as if they should be sought after or avoided. Moreover, the difficulty also bears on the internal senses in which I seem to have discovered faults—for example, when someone, misled by the gratifying flavor of a certain food, consumes the poison concealed within. But, to be sure, in that situation the person is urged on by nature toward seeking that in which the gratifying flavor consisted, not, however, toward seeking the poison about which he is ignorant. Thus nothing more can be concluded from this example than that this nature is not omniscient: this is not astonishing because, since a man is a limited thing, there is nothing else consonant with him but a nature of limited perfection.

But certainly we err, and not infrequently, even as regards those 143 things toward which we are urged on by nature: as when the sick seek drink or food, which a short time afterward is harmful to them. Perhaps in this case it will be said that they err because their nature is corrupted. However, this reply does not take away the difficulty because a sick man is no less truly God's creature than a healthy man, and consequently it seems no less contradictory for God to bestow a deceiving nature upon the sick man. But let us pursue this matter. A clock, for example, is assembled from wheels and weights; moreover, it no less completely observes all the laws of nature when it is badly made and fails to indicate the correct time than when it satisfies the wishes of the craftsman in every respect. Suppose now I were to consider the body of a man insofar as it is a particular skillful contrivance made from bones, nerves, muscles, veins, blood, and skin. Suppose furthermore that I considered it so composed and adapted that, even if no mind were to exist in it, it nevertheless would have all the same motions that now occur in a man's body, not from the control of his will, and hence not on account of his mind. On these suppositions there are similarities to the clock. Thus I easily recognize that it would be natural for the man, when he has no defect in him, to be moved by dryness in the throat toward taking a drink useful to himself; but I furthermore also easily recognize that if, for example, he suffered from dropsy, it would be equally natural for him both to suffer that dryness in the throat that his mind customarily concludes is a sensation of thirst, and also to be so disposed in his nerves and remaining parts by this dryness that he takes a drink, which increases the disease. In addition, although in looking to a preconceived use of the clock I can say that, when it fails to indicate the hours correctly, it diverges from its nature; and although, in the same way, by considering the skillful contrivance of the human body, as it were, in comparison to the motions normally in it, I can also conclude that it diverges from its nature if it has a dry throat when drink is not beneficial to its conservation; nevertheless, I sufficiently recognize that this last meaning of "nature" differs much from the other meaning of "nature": for this last meaning of "nature" is nothing but a denomination by my thinking due to my comparing the sick man and the badly made clock with the idea of a healthy man and the idea of a correctly made clock, and it is extrinsic to the things spoken about; by the other meaning of "nature" I indeed understand something that truly is in things, and accordingly it contains something of the truth.

But certainly, as regards the body with dropsy, even if it is 144 only an extrinsic denomination when it is said that its nature is corrupted because it has a dry throat but does not need drink, nevertheless it is not a pure denomination as regards the composite, that is, as regards the mind united to such a body; rather it is a true error of nature that this composite is thirsty when drink is harmful to it; and accordingly it here remains to be inquired how the goodness of God does not prevent the sick man's nature, thus understood, from being deceiving.

First of all, I call attention to the fact that there is a great 145 difference between the mind and body in that body of its nature is always divisible, but the mind, however, is manifestly indivisible; for undoubtedly, when I consider the mind, or myself, insofar as I am only a thinking thing, I can distinguish no parts, but rather understand that I manifestly am one and an entire thing; and although the entire mind seems united to the entire body, nevertheless, when a foot or any other part of the body is cut off, nothing is therefore known to be taken away from my mind; moreover, even the faculties of willing, sensing, imagining, and so on, cannot be said to be parts of the mind, because it is one and the same mind that wills, senses, and understands. Indeed, on the contrary, I can think of no corporeal or extended thing that in my thinking I may not easily divide into parts, and from this very fact I understand that a corporeal or extended thing is divisible; and this alone would suffice to teach me that mind is altogether diverse from body if I did not as yet sufficiently well know it on other grounds.

Next, I call attention to the fact that the mind is not im- 146 mediately affected by all parts of the body, but only by the brain, or perhaps even by only one very small part of it, namely, by the part in which it is said that the common sense exists. Every time this part of the brain is disposed in the same way, it displays the same thing to the mind even though the remaining parts of the body can in the meanwhile assume different conditions. This is proved by numerous experiments it is not germane to list here.

Furthermore, I call attention to the fact that it is the nature 147 of the body that no part of it can be moved by another part that is somewhat distant from it unless it can also be moved in the same manner by whatever parts lie in between even though that more distant part does nothing. Thus, for example, in the chord ABCD, if its last part, D, is pulled, the first part, A, will not be moved in any way differently from how it could also be moved if one of the intermediate parts B or C were pulled and the last part, D, remained unmoved. By similar reasoning, when I feel the pain of my foot, physics has taught me that that sensation is brought about by means of the nerves spread out through the foot. Physics has also taught me that these nerves, which resemble strings, extend continuously from the foot to the brain and that, when they are pulled in the foot, they also pull the inmost parts of the brain to which they extend, and excite in these parts a particular motion that has been instituted by nature so that it affects the mind with a sensation of a pain existing, as it were, in the foot. But since those nerves must pass through the shinbone, legs, loins, back, and neck to come from the foot to the brain, it can occur that, although no part of the nerves in the foot is touched, but just the intermediate part, manifestly the same motion will take place in the brain as results from a foot in bad condition, and from this it will necessarily result that the mind feels the same pain.

148   Last, I call attention to the fact that since each of the motions that occur in that part of the brain that immediately affects the mind carries but one particular sensation to the brain, we can think of nothing better than if, from among all the sensations a particular motion can carry, it carries the one that conduces in the greatest way and most frequently to the conservation of a healthy man. Moreover, experience shows that all the senses bestowed upon us by nature are such; and accordingly, manifestly nothing is found in them that does not show the power and goodness of God. Thus, for example, when the nerves in the foot are violently and abnormally moved, that motion of the nerves through the marrow of the spine of the back reaches to the inmost part of the brain, where it provides a sign to the mind to sense something, namely, the pain existing, as it were, in the foot; and by this sign the mind is roused to rid itself as much as it can of the cause of the pain—for example, to rid itself of that which is injurious to the foot. Certainly, the nature of man could have been so constituted by God that the same motion in the

brain that signifies to the mind a pain existing, as it were, in the foot would display any other thing you choose to name—for example, that motion could have displayed itself to the mind either insofar as it is a motion in the brain, or insofar as it is a motion in the foot, or insofar as it is a motion in the intermediate places; finally, that same motion could have displayed anything else whatsoever to the mind; but none of these other things would lead as well to the conservation of the body. In the same way, when we require drink there arises a dryness in the throat, moving the nerves of the throat, which in turn move the inner parts of the brain; and this motion affects the mind with the sensation of thirst, because nothing in this entire affair is more useful for us to know than that by drinking we help conserve our healthy condition; and it is the same in other cases.

From these things it is altogether manifest that, despite the immense goodness of God, the nature of man, since it is composed from mind and body, cannot fail to be occasionally deceiving. For if some cause that is not in the foot, but either is in another part of the body through which the nerves extend from the foot to the brain, or is even in the brain itself, excites what is manifestly the same motion that is customarily excited by a foot in bad condition, then pain will be felt as if it were in the foot, and sense naturally will be deceived. This is so for the following reason: since that same motion can only cause the same sensation all the time, and since that sensation customarily proceeds much more frequently from a cause that injures the foot rather than from a cause existing somewhere else, it is consonant with reason that it always display a pain in the foot rather than a pain in another part of the body. And if in certain abnormal situations dryness of the throat is caused to occur when drink is not conducive to the healthy condition of the body, as happens in the case of the victim of dropsy, it is still far better that the sense of thirst deceives us in that case than if, on the contrary, it would always deceive us even when the body is well; and the same is true of the other senses.

And this consideration helps very much, not only so that I may call attention to all the errors to which my nature is liable, but also so that I may easily correct or avoid them. For undoubtedly, since I know that all the senses have reference to the advantage of the body, and much more frequently indicate the true rather than the false; and since I can nearly always use most of them in examining the same matter; and since, moreover, I can use memory, which connects present things with preceding ones; and since I can use the intellect, which now has seen through all the causes of making errors: I should, accordingly, no longer fear that the things daily displayed by the senses are false. On the contrary, the hyperbolical doubts of the past days ought to be expelled with laughter. I ought particularly to expel that general doubt about my not distinguishing sleeping from waking; for now I notice the very large difference that separates the two of them—namely, that what occurs in sleep is never conjoined by memory with all the remaining actions of life as are the things that occur to one awake; for undoubtedly, if while I am awake someone should suddenly appear to me and immediately afterward, as happens in dreams, disappear in such a way that I would not see whence he had come or where he went, I would not unreasonably judge him to be a specter, or better, to be a phantasm depicted in my brain, rather than a real man. And since those things do indeed occur about which I distinctly notice whence and when they come to me, and since I completely connect the perception of them with the rest of my life, I am clearly certain that they occur not to one dreaming, but to one awake. Moreover, I should not doubt even in the slightest concerning the truth of these same things if, after I have employed all the senses, memory, and intellect to examine them, they do not report anything to me that clashes with the others. For from the fact that God is not deceiving, it assuredly follows that I am not deceived in such matters. But since the exigency of practice does not always permit a delay in which to make such accurate examination, it must be confessed that human life is very often liable to errors concerning particular things, and the weakness of our nature should be recognized.

APPENDIX

REASONS PROVING THE EXISTENCE OF GOD

Introduction

This selection from "Replies to the Second Objections" to the *Meditations* is not easily accessible taken on its own. However, when the definitions contained in it are read in connection with the *Discourse* and especially the *Meditations*, then the definitions provide an excellent key to crucial terminology used by Descartes in the formulation of his metaphysics. I have explained these definitions at some length in my introductory essays to the *Discourse* and *Meditations*, and I refer the reader to those discussions.

SOURCE FOR THE LATIN TEXT

This selection is from "Replies to the Second Objections," which was first published in Paris in 1641 along with the *Meditations* and various objections to the *Meditations* and replies.* It was again published in 1642 in Amsterdam by Louis Elzevir as part of a new, second edition of the *Meditations* and "Objections and Replies." Adam and Tannery follow the 1642 text, and my translation is based on their presentation.†

---

* The "Second Objections" were gathered by Père Marin Mersenne from various theologians and philosophers (*Meditations, Oeuvres*, vol. IX–1, p. 102).

† *Meditationes, Oeuvres*, vol. VII, pp. v–xviii.

1 Reasons Proving the Existence of God and the Distinction of the Soul from the Body

arranged in geometrical order

1

2 DEFINITIONS

3   I. By the name of *thought* I comprise each thing that is in us in such a way that we are immediately conscious of it. Thus all the operations of the will, intellect, imagination, and senses are thoughts. But I added *immediately* in order to exclude those things that are the consequences of these, such as voluntary motion, which indeed has thought as its principle but nevertheless is not itself thought.

4   II. By the name of *idea* I understand that form of any thought through the immediate perception of which I am conscious of that very same thought; so that I am unable to express anything in words, while understanding what I say, without this very fact making it certain that there exists in me an idea of what is signified by those words. And thus I do not call only images depicted in the fantasy ideas; on the contrary, I here emphatically do not call them ideas insofar as they are in the corporeal fantasy—that is, insofar as they are depicted in some part of the brain—but I call them ideas only insofar as they inform the mind itself that is turned toward that part of the brain.

5   III. By *the objective reality of an idea* I understand the being

of the thing represented through the idea, insofar as it exists in the idea; and in the same way it is possible to speak of objective perfection or objective artifice, and so on. For whatever we perceive as though in the objects of our ideas, those same things exist in our ideas objectively.

IV. The same things are said to exist *formally* in the objects 6 of ideas when they are in these objects in the manner we perceive them, and *eminently*, when indeed they are not such, but yet can substitute for such.

V. Each thing is called a *substance* in which there immediately 7 inheres, as in a subject, or through which there exists, anything we perceive—that is, any property, or quality, or attribute of which there is a real idea in us. Nor have we any other idea of this very substance precisely taken except that it is a thing in which this something that we perceive or that is objectively in any of our ideas formally or eminently exists, since it is manifest to the natural light that nothing can be a real attribute of nothing.

VI. The substance in which thought immediately inheres is 8 called *mind*; moreover, I speak here of mind rather than soul, because the name "soul" is equivocal, and often it is used for something corporeal.

VII. The substance that is the immediate subject of local extension, and of the accidents that presuppose extension, such as figure, position, local motion, and so on, is called *body*. Whether indeed it is one and the same substance that is called mind and body, or whether they are two diverse substances must be inquired into afterward.

VIII. The substance that we understand to be most perfect and 10 in which we manifestly conceive nothing that involves any defect or limitation of perfection is called *God*.

IX. When we say that something is contained in the nature 11 or concept of anything, it is the same as if we were to say that it is true of that thing, or can be affirmed of that thing.

X. Two substances are said to be really distinct when each can 12 exist without the other.

13 ## POSTULATES

14   I ask, first, that the readers notice how weak are the reasons on account of which they have up until this time believed in the senses, and how uncertain all the judgments they have built upon them; and that they review these considerations for so long a time and so often that they finally acquire the habit of no longer trusting the senses too much. For this I consider required in order to perceive the certainty of metaphysical things.

15   Second, I ask the readers to consider the mind proper, and all its attributes—which they shall discern they cannot doubt even though they suppose false everything they ever received from their senses; and I ask them not to stop considering it until they have acquired the habit of clearly perceiving it, and of believing it is easier to know than all corporeal things.

16   Third, I ask them to ponder diligently the self-evident propositions they will find within themselves, such as: *that the same thing cannot at the same time be and not be; that nothing cannot be the efficient cause of anything,* and the like; and thus the readers may exercise a perspicuity of intellect pure and freed from the senses; for this perspicuity of intellect has been placed in them by nature, but the appearances of the senses are wont to confuse it to the greatest extent possible. And by this procedure the truth of the axioms that follow will easily become known to them.

17   Fourth, I ask that they examine the ideas of those natures that contain the combination of many attributes together: such as the nature of the triangle, of the square, or of another figure; and likewise, the nature of the mind and the nature of body; and above all, the nature of God, or the most perfect being. And I ask them to observe that everything we perceive contained in these natures can be truly affirmed of them. Thus, because the equality of its three angles to two right angles is contained in the nature of the triangle, and because divisibility is contained in the nature of body or of an extended thing (for we conceive no extended thing so small that we cannot at least in thought divide it), it is true to say that the three angles of every triangle are equal to two right angles, and that every body is divisible.

18   Fifth, I ask that they dwell long and intensely in contemplating

the nature of the most perfect being; and that, among other things, they consider that possible existence is indeed contained in the ideas of all other natures, whereas not merely possible, but altogether necessary existence is contained in the idea of God. And from this alone, and without any process of reasoning, they will recognize that God exists; and this will be no less self-evident to them than that the number 2 is even and the number 3 is odd, and the like. For some things are self-evident to particular people that are understood by others only through a process of reasoning.

Sixth, I ask them that, by carefully scrutinizing all the examples 19 of clear and distinct perception, and likewise of obscure and confused perception, that I have enumerated in my *Meditations*, they accustom themselves to distinguish betwen things that they know and obscure things; for this is more easily learned from examples than rules, and I think I have explained therein all the examples which pertain to this matter, or at least, have touched on all of them.

Seventh, and finally, I ask that they notice that they have never 20 found falsity in things clearly perceived, and, on the contrary, never discovered truth, save by chance, in things obscurely comprehended. And they should consider it manifestly unreasonable, because of either the mere prejudices of the senses or hypotheses containing something unknown, to call into doubt things clearly and distinctly perceived by the pure intellect. And thus they will easily admit the following axioms as true and indubitable. However, I indeed admit that many of these could have been much better explained, and should have been propounded as theorems rather than axioms, had I intended to be more exact.

AXIOMS OR COMMON NOTIONS 21

I. Nothing exists concerning which it is not possible to inquire 22 into the cause why it exists. For this can be asked even about God himself, not that God stands in want of a cause, but because the very immensity of his nature is the cause or reason why he stands in no want of a cause in order to exist.

II. The present time does not depend upon the proximately 23 preceding time; and accordingly, no less a cause is required to conserve a thing than to produce it in the first place.

III. There is not any thing, nor any actually existing perfec- 24 tion of a thing, which can have nothing, that is, have something that is nonexisting, for the cause of its existence.

25 IV. Whatever reality or perfection is in any thing, it is formally or eminently in the first and adequate cause of the thing.

26 V. From this it follows also that the objective reality of our ideas requires a cause in which this same reality is contained, not merely objectively, but formally or eminently. And it must be noted that so necessary is the admission of this axiom that upon this one axiom depends the knowledge of all things, sensible and insensible. For example, whence do we know that heaven exists? Is it because we see it? But this seeing does not reach the mind except insofar as it is an idea; an idea, I say, inhering in the mind itself, not an image depicted in the corporeal fantasy. And yet we cannot judge that heaven exists on the basis of this idea unless it be because every idea must have a really existing cause of its objective reality, and we can judge this cause to be this very heaven; and so forth with the other ideas.

27 VI. There are different grades of reality or of being; for substance has more reality than an accident or a mode, and infinite substance has more reality than a finite substance. And consequently there is more objective reality in the idea of substance than in the idea of an accident; and there is more objective reality in the idea of an infinite substance than in the idea of a finite substance.

28 VII. The will of a thinking thing is born, voluntarily indeed and freely (for this is of the essence of the will), but nonetheless infallibly, toward a good clearly known to it; and consequently if it knows any perfections that it lacks, it will immediately give them to itself, if they are in its power.

29 VIII. Whatever can effect the greater or more difficult can also effect what is less.

30 IX. It is greater to create or conserve substance than the attributes or properties of substance; however, it is not greater to create than to conserve the same thing, as has already been said.

31 X. In the idea of each thing, or in the concept of it, existence is contained, because we can conceive nothing except under the character of existing; that is, possible or contingent existence is contained in the concept of a limited thing, but necessary and perfect existence is contained in the concept of the most perfect being.

[PROPOSITIONS]

PROPOSITION I
*The existence of God is known from the
sole consideration of his nature.*

32

Demonstration

33

To say something is contained in the nature or concept of anything is the same as to say that it is true of that thing (by definition IX). But necessary existence is contained in the concept of
God (by axiom X). Therefore is it true to say of God that necessary existence is in him, or that he exists.

34

And this is the syllogism that was at issue in my *response to
the sixth objection* made above; and the conclusion of this syllogism can be self-evident to those who are freed from prejudices, as
has been said in the fifth postulate; but because it is not easy to
attain to such great perspicacity, we shall seek for the same thing in
other ways.

35

PROPOSITION II
*The existence of God is demonstrated a posteriori
from the single fact that the idea of him is in us.*

36

Demonstration

37

The objective reality of any of our ideas requires a cause in
which this same reality is contained not only objectively, but
formally or eminently (by axiom V). Moreover, we have the idea
of God (by definition II & VIII), and the objective reality of this
idea is not contained in us either formally or eminently (by axiom
VI), nor can it be contained in any other thing except God himself
(by definition VIII). Therefore this idea of God, which is in us,
requires God for its cause, and God, accordingly, exists (by
axiom III).

38

39
PROPOSITION III
*The existence of God is also demonstrated from
the fact that we ourselves exist having the
idea of him.*

40 Demonstration

41 If I were to have the force for conserving myself, so much the more would I also have the force for giving myself the perfections lacking to me (by axioms VIII & IX); for these perfections are only attributes of a substance, and I, however, am a substance. But I do not have the force for giving myself these perfections; for otherwise I would already have them (by axiom VII). Therefore I do not have the force for conserving myself.

42 Next, I cannot exist unless I am conserved as long as I exist— conserved either by myself, if indeed I have this force, or by something else that has this force (by axioms I & II). But I exist, and nevertheless I do not have the force of conserving myself, as already has been proved beforehand. Therefore I am conserved by another.

43 Furthermore, that by which I am conserved has in itself formally or eminently everything that is in me (by axiom IV). However, there is in me a perception of many perfections that I lack, and at the same time there is in me a perception of the idea of God (by definitions II & VIII). Therefore the perception of these same things is also in that by which I am conserved.

44 Finally, that same thing by which I am conserved cannot have a perception of any perfections that it lacks or does not have in itself formally or eminently (by axiom VII). For since it has the force for conserving me, as already has been said, so much the more would it have the force of giving those same things to itself if they were lacking to it (by axioms VIII & IX). Moreover, it has a perception of all those things that are lacking to me, and that I conceive capable of being in God alone, as has recently been proved. Therefore it has all those things formally or eminently in itself, and thus it is God.

COROLLARY

*God created the heaven and the earth and everything
in them: and in addition, he can bring about whatever
we clearly perceive as we perceive it.*

45

Demonstration

46

All these things clearly follow from the preceding proposition. 47
For therein the existence of God has been proved from the fact
that something must exist in which is formally or eminently contained all the perfections of which we have any idea. But we have
the idea of so great a power that the thing in which this power
exists has alone created heaven and earth and can bring about
everything I understand to be possible. Therefore, together with
the existence of God, all these things are also proved about him.

PROPOSITION IV

Mind and body are really distinct.

48

Demonstration

49

Whatever we clearly perceive, God is able to do it as we perceive 50
it (by the preceding corollary). But we clearly perceive the mind,
that is, thinking substance, without the body, that is, without any
extended substance (by the second postulate); and vice versa, we
clearly perceive body without mind (as everyone easily concedes).
Therefore, at least by divine power, mind can be without body, and
body without mind.

For certainly, substances that can be one without the other are 51
really distinct (by definition X). But mind and body are substances (by definitions V, VI, & VII), and one can be without the
other (as has just been proved). Therefore mind and body are
really distinct.

And it must be noted that I here used divine power as a means, 52
not because some extraordinary force is required to separate the
mind from the body, but because, since I have dealt with God
alone in what preceded, I had nothing else I could use as means.
Moreover, for us to recognize that two things are really distinct,
the power by which they are separated is not of concern.

Notes

RULES

1. *Regulae ad directionem ingenii, Oeuvres,* vol. X, pp. 486–488.
2. *Ibid.;* cf. R 27.
3. R 86–93, D 52–57, M 145–149. For fuller statements, see *Traité de l'homme, Oeuvres,* vol. XI (1967), pp. 3–215; *Dioptrique, Oeuvres,* vol. VI, (1965), esp. pp. 109–114; *Description du corps humain, Oeuvres,* vol. XI, (1967), pp. 219–290.
4. R 132–154.
5. R 111, 114.
6. R 111, 114.
7. R 111, 114.
8. See pp. 111–113, 176–177.
9. R 103.
10. See pp. 170–172.
11. R 22.
12. R 25.
13. R 7, 14; D 24. The topics of knowledge, probability, verisimilitude, obstinacy, precipitation, and syllogistic reasoning were interrelated in the debates between the ancient Skeptics and the Stoics; see Cicero, *Academica* (Cambridge, Mass.: Harvard University Press, 1961). Cf. Augustine, *Contra academicos, Oeuvres de Saint Augustin,* vol. 4 (Paris: Desclée de Brouwer et Cⁱᵉ, 1948); English translation by Patricia Garvey, R.S.M., *Against the Academicians* (Milwaukee: Marquette University Press, 1973).
14. M 145.
15. Descartes uses *respectus* in R 35. I have translated *respectus,* which literally means "looking back," as "relation." Descartes prefers the appositive expression *proportiones sive habitudines; cf.* R 38, 130. I have rendered this phrase as "proportions or relations," and a com-

parison of R 35 and 130 will justify this rendering. While relations or proportions may apply beyond mathematical contexts, proportions are perspicuously manifest in mathematical contexts; cf. Bonaventure, *Itinerarium mentis in Deum, Opera omnia,* vol. XII (Paris: Ludovicus Vives, 1868), pp. 7–9; English translation by George Boas, *The Mind's Road to God* (Indianapolis, Ind.: Bobbs Merrill, 1953), pp. 16–20.

16. R 98.

17. Re 22–31.

18. Thomas Aquinas, *De ente et essentia,* ed. M. D. Rolland Gosselin, O.P., *Revue des sciences philosophiques et théologiques* (Kain, Belgium: Le Saulchoir, 1926), esp. pp. 12–14; English translation by Robert Goodwin, *Selected Writing of St. Thomas Aquinas* (Indianapolis, Ind.: Bobbs Merrill, 1965), esp. pp. 40–41. Aquinas does not deny that body must have three dimensions. However, he maintains that body may have further perfections, such as in man, who has both a sensitive and an intellectual nature. Thus, according to Aquinas, "body" need not be restricted to designating what has three dimensions but may refer to a thing that has a "form" such that three dimensions can be designated in it, whatever that form may be and whether or not there can arise from the form some further perfection. Descartes insists that a subject or substance can be understood only through its essential attribute and, in particular, that body can be understood only through extension, so that there can be no further "form" in body. Hence it follows that whatever else can be predicated of body must be predicated through extension—that is, it must necessarily presuppose extension. However, Descartes will also argue that thinking can be conceived to exist without presupposing any extension; hence thinking cannot be predicated through extension, and therefore it cannot be predicated of the same subject or substance of which extension is predicated. Thus man is a composite of two substances.

19. See pp. 104–106.

DISCOURSE

1. "Secundae responsiones," *Oeuvres,* vol. VII, pp. 155–156: "Analysis shows the true way in which the matter is methodically, and as it were a priori, discovered; so that, if the reader wishes to attend sufficiently to everything, he will understand the matter and render it his own no less than if he had discerned it himself. . . . Synthesis, on the other hand, takes the opposite way, which is, as it were, pursued a posteriori (although often the proof itself is in this respect more a priori than in analysis). And indeed synthesis clearly demonstrates what is concluded, and it uses a long series of definitions, postulates, axioms,

theorems, and problems . . . but synthesis does not satisfy as analysis does, nor does it appease the minds of those desirous of learning, since it does not teach the manner in which the matter was discovered."

2. *Ibid.*, p. 156.

3. D 40.

4. Descartes had an inchoate doctrine concerning the distinction of substances as early as the *Rules*; see pp. 18–20.

5. D 42.

6. "Sextae responsiones," *Oeuvres*, vol. VII, p. 436: "Nor is it necessary to inquire into the manner in which God from all eternity might have made it untrue that twice 4 is 8, and so on. I admit it cannot be understood by us. Yet because I understand, on the other hand, that nothing in any category of being can have existence unless it depends upon God, and that it would have been very easy for him to institute some things such that we men could not understand that they could be different from the way they are, it would be unreasonable, because we do not understand nor recognize that we ought to understand, to doubt about what we rightly understand. In like manner, neither should it be thought that the eternal truths depend upon the human intellect or upon other existing things, but they depend only upon God, who, as the highest legislator, instituted them from all eternity."

7. D 46.

MEDITATIONS

1. This matter has been discussed above; see pp. 104–106.

2. See p. 102 and *Discourse*, n. 1, above.

3. M 26.

4. M 26.

5. Cicero, *Academica* (Cambridge, Mass: Harvard University Press, 1961), pp. 526–530.

6. *Ibid.*, p. 576.

7. See pp. 104–106.

8. See pp. 106–110.

9. See pp. 111–113.

Conceptual Index

The purpose of this conceptual index is to help the reader discern the structure of Descartes's philosophy, particularly the many interrelations between the theory of knowledge and the metaphysics. The basic structure of his philosophy is indicated by the major headings and subdivisions (outlined below); similarly, the role of the more detailed conceptions can be inferred from their location. Where the work cited is not included in this volume, a translation of a crucial passage is often provided. References to such works are made by the following abbreviations, plus page numbers:

P = *Principles of Philosophy*, together with the part and principle number
OR = "Objections and Replies"
N = *Notes on a Program**

A glance at the major headings shows their emphasis: I–IV, key elements in the theory of knowledge; V, the metaphysical question of the nature of the thing to be known, as well as the epistemic question of how to proceed in order to know its nature; VI–VII, the special metaphysical question concerning man's nature and the relation of his various functions to the attainment of knowledge; VIII–IX, the special significance and demands of metaphysical certitude, as well as the procedures for attaining such certitude about God and the nature of the human mind.

---

* *Principia philosophiae, Oeuvres*, vol. VIII–1 (1964), pp. 1–353; "Objectiones doctorum aliquot virorum in praecedentes meditationes cum responsionibus authoris," *Oeuvres*, vol. VII (1964), pp. 91–603; *Notae in programma, Oeuvres*, vol. VIII–2 (1965), pp. 340–369.

I. KNOWLEDGE: CERTAIN AND EVIDENT COGNITION

Knowledge of self is first and most certain to one philosophizing in an orderly manner, P1, VII, pp. 6–7. Suggestion of a metaphysical doubt about knowledge of self, M 57; cf. P1, VII, pp. 6–7, with P1, XIII, pp. 9–10. Certainty and evidence of God vis-à-vis certainty and evidence of mathematics, M 6. Mathematics can be doubted, D 40; M 33–34; P1, V, p. 6. In context of principal proof of God's existence in the Third Meditation (see M 19, 53–91; cf. D 40–43): God is intuited, M 91; nothing is more certain and evident than God, M 93. In context of "new" proof for God's existence in Fifth Meditation (see M 21, 109–125; cf. D 44): existence of God is at least as certain as mathematical truths before a proof of God's existence, M 116, D 44; how certainty and truth of every science depend solely on cognition of true God, M 122–125; D 46; P1, XIII, pp. 9–10.

II. SOURCES OF COGNITION: EXPERIENCE AND DEDUCTION

Experience and deduction as sources of cognition, R 8. Definition of experience and relation to intuition, R 103. Experience and simple natures, R 55, 62, 96–111. See III.B, Deduction.

III. OPERATIONS BY WHICH KNOWLEDGE IS ATTAINED: INTUITION AND DEDUCTION

Intuition and deduction are only paths to knowledge, R 19–20, 65. Intuition and deduction are acts of intellect, R 15. Intuition and deduction are native to human intellect, R 23. Intuition and deduction require direction by method, R 22–23.

A. INTUITION

Definition, R 16; cf. R 17, and definition of experience, R 103. Intuition as certain and evident, R 18. Intuition and a clear and distinct proposition, R 79. Reducibility of deduction to intuition, R 19. Intuition and enumeration, R 46. Intuition and simple natures, R 37. Intuition and rational connections (discursus), R 18. Intuition extends to simple natures, necessary connections, and what intellect experiences in self or "corporeal fantasy," R 106. Falsity impossible only in intuition of simple things or combinations of them, R 115; cf. entries regarding questions under V.B.4, Intuition, Deduction, and Questions. No effort to cognize simple natures but only to separate them out, R 107; cf. Perspicacity defined, under IV, Method for Acquiring Knowledge. Intellect can be helped to intuit by sense, memory, and imagination, R 83.   When image is not a help to intuition, R 95, 98.   Examples of intuition without image, R 98.   Examples of intuition with image, R 70.   God is intuited, M 91.

B. DEDUCTION

Definition, R 19.   Deduction and mistakes, R 8, 105.   Deduction is necessary deduction, R 105.   Deduction, unlike syllogistic formulas, yields new knowledge, R 75–76; *cf.* D 24.   Deduction should proceed from objects of intuition, R 37.   Deduction involves movement of mind, R 19.   No movement of mind in deduction as performed, R 79.   Deduction is certain but not evident, R 19.   Reducibility of deduction to intuition, R 19, 79.   Same object as known by intuition and deduction, R 19.   Deduction not reduced to intuition called enumeration or induction, R 19, 46.   Artful deduction and sagacity, R 65; *cf.* sagacity, R 77.   Deduction alone allows us to compare things so as to be certain of their truth, R 105; *cf.* impulse and conjecture, R 104, *and entries regarding* comparisons *and* proportions *under* V.B.3, Deduction of Complicated Things from Simple Natures.

IV. METHOD FOR ACQUIRING KNOWLEDGE

Definition of true method, R 22, D 23.   Completeness criteria for method, R 23.   Method and limits of human knowledge, R 22–23, 54.   Method directs intuition and deduction, R 23.   Principles of method inborn, R 24.   Method explains first rudiments of human reason and extends to all subject matters, R 25.   Method as universal mathematics, R 25–26.   Universal mathematics as preparation for higher sciences, R 27.   Method draws on geometry and algebra, R 26, D 24.   Rules of method replace rules of logic, D 24.   Rules of method listed, D 25–28, and more specifically, R 31, 41 (enumeration), 64 (perspicacity), 71 (sagacity), 77, 83.   Enumeration called induction, R 45.   Enumeration defined, R 45.   Enumeration must be sufficient, R 46–47.   Sufficient enumeration, completeness, and distinctness, R 48.   Sufficient enumeration and order, R 49.   When enumeration required, R 46.   Perspicacity defined, R 66; *cf. entries regarding* questions *under* V.B.4, Intuition, Deduction, and Questions.

V. THINGS TO BE KNOWN AND THE ORDER IN COMING TO KNOW THEM

In respect to order of cognition, things regarded differently than as they truly exist, R 97, D 27.

A. Things to Be Known

Things to be known are simple or complicated, R 31. Things to be known can be simple and unitary although in order of cognition composed of single natures, R 97. Even *I think, therefore I am* composed from simple natures, P1, X, p. 8.

B. Order in Coming to Know Things

Intellect must divide a thing into single natures, R 97. Often easier to attend to the union of simple natures, R 102. Simple natures better known than union of them, R 102. To know things, we must consider spontaneously obvious things, the manner of deducing things, and what is deduced, R 85.

1. Simple Natures

Simple natures are self-evident objects of intuition, R 37. Falsity impossible only in intuition of simple natures and their combinations, R 115; *cf. entries regarding* questions *under* V.B.4, Intuition, Deduction, and Questions. Simple natures purely spiritual, purely material, or common, R 62, 98. Definition and examples of material and spiritual, R 98. Definition and examples of common, R 98, Re 21–31. Simple natures include privations of simple natures, R 99.

2. Composite Natures

Relation of composite to simple natures, R 62, 102. Falsity possible only in composite natures composed by intellect, R 62, 103. Falsity impossible in intuition of simple natures or combinations of them, R 115; *cf. entries regarding* questions *under* V.B.4, Intuition, Deduction, and Questions. *See also entries regarding* substance, subject, *and* composite entities *under* IX.C, Mind and Body as Really Distinct Substances.

3. Deduction of Complicated Things from Simple Natures

Few pure and simple natures in series leading to things to be known, R 37. Only deduction allows us to compose things in such a way that we are certain of their truth, R 105; *cf.* impulse and conjecture, R 104. Absolute is pure and simple nature relevant to solving questions, R 34. Examples of absolute, R 34; *cf.* simple and more difficult comparisons and proportions, R 130. Relative is deduced from absolute according to a series, R 35. Relative participates in absolute nature, R 35. Relations (*respectus*) contained in concept of relative things, R. 35. Things involving relations or proportions, R 130–133. Connections between simple natures are necessary or contingent, R 101.   Necessity explained, R 101.   Contingent connections as absence of any necessary connections, R 101.

4. Intuition, Deduction, and Questions

What can be be known are simple propositions and questions, R 111. Questions are everything in which truth or falsity is found, R 114. Simple propositions intuited, R 111.   Falsity impossible only in intuition of simple things or combinations of them, R 115.   Simple things become questions when we reflect on them, R 115; cf. Socrates's doubt as question, R 115, and explication of self as immediately known, M 46–52.   Only rules for simple propositions are those governing perspicacity and sagacity, R 111; cf. R 111 with R 64, 66.   Questions are either perfectly or imperfectly understood, R 111.   Location (actual or intended) of rules governing both sorts of questions, R 111. Signs of perfectly understood questions, R 111; cf. entries regarding comparisons and proportions under V.B.3, Deduction of Complicated Things from Simple Natures.

VI. HUMAN INTELLECT AND KNOWLEDGE: ROLE OF SENSE, MEMORY, AND IMAGINATION; BODY–MIND COMPOSITE AND INNATE IDEAS

Intellect alone capable of knowledge, R 61.   Intellect helped or impeded by three other faculties: sense, memory, and imagination, R 61; cf. R 57, and entries regarding faculty and innateness under VI.C, Body-Mind Composite, Primacy of Intellect, and Innate Ideas.   Need to study how intellect can be helped or impeded by these facutlies, R 57, 61.

A. INTELLECT

Thinking thing (res cogitans), intellect (intellectus), mind (mens), soul(animus), and reason (ratio) are equivalent, M 43.   Soul (anima) and mind (mens) used equivalently in context of early part of Meditations, cf. M 3 with M 9.   Soul (anima) can carry a suggestion of corporeality, Re 8; N, p. 347; OR, pp. 355–356.   Descartes prefers mind to soul (anima), Re 8; N, p. 347; OR, p. 356.   When Descartes distinguishes a concept of himself that includes no reference to corporeal things, he uses the term animus to designate himself, M 33–34; cf. the distinction between anima and animus in Lucretius, De rerum natura I, 132.   Intellect alone capable of perceiving truth, R 85.   Reason or good sense is ability to distinguish true from false, D 3.   Intuition and deduction are the only operations whereby intellect can attain to truth, R 15, 19–20.   No cognitions more obscure than others, R 109, D 29. All truths discerned with equal facility in whatever subject matter, R 67.   All truths discerned with same act of mind, R 67.   Intellect cannot apprehend false under form of truth, OR, p. 378; *cf.* mistakes, R 8, 67, 105; impulse and conjecture, R 104; definition of experience, R 103.

B. Intellect and the Role of Sense, Memory, and Imagination

"Suppositions" concerning faculties in the body-mind composite that contribute to knowing, R 83–95.   Development and proof of these suppositions, M 18, 41–52, 127–150.   Intellect is knowing force (*vis cognoscens*), R 94–95; *cf.* Definition of faculty *under* VI.C, Body-Mind Composite, Primacy of Intellect, and Innate Ideas. Knowing force is purely spiritual and distinct from body, R 94.   Knowing force is one thing whether it applies itself to the common sense and corporeal fantasy or whether it receives figures from the common sense and corporeal fantasy (*phantasia*), R 94; *cf.* M 51–52.   Common sense (*sensus communis*) is part of body, R 91; *cf.* D 57.   Common sense assumes different figures from objects affecting external sense organs, R 91. Common sense impresses figures derived from the external senses on fantasy, R 92.   Fantasy (*phantasia vel imaginatio*) is part of the body, R 92.   Fantasy as part of the body lays the basis for corporeal memories and imaginations, R 92, D 57.   Sensing is application of knowing force to common sense and corporeal fantasy, R 94.   Remembering is application of knowing force to the imagination already formed with different figures, R 94.   To imagine or to conceive (*imaginari vel concipere*) is an application of knowing force to the imagination (*phantasiam*) to devise new figures, R 94.   In applying itself to fantasy to devise new figures, knowing force is properly called native talent or native wit (*ingenium*), R 94.   Knowing force is said to understand (*intelligere*) when it acts alone, R 94.   Knowing force called pure intellect (*intellectus purus*) when it acts alone, R 94.   Imagining is appropriate to corporeal things, R 95.   Imagining is appropriate only to corporeal things, R 95, D 45.   For interesting application of imagining, conceiving, or native wit to aid reasoning about extension both generally and specifically, *see* R 132–181. (The discussion of R 135–140 has interesting implications for Descartes's metaphysics. By pressing the point that the subject of extension can be conceived only through its extension, Descartes is paving the way for his later doctrine that a substance can be conceived only through an essential property and that since extension can be conceived without thinking and vice versa, the substance that is extended is different, i.e., diverse, from the substance that thinks. *See* IX.C, Mind and Body as Really Distinct Substances.) Even the extension of specific bodies, and extension generally, are not perceived by imagining, but only because they are understood by the mind, intellect, or faculty of judging, M 47–52. When intellect acts on things in which there is nothing corporeal or similar to the corporeal, it is impeded by sense and imagination, R 95. Soul cannot be imagined, D 45, M 43–52. God and self are perceived by same faculty of mind, M 90; *cf.* D 41, 45. Difference between pure understanding and imagining, M 128.

C. BODY-MIND COMPOSITE, PRIMACY OF INTELLECT, AND INNATE IDEAS

Definition of simple entity, N, p. 350. Definition of composite entity, N, p. 350. Man is composite from thinking and extension, N, p. 351; *cf. entries regarding* subject *and* substance *under* IX.C, Mind and Body as Really Distinct Substances. Common sense (*sensus communis*) is part of body, R 91; *cf.* D 57. Common sense assumes different figures from objects affecting the external sense organs, R 91. Figure in the external sense organ is transferred in an instant without motion of any real entity from the external sense organ to the common sense, R 91. All sensations from external things—light, texture, color, figure—operate only by changing the figuration of external organs and by effecting a change of figure in common sense, R 88, D 57. Fantasy is a genuine part of body, R 92. Common sense impresses figures received from external objects on fantasy, R 92. Figures impressed on fantasy lay basis for corporeal memories and imaginations, R 92, D 57. Light, texture, color, and so on, as well as the figures of external bodies, are represented only through figures, R 88–90, 133. Figures in common sense and corporeal fantasy do not correspond exactly to the figures of external objects, R 103, M 141. Sensations called flavors, smells, sounds, colors, and so on, represent nothing posited outside thought, P1, LXXI, pp. 35–36. Body is perceived only by intellect, and senses cannot distinguish one body from another, OR, pp. 132–133. "Everything in our ideas is innate in the mind or faculty of thinking, with the sole exception of circumstances that refer to experience, that is, when we judge that these or those ideas that we presently have in our thought are to be referred to objects that exist outside ourselves—not because those things transmitted these ideas to our mind through the organs of sense, but because they sent something that gives the mind the occasion, through its innate faculty, to form these ideas at this time rather than another," N, pp. 358–359. Definition of faculty: "to exist in faculty is not to exist in act, but only to exist in potency, for the name of 'faculty' designates nothing but potential existence," N, p. 361. "When we say that any idea is innate in us we do not mean that it is always present to us—in this sense no idea would be innate—but we mean only that we have in us a faculty of summoning it up," OR, p. 189. "To be sure, nothing from external objects comes to our mind through the organs of the senses save certain corporeal motions . . . but indeed not even these motions nor the figures that arise from them are conceived by us as they are in the organs of the senses, as I amply explained in the *Dioptrics*. From which it follows that these ideas of motion and figure are innate in us. And so much more innate are the ideas of pain, colors, sounds, and the like, so that our mind can, on the occasion of certain corporeal motions, exhibit these ideas to itself; for these ideas have no similarity to corporeal motions," N, p. 359. Not even ideas of simplest figures make their way to the mind by means of the senses, OR, pp. 381–382.

VII. WILL AND ERROR

In addition to intellect, mind has a faculty of willing, M 100. Faculty of willing is liberty of deciding (*libertas arbitrii*), M 100. Formal nature of willing, M 100, 106. Mind can avoid error by using its proper liberty to withhold assent, *cf.* M 26 *with* M 35–36, 107–108. Avoidance of error and the natural light of reason, M 62. Natural impulses can be misleading and conflict with evidence of reason, M 62–65, 133, 141; *cf.* definition of experience, R 103; *cf. also* R 104.

VIII. QUEST FOR METAPHYSICAL CERTITUDE

Metaphysical certitude vs. moral assurance, D 46; M 57; P4, CCVI, pp. 328–329. General doubt until we know origins of reason, D 46; *cf.* consequence of the possibility of a deceiving deity, M 33, and of no God at all, M 34. The method and the *Meditations*, M 5, 9, 14. Assent must be withheld from everything not certain and indubitable, D 40, M 26. Senses are insufficient evidence for basic physical judgments, M 28 (small and more-distant objects), 133, 141. Sense qualities not known to be images of things, M 65; *see also* VI.C, Body-Mind Composite, Primacy of Intellect, and Innate Ideas. Mathematics can be doubted because of the possibility of paralogisms, D 40; P1, V, p. 6. Mathematics can be doubted because of doubt about origins of reason, M 33–34, 57. Supposition of evil genius as a way of reminding oneself of the maxim to withhold assent from everything uncertain and dubitable, M 36, 57.

IX. METAPHYSICAL KNOWLEDGE

I think, therefore I am as first principle of a philosophy, *D* 40; *cf. I am, I exist* as axiom (*pronunciatum*), *M* 40. Clarity and distinctness as universal mark of truth, *D* 42, *M* 55. In *Meditations* no immediate claim of a substantial (real) distinction between mind and body, *M* 11, 18, 44. Suggestion of a doubt even about knowledge of self, *M* 57; *cf.* P1, VII, pp. 6–7, with P1, XIII, pp. 9–10. Principal proof of God's existence is in the Third Meditation, *M* 19; *cf. D* 43. "New" argument in the Fifth Meditation, *M* 21; *cf. D* 44.

A. ELEMENTS IN THE PRINCIPAL PROOF OF GOD'S EXISTENCE

General axioms governing causation, *Re* 16, 22–24; *M* 67. From the principle that the effect derives its reality from the cause, it follows that (1) nothing comes from nothing and (2) it is impossible that the more perfect comes from the less perfect, *M* 67. Things thought about can be assigned degrees of reality, *Re* 27. Ideas alone have objective realities, *M* 67; *Re* 5; OR, pp. 102–103. Definition of idea, *Re* 4. Definition of objective reality of idea, *Re* 5. Degree of objective reality in an idea depends on degree of reality in things represented, *M* 66, *Re* 27. Objective realities in ideas require a cause that is not merely an objective reality, *M* 67, *Re* 26. Ideas or objective realities representing whatever is dubious do not reveal their true origins, *M* 60. Dubious ideas provide us no basis for knowing that they do not proceed from what is in the self formally or eminently, *M* 60, 69–73. Definition of formal, *Re* 6. Definition of eminent *Re* 6. Objective reality represented in idea of God, *M* 74. Objective reality in idea of God must proceed from God, *M* 74–91, 93.

B. FEATURES OF THE "NEW" ARGUMENT IN THE FIFTH MEDITATION

The "new" proof is at least as certain as mathematical truths were before a proof of God's existence, *M* 116; *cf. D* 44. How certainty and truth of every science depends on a cognition of God, *M* 122–125; *cf. D* 46; P1, XIII, pp. 9–10.

C. MIND AND BODY AS REALLY DISTINCT SUBSTANCES

Ability to distinguish created substances not assumed until there is a divine guarantee of clear and distinct ideas, *M* 18, 44, 135. Definition of substance, *Re* 7. Definition of mind as substance, *Re* 8.